ICFA Continuing Education
Managing Emerging Market Portfolios

September 28-29, 1993
San Francisco, California

Horace W. Brock
Lyle H. Davis, CFA
Arjun Divecha
Marc Faber
David H. Gill
Teresa E. Goodale
René T. Goupillaud
Josephine S. Jimenez, CFA
Donald M. Krueger, CFA, *Moderator*
Patrick O'Brien

Jeremy Paulson-Ellis
Alexander Peña
Francisco Portillejo
John F.H. Purcell
Gary S. Schieneman
Andrew Summers
Jayant S. Tata
Rudolf van der Bijl
Shaw B. Wagener, CFA
Marc Wenhammar

Edited by John W. Peavy III, CFA

Jointly sponsored by AIMR and the
Center for Emerging Markets, Research Foundation of the ICFA

AIMR Education Steering Committee 1993–94

Ian R. O'Reilly, CFA, *Co-Chairman*
  Toronto, Ontario, Canada

Eliot P. Williams, CFA, *Co-Chairman*
  Windsor, Connecticut

Abby Joseph Cohen, CFA
  New York, New York

Lea B. Hansen, CFA
  Toronto, Ontario, Canada

Charles F. O'Connell, CFA
  Chicago, Illinois

Frank K. Reilly, CFA
  Notre Dame, Indiana

Donald L. Tuttle, CFA
  Charlottesville, Virginia

To obtain an AIMR Publications Catalog or to order additional copies of this publication, turn to page 143 or contact:

AIMR Publications Sales Department
P.O. Box 7947
Charlottesville, VA 22906
U.S.A.
Telephone: 804/980-3647
Fax: 804/977-0350

The Association for Investment Management and Research comprises the Institute of Chartered Financial Analysts and the Financial Analysts Federation.

© 1994, Association for Investment Management and Research

All rights reserved. No part of this publication may be reproduced, stored in a retrieval system, or transmitted, in any form or by any means, electronic, mechanical, photocopying, recording, or otherwise, without the prior written permission of the copyright holder.

This publication is designed to provide accurate and authoritative information in regard to the subject matter covered. It is sold with the understanding that the publisher is not engaged in rendering legal, accounting, or other professional service. If legal advice or other expert assistance is required, the services of a competent professional should be sought.

ISBN 1-879087-37-5

Printed in the United States of America

February 1994

Table of Contents

Foreword . . . . **vii**
    Katrina F. Sherrerd, CFA

Biographies of Speakers . . . . **viii**

Managing Emerging Market Portfolios: An Overview **1**
    John W. Peavy III, CFA

Introducing Emerging Markets **8**
    Jeremy Paulson-Ellis

Top-Down Investing in Emerging Markets **19**
    Lyle H. Davis, CFA

Bottom-Up Investing in Emerging Markets **29**
    Shaw B. Wagener, CFA

Valuation Techniques for Emerging Market Securities **33**
    Donald M. Krueger, CFA

The Research Challenge: Analyzing the Numbers **40**
    Gary S. Schieneman

The Research Challenge **45**
    Josephine S. Jimenez, CFA

Building and Administering Country Funds **49**
    David H. Gill

Managing Emerging Market Fixed-Income Portfolios **58**
    Marc Wenhammar

Emerging Markets from a European Perspective **66**
    Patrick O'Brien

Investing in Emerging Market Currencies **69**
    Francisco Portillejo

Political Considerations in Emerging Markets Analysis **72**
    John F.H. Purcell

(continued on next page)

Regulatory Environments in Emerging Markets **80**
    Rudolf van der Bijl

Trading and Execution in Emerging Markets **92**
    Alexander Peña

Settlement, Custody, and Regulatory Challenges in Emerging Markets **101**
    Andrew Summers

Understanding Emerging Market Life Cycles **106**
    Marc Faber

Adventures of the Russell 20–20 . . . . **121**
    Teresa E. Goodale

Trends in Emerging Markets **125**
    Jayant S. Tata

Emerging Markets Allocation: The Plan Sponsor's View **127**
    René T. Goupillaud

Choosing an Emerging Markets Benchmark **131**
    Arjun Divecha

Self-Evaluation Examination
    Questions **137**
    Answers **140**

Order Form **143**

Selected AIMR Publications **144**

ICFA Board of Trustees, 1993–94

Eliot P. Williams, CFA, Chairman
  Boston, Massachusetts
Brian F. Wruble, CFA, Vice Chairman
  Philadelphia, Pennsylvania
Charles D. Ellis, CFA, AIMR Chairman
  Greenwich, Connecticut
John L. Maginn, CFA, AIMR Vice Chairman
  Omaha, Nebraska
Abby Joseph Cohen, CFA
  New York, New York
Thomas L. Hansberger, CFA
  Ft. Lauderdale, Florida

Frederick L. Muller, CFA
  Atlanta, Georgia
Ian R. O'Reilly, CFA
  Toronto, Ontario, Canada
Norton H. Reamer, CFA
  Boston, Massachusetts
Frank K. Reilly, CFA
  Notre Dame, Indiana
Guy G. Rutherfurd, Jr., CFA
  New York, New York

AIMR Council on Education and Research

Ian R. O'Reilly, CFA, *Chairman*
  Toronto, Ontario, Canada
Keith P. Ambachtsheer
  Toronto, Ontario, Canada
Gary P. Brinson, CFA
  Chicago, Illinois
Charles D. Ellis, CFA
  Greenwich, Connecticut
H. Russell Fogler
  Gainesville, Florida
W. Van Harlow III, CFA
  Boston, Massachusetts
Lawrence E. Harris
  Los Angeles, California
Martin L. Leibowitz
  New York, New York

Roger F. Murray
  Wolfeboro, New Hampshire
John W. Peavy III, CFA
  Dallas, Texas
André F. Perold
  Boston, Massachusetts
Frank K. Reilly, CFA
  Notre Dame, Indiana
Stephen A. Ross
  New Haven, Connecticut
Eugene C. Sit, CFA
  Minneapolis, Minnesota
Bruno Solnik
  Jouy-en-Josas Cedex, France
James R. Vertin, CFA
  Menlo Park, California

Management Committee

Thomas A. Bowman, CFA
  Executive Vice President
Michael S. Caccese
  Senior Vice President and General Counsel
Katrina F. Sherrerd, CFA
  Senior Vice President

Donald L. Tuttle, CFA
  Senior Vice President
Raymond J. DeAngelo
  Vice President
Jane P. Birckhead, CPA
  Treasurer and Controller

Foreword

The theme running through the presentations in this proceedings from the seminar on *Managing Emerging Market Portfolios* is that interest in emerging market investing is booming. This theme is not surprising, as the authors make clear, because these markets have historically provided superior returns and excellent diversification.

The authors of these presentations also make clear, however, that emerging markets are not like developed markets, and the investor in these markets must be cautious. Information may be difficult to obtain, and when obtained, may need careful scrutiny before the analyst can apply the usual evaluation models to it. Low liquidity can put constraints on choices in certain markets, regulations should be carefully examined, and execution may take more careful timing and effort than in the developed markets. Moreover, investors must watch the markets carefully and constantly. Returns can be volatile, and the asset class is not static, as countries and markets move in, up, and out.

These presentations offer important insights into evaluating the countries and companies *within* emerging markets and insights into choosing among the investment vehicles available in the markets—from fixed-income sovereign bonds to emerging market equity funds to packing up and moving to Shanghai.

AIMR wishes to thank all the participants in this seminar for assisting in the preparation of the proceedings. Because of the nature of the subject matter, participants were scattered around the globe; thus, we are particularly grateful for the timely replies to our questions and pleas for help. Special thanks go to Donald Krueger, CFA, the moderator of the seminar, and to John Peavy, CFA, who served as the book editor, authored the "Overview," and prepared the self-examination questions and answers.

We also thank the speakers who so ably participated in this seminar: Horace W. ("Woody") Brock, Strategic Economic Decisions, who was unable to prepare a written version of his presentation for this proceedings; Lyle H. Davis, CFA, Boston International Advisors; Arjun Divecha, Grantham, Mayo, Van Otterloo & Company (formerly with BARRA); Marc Faber, Marc Faber, Ltd.; David H. Gill, Morgan Stanley Emerging Markets Fund; Teresa E. Goodale, AT&T Investment Management Corporation; René T. Goupillaud, ARCO Investment Management Company; Josephine S. Jimenez, CFA, Montgomery Emerging Markets Fund; Donald M. Krueger, CFA, Soros Fund Management Company (formerly with Templeton Investment Counsel); Patrick O'Brien, Swiss Bank Corporation; Jeremy Paulson-Ellis, Genesis Investment Management; Alexander Peña, Morgan Stanley & Company; Francisco Portillejo, Swiss Bank Corporation; John F.H. Purcell, Salomon Brothers Inc; Gary S. Schieneman, Smith New Court; Andrew Summers, Morgan Stanley & Company; Jayant S. Tata, International Finance Corporation; Rudolf van der Bijl, International Finance Corporation; Shaw B. Wagener, CFA, Capital International; and Marc Wenhammar, Latin American Securities.

Katrina F. Sherrerd, CFA
Senior Vice President
Publications and Research

Biographies of Speakers

Horace W. ("Woody") Brock is founder and president of Strategic Economic Decisions. Previously, he was a senior member of Stanford Research Institute's International Management and Economics Group. His commentaries on the world economy have appeared in the *New York Times* and the *International Herald Tribune*. Dr. Brock holds five degrees from Harvard and Princeton Universities and has taught at both.

Lyle H. Davis, CFA, as a founder and managing director of Boston International Advisors, is primarily responsible for client communication and general business management. He serves as chair of the Investment Committee and as president of the firm. Mr. Davis began his career at John Hancock Mutual Life Insurance Company, where he was an investment analyst, portfolio manager, and investment strategist. He later joined State Street Bank and Trust Company and served as the chief investment officer and head of the institutional investment area. Mr. Davis holds an A.B. in U.S. history from Cornell University and an M.B.A. from the University of Virginia.

Arjun Divecha serves as managing director of Grantham, Mayo, Van Otterloo & Company. Previously, he held various positions at BARRA, in product development, marketing, and client support, in managing the development of BARRA's emerging markets and Korean models, and as managing director. Mr. Divecha received his undergraduate degree in aerospace engineering from the Indian Institute of Technology in Bombay and his M.B.A. from Cornell University.

Marc Faber is managing director of Marc Faber, Ltd. Previously, he was the managing director of Drexel Burnham Lambert (Hong Kong), Ltd., and he has also worked for White Weld & Company, Ltd., in New York, Zurich, and Hong Kong. Dr. Faber writes commentary on the capital markets and is the author of *The Great Money Illusion: The Confusion of the Confusions* (Hong Kong: Longman Group, 1989). He is the investment manager for the Iconoclastic International Fund, a fund that invests in unusual situations. He is also the editor of the *Gloom, Boom & Doom Report*, a newsletter that focuses on unusual opportunities in emerging markets. Dr. Faber holds a Ph.D. degree in economics from the University of Zurich.

David H. Gill is a director of Morgan Stanley's Emerging Markets Fund and former director of Capital Markets at the International Finance Corporation. Mr. Gill is a member of the Capital Markets Committee of the Inter-American Investment Corporation, of the Advisory Council of the Investment Management Company, Chile, S.A., of the International Advisory Committee of Banon Surinvest, S.A., and of the International Advisory Council of the Thailand Fund. He serves as a director of the Thai Fund, the Latin American Discovery Fund, the Mauritius Fund, Ltd., and the Commonwealth Equity Fund.

Teresa E. Goodale is vice president of the international area at AT&T Investment Management Corporation. She is responsible for the direction, planning, and surveillance of the international equity asset class of the AT&T Pension Trust. Ms. Goodale received her B.S. degree in finance from the University of Illinois and her M.B.A. from Pace University.

René T. Goupillaud serves as director of outside investments at ARCO Investment Management Company. His responsibilities for overseeing all externally managed assets include U.S. and international equities, U.S. and international fixed-income investing, currency hedging, real estate, and private equity. Mr. Goupillaud was in private law practice before joining ARCO in 1979. He holds B.A. and J.D. degrees from the University of Oklahoma and an M.B.A from the University of California at Los Angeles.

Josephine S. Jimenez, CFA, is managing director of the Montgomery Emerging Markets Fund, an open-end, no-load mutual fund with investments in 20 countries. She has also served as director of research and portfolio manager of investments in Latin America, the Philippines, the Middle East, and Europe, and she is the developer of a model for selecting stocks in hyperinflationary environments. Ms. Jimenez received a master's degree in investment management from the Massachusetts Institute of Technology.

Donald M. Krueger, CFA, is with Soros Fund Management Company. Previously, he served as vice president of portfolio management and research at Templeton Investment Counsel. Prior to joining Templeton, Mr. Krueger was a global analyst/portfolio manager for Capital Research and Management

Company, established a Japanese equity research organization at Wertheim Schroder, and was a senior vice president with Sanyo Securities America. While at Capital Research and Management, Mr. Krueger was selected by *Institutional Investor* magazine as one of the top ten buy-side analysts in the United States. He received a bachelor's degree in economics from the University of Rochester and an M.B.A. from the Harvard Graduate School of Business Administration.

Patrick O'Brien is a director of Swiss Bank Corporation's Emerging Markets Group, which handles the distribution of emerging market products throughout Europe and the Far East. Before joining Swiss Bank, Mr. O'Brien worked at Citicorp Investment Bank's Corporate Finance Distribution Unit focusing chiefly on structured transactions in South America. He has an L.L.B. degree from University College, London, and is a barrister at law.

Jeremy Paulson-Ellis is chairman of Genesis Investment Management, a specialist investment management firm in emerging markets. Previously, he served as chairman of Vickers de Costa, Ltd., after it was acquired by Citicorp and as investment director at Genesis. Mr. Paulson-Ellis began his career with Vickers—as an analyst covering European stock markets and companies, in charge of Vickers' Japanese business, and later as founder of the firm's Tokyo branch. Mr. Paulson-Ellis was educated at Sherborne School.

John W. Peavy III, CFA, is the Mary Jo Vaughn Rauscher Professor of Financial Investments and former chairman of the Department of Finance in the Edwin L. Cox School of Business at Southern Methodist University (S.M.U.). He is also on the faculty of the Southwestern Graduate School of Banking at S.M.U. Dr. Peavy serves as research director of the Research Foundation of the ICFA and as vice chairman of the ICFA Candidate Curriculum Committee. He is the executive editor of *The CFA Digest* and serves on the editorial boards of the *Financial Analysts Journal* and the *Review of Business and Economic Research*. He has published four books and authored over 50 refereed journal articles. Dr. Peavy has received the Rotunda Award for distinguished teaching and the Faculty Research Excellence Award at S.M.U. He holds a B.B.A. from S.M.U., an M.B.A. from the Wharton School at the University of Pennsylvania, and a Ph.D. from the University of Texas at Arlington. He also holds the Chartered Life Underwriter and Chartered Financial Consultant designations.

Alexander Peña is head of emerging markets trading at Morgan Stanley & Company. Before joining Morgan Stanley, he worked for Baring Securities in New York, Mexico, and Argentina in both sales and research. Mr. Peña holds a B.A. degree in Spanish and Latin American studies, with a concentration in economics, from Columbia University.

Francisco Portillejo currently serves as director, Capital Markets and Treasury, Latin American Coverage, at Swiss Bank Corporation. He previously served Swiss Bank as director of European foreign exchange marketing. Prior to joining Swiss Bank, Mr. Portillejo worked for Devon Systems International as senior technical consultant for Europe, as marketing and sales manager for Europe, and as director of European operations. He received a bachelor's degree in electronics from the Ecole d'Enseignement Technique de l'Air, a computer science specialization from the French Aerospace Institute, and a computer science degree in aerospace engineering from the Centre d'Expérimentation Aéronautique.

John F.H. Purcell, the director of Emerging Markets at Salomon Brothers, also heads the Sovereign Credit Assessment Group. Prior to joining Salomon Brothers, Dr. Purcell was vice president at Bankers Trust Company in charge of Latin American political assessment in the International Economics Group. He has also been a consultant to the Rockefeller Foundation on U.S.–Mexico relations. Dr. Purcell received his B.A. degree from Harvard University and his M.A. and Ph.D. degrees in political science from the University of California at Los Angeles.

Gary S. Schieneman is vice president and director of Latin American Research at Smith New Court. Before joining Smith New Court, Mr. Schieneman held a number of financial management positions in the United States and Europe with Mobil Oil Corporation, was an international services partner at Arthur Young, and was a vice president and senior international accounting analyst at Prudential-Bache Securities. Mr. Schieneman is an adjunct professor of accounting at New York University Graduate School of Business Administration and a frequent lecturer on international accounting issues. He holds a B.S. from the University of Illinois and an M.B.A. from New York University. He is also a Certified Public Accountant.

Andrew Summers serves as a principal of Morgan Stanley & Company. After several years of experience in international administration in London, he joined Morgan Stanley Asset Management to take responsibility for international operations. Mr. Summers graduated from St. Andrew's University, Scotland, with a B.Sc. in applied mathematics. He is a Chartered Accountant with the Scottish Institute.

Jayant S. Tata is head of the International Securities Group at the International Finance Corporation (IFC). He previously served as division manager in the Capital Markets Department and in the International Securities Group at the IFC. Prior to joining the IFC, Mr. Tata was a trustee at Batterymarch Financial Management, where he was responsible for managing the firm's emerging market funds. He has also served as vice president of corporate finance at the Prudential Insurance Company. Mr. Tata has a B.A. degree from New York University and M.A. and M.B.A. degrees from the University of Pennsylvania.

Rudolf van der Bijl serves as principal investment officer of the International Finance Corporation. Previously, he was manager of advisory and technical assistance in the IFC's Capital Markets Department, the private-sector-development affiliate of the World Bank. Mr. van der Bijl's work has dealt with advice to the IFC's regional capital markets divisions, relationships with other organizations, commercial banking, venture capital, and emerging securities markets. He has been active in investment and technical assistance and in advisory projects concerning capital market development in more than 50 countries. Mr. van der Bijl holds a degree in business administration from the University of Munich.

Shaw B. Wagener, CFA, serves as vice president and a director of Capital International and as chairman of Capital International's Emerging Markets Investment Subcommittee. He also serves as a Capital International regional portfolio manager, investing in Latin American equity and fixed-income securities. Mr. Wagener previously served as the head of equity trading at Capital Research and Management Company. He is a graduate of Claremont McKenna College with a B.A. in international relations.

Marc Wenhammar is the head of the fixed-income operations at Latin American Securities (London), a joint venture between Foreign & Colonial Management and Banco de Investimentos Garantia. He is also manager of the Latin American Extra Yield Fund and the Latin American Corporate Bond Fund. Mr. Wenhammar previously worked as an advisor and consultant for foreign investment promotion and implementation (joint ventures, direct investment, technology transfers) in Mexico. He received a master's degree in finance and a postgraduate degree in international trade from the University of Paris.

Managing Emerging Market Portfolios: An Overview

John W. Peavy III, CFA
Mary Jo Vaughn Rauscher Professor of Financial Investments
Edwin L. Cox School of Business, Southern Methodist University
Research Director, Research Foundation of the ICFA

Industry experts estimate that between $15 billion and $25 billion is invested in the marketable securities of emerging markets. That amount is up from $500 million only ten years ago, and the expectation is that $150 billion of foreign capital will flow into emerging markets by the end of the century.

Emerging market investments have become increasingly attractive to investors because of their handsome returns and overall diversification benefits. The low correlation of emerging markets with each other and, as a group, with developed markets provides the potential for enhancing the return and reducing the risk of the total portfolio. Many investors and prospective investors in emerging markets proceed with caution, however; they recognize that the risks must be carefully evaluated and understood. These investors must cope with high market volatility, economic and political instability, dramatic currency swings, illiquidity and high transaction costs, rapid and unpredictable growth, constant change, and a limited amount of reliable information. For most investors, investing in only one or a few emerging markets is an excessively risky approach; annual standard deviations of returns often exceed 50 percent, which is high enough to cause even the most venturesome investor to pause.

Fortunately, however, emerging market investments reap enormous diversification benefits. Whereas the individual emerging markets are characterized by substantial risk, a diversified portfolio of stocks representing a cross-section of many emerging countries possesses only a modest degree of risk. A remarkable statistic is that the 22.2 percent annual standard deviation of returns of the IFC (International Finance Corporation) Global Composite Index for the last five years is only slightly greater than the historical yearly standard deviation for U.S. stocks. Further diversification benefits exist when emerging market assets are combined with other asset classes. Thus, the surging popularity of investing in this newly recognized asset class is built on a strong foundation of attractive and empirically documented risk and return characteristics.

What Are Emerging Markets?

Although the term "emerging markets" was introduced only recently, it has become a widely recognized investment alternative, among both institutional and individual investors. So prominent is the concet of emerging markets that these investments have recently become accepted as a new asset class by many of the world's most successful investors. Unfortunately, however, no universally accepted definition of an emerging market exists, nor does a consensus about which countries merit the "emerging" status. Thirty years ago, Japan was an emerging market, and only slightly more than a century has passed since the United States was considered to be an emerging market. Presently, of course, both Japan and the United States are highly developed markets. The key message of these facts is that the composition of the emerging market universe is in a continual state of flux. Today's emerging market may be tomorrow's vibrant economy—thus, the attractiveness and excitement of this important new asset class.

The World Bank, by far the largest investor in these markets, defines a developing country as one having a per capita GNP of less than US$7,910. Only a handful of the many countries that can be called developing, however, can justly claim the emerging title. "Emerging" implies change and growth, both of which can occur only as the people of a country aspire and drive for improved economic, social, and political standards. Investors strive to identify the new emerging markets among the developing countries and invest in those markets, but they tend to shun those markets that do not possess the important traits that class them as emerging.

Once identified, to attract the attention and capital of foreign investors, an emerging market must also be investable. Although developing countries contain approximately 85 percent of the world's population, they represent only about 6 percent of the world's stock market capitalization. This disproportionate population–capitalization mix vividly illustrates the future growth potential for stocks in developing lands, but it also indicates the incredible selectivity that must accompany investments in these markets. The IFC, the senior compiler of emerging market returns, includes the stocks of only 18 emerging countries in its Investable Index. Furthermore, only 2 of those countries, Malaysia and Mexico, account for more than 50 percent of the IFC Investable Index. Obviously, the serious investor might question the diversification benefits of such a concentrated grouping.

Regardless of how they are defined, emerging markets have captured the attention and scrutiny of countless investors. No longer are the securities of these growing areas considered off-limits because of excessive risk. Rather, the allure of their rapid growth and unusually attractive diversification benefits has caused these assets to be warmly embraced by investors worldwide.

Significant differences exist among emerging markets, but as a group, they share one primary similarity—change. Through improved communications, individuals all over the world have seen the rewards of economic growth, and they want to participate. Only through continued change and improvement, however, can economic growth and the associated rewards persist. Jeremy Paulson-Ellis indicates that the structural changes occurring in the emerging economies are brought about by development and by political change and reform. Evolutionary changes are being driven by the rising aspirations of people and by demographics. These changes provide the environment for growth, and growth, in turn, leads to profitable opportunities for investors. Thus, Paulson-Ellis posits that the overriding motivation pushing investors toward emerging markets is the desire to add value at the edge of a conventional world index for some period by a reasonable margin.

Of course, risks accompany these opportunities, but investors can foster success by seeking out economies that have or will soon have political stability, open markets, policies that encourage growth, strong institutional structures, clearly defined investment rules, equitable taxation, market liquidity, and satisfactory intermediaries. According to Paulson-Ellis, if investors choose to invest in emerging markets, they will share in the opportunities, and the rewards will be considerable.

Investment Strategies in Emerging Markets

The provocative nature of investing in emerging markets is largely attributable to the wide spectrum of pros and cons associated with these assets. On the one hand, the high investment returns from these securities compare favorably with almost any other asset group, and the diversification benefits within the asset class and among other classes are substantial. On the other hand, investing in these diverse assets can be treacherous to the unsuspecting investor. The investments are laden with the significant risks of high volatility, limited liquidity, expensive trading costs, and poor information availability.

All in all, however, the advantages are so substantial that to neglect investing in these assets seems irresponsible. Consequently, to pursue these handsome returns, an investor must carefully diversify risk, reduce transaction costs, and enhance information flows, or else be prepared to suffer the consequences—sizable losses. In actively seeking the rewards of emerging market investing, an investor should employ an organized and proven research strategy. As with domestic investments, either a properly implemented top-down or bottom-up approach (or some combination) can enable the investor to achieve desirable returns while holding risk to an acceptable level.

Top-Down Investing

Given the return–risk profiles of individual emerging markets, a strategy of proper diversification among the markets is imperative. A top-down strategy may be used to identify the most attractive emerging markets and to determine the appropriate investment weighting for each market. In this approach, the key decision is not identifying the individual stocks to compose an emerging markets portfolio but, rather, ascertaining the respective weights to be assigned to the investments in each market.

Once the weights are estimated, either index funds or individually selected securities can be used to complete the portfolio. Lyle Davis suggests considering several alternative weighting schemes to design the final portfolio. The primary schemes involve capitalization weights, GNP weights, trading weights, equal weights, minimum risk, or forecasted returns. Each approach has its peculiar advantages and disadvantages. Consequently, Davis uses an optimizer to aid in the selection among the weighting alternatives. His results endorse a weighting scheme based on forecasted returns for the individual markets; Davis stresses, however, that this approach is highly sensitive to the accuracy of the estimated returns.

Among the alternative schemes, the weighting approach using historical trading weights produced dismal return–risk results. The primary reason is that the disproportionate trading volumes among these markets lead to huge portfolio concentrations in the most actively traded markets, which diminishes the diversification benefit. Davis cautions the investor to avoid concentrations in the markets and heed the crucial mandate to diversify.

Bottom-Up Investing

Fundamental analysis can be particularly effective in emerging markets because the markets are less efficient than developed markets and are relatively uncorrelated with other markets, because company performance can vary from market performance, and because research on individual companies can add significant value. Selecting individual stocks requires a healthy dose of top-down knowledge, but this knowledge is used to pick attractive companies, not countries. Note that top-down investing and bottom-up investing are not mutually exclusive. In fact, emerging market investing may be the ideal arena for these two approaches to work effectively in concert.

Shaw Wagener cites several factors common to successful bottom-up investing in emerging markets and suggests that the greatest opportunities may lie in companies that provide infrastructure to the developing nations, such as energy, power, and telecommunications companies. Among these potential investments, however, the company's country environment and management quality are crucial.

Moreover, unlike developed markets, the focus in emerging markets should be absolute valuation rather than relative values. These markets swing dramatically from undervalued to overvalued, so buying a stock that is cheap relative to its own market is dangerous, particularly when the market is overvalued.

Valuation Techniques and Research

Investing in emerging markets in recent years has yielded particularly attractive returns to the diligent and knowledgeable analyst. Donald Krueger warns, however, that performing diligent research in the emerging markets is not without difficulties. He identifies four major problems that confront outside investors. These problems revolve around the quantity and quality of information about the markets and the companies in the markets, currency uncertainties, political instability, and misleading value measures.

Foremost among these concerns is the lack of reliable information. Krueger believes that information providers in emerging markets do not understand what kind of information a fundamental analyst wants. In many cases, balance sheet information is unavailable because the focus in the emerging markets is typically on income statements. Yet in emerging market investing, balance sheet data are more important than income statement analysis in making investment choices. Consequently, the emerging markets analyst may lack significant information and should proceed with caution in making investment decisions.

Krueger also points out the pitfalls of using earnings ratios and book values to select among securities in emerging markets. Reporting standards vary considerably from country to country and sometimes even within a country. The conventional wisdom of purchasing securities based on levels of P/E ratios or price-to-book ratios does not hold in emerging markets because of the variety of ways these ratios are calculated among the various countries. Before entering an emerging country, an investor should search for good data sources and examine the accounting characteristics of the country. As a final comment, Krueger reminds investors that successful investing in emerging markets requires conscientiously applied common sense.

Gary Schieneman elaborates on the accounting issues that confront the emerging market analyst. Although emerging markets may sometimes be more effectively evaluated by using macroeconomic information than by analyzing fundamentals, selecting the most attractive individual securities in these markets requires fundamental analysis.

Of the myriad of accounting issues confronting the emerging markets investor, the most important is accounting for inflation. The inflation issue may be particularly troublesome in those countries that do not use price indexing.

In performing fundamental analysis, analysts frequently want to convert financial information to U.S. generally accepted accounting principles, but as Schieneman warns, such a conversion may not be correct and often is not feasible because of data unavailability. More important than restating data is understanding the differences in accounting approaches. Understanding the differences provides important insights into the quality of earnings, which will help the investor make a reasoned investment decision.

Further elaboration on the uniqueness of researching emerging markets is provided by Josephine Jimenez. She discusses three important aspects of the research in emerging markets: how and where to obtain information, what is involved in analyzing companies and markets, and how value is defined. Information for company valuations must be gathered from various published sources, participants in the local markets, and most importantly, country and company visits. Jimenez supports Schieneman's admonition that care must be exercised in interpreting the accounting information. Jimenez recommends that the analyst build a proprietary data base on emerging market securities. Once compiled, these data can be imputed into optimization models to value and compare investment opportunities.

Country Funds

The inability of most investors to invest directly in emerging market securities opens the opportunity for professionally managed funds composed of these assets. One of the oldest and most popular avenues for this kind of investing is the closed-end country fund. David Gill summarizes the reasons for investing in emerging market funds and discusses important aspects of setting up, administering, and monitoring such funds.

Gill emphasizes the importance of "doing it right" at a country fund; he demonstrates that a high-quality fund will sell at higher prices (that is, a higher premium to or lower discount from net asset value) than one of questionable quality.

For the investor, the choices among country funds are many; for example, nearly 30 China funds exist. Therefore, the investor must carefully evaluate the key characteristics of a fund before investing.

Asset Options in Emerging Markets

Discussions of investing in emerging market securities typically focus on equities; after all, the equity securities from these markets have provided the attractive rates of return in recent years. Other investment alternatives exist, however—debt, currency, and direct investment (for example, entrepreneurship and venture capital are mentioned by several authors, among them, Marc Faber and Jayant Tata). Foremost of these investment forms are debt securities.

Fixed-Income Securities

A large factor in the appeal of emerging market debt, and a topic to which the authors of these presentations frequently refer, is the Brady plan. Introduced in 1989, the Brady plan, which was accepted by both the International Monetary Fund and the World Bank, allows debtor countries to exchange loans for bonds, known as Brady bonds. The debtor countries receive some relief from their debt through partial debt forgiveness, lower interest rates, and extended maturities. In return, they agree to reduce their inflation rates, public-sector borrowing, and trade deficits. Many emerging markets—in particular, Argentina, Brazil, Mexico, and Venezuela—have huge amounts of debt in dollar-denominated restructured bonds. This debt presents some attractive investment opportunities. Moreover, currency is often not an issue with Brady bonds because the bulk of the debt is denominated in U.S. dollars.

Brady bonds are Euro-issues; they are not custodied in the country of issuance. These bonds are among the largest trading issues in the Eurobond market; in particular, bonds created from Mexico's restructured debt are regularly the most actively traded Eurobonds.

Brady bonds differ greatly from most emerging market or foreign equity investments because the costs of trading are generally small. Although some Eurocurrency and local market debt instruments are available in the emerging markets, Brady bonds are a larger part of the total emerging market debt universe than the other forms.

At an estimated $400 billion, emerging market debt has become a fertile arena for many investors. In recommending that investors carefully consider emerging market debt securities, Marc Wenhammar cites the debt's four key attractions: high rates of return, debt's new-asset-class characteristics (offering significant diversification benefits), improving creditworthiness of the countries, and prospects for sustainable growth. Wenhammar points out that, as recently as 1988, the only fixed-income investment instruments in these markets were bank loans and domestic debt. Now, especially with the surge in Eurobond issues and Brady bonds, this developing asset class has become a diverse and attractive investment outlet for many investors.

To capture the advantages of investing in emerging market debt securities, an investor must establish a realistic investment objective, perform research to evaluate credit and marketability risks, diversify among issues and markets, understand the nuances of buying and selling these issues, and maintain close contact with the various debt markets. Because of rapid value swings in the markets, neglecting any one of these activities can translate into substantial losses.

Patrick O'Brien testifies further to the popularity and growth of emerging market fixed-income investments. Taking a European perspective, he observes a soaring interest in Eurobonds and an increasing popularity of Latin American debt among European investors. Although U.S. investors dominate the emerging markets' debt markets, predictions are that European and Asian investors will occupy a growing presence in these markets. The consequence is likely to be a reduction in the cost of funds for emerging market borrowers.

Currency

Although much smaller in size and trading volume than the equities and fixed-income securities of emerging markets, the currencies of these developing countries are evolving as a legitimate investment outlet. Risks remain high among these investments, however, and because of the limited derivative products, investing in emerging market currencies typically involves taking total currency risk.

To reduce these risks, Francisco Portillejo contends, the international investor must investigate local economic, political, and monetary policies, evaluate the degree of governmental currency regulation, and select an appropriate counterparty. He also argues that, in order for the emerging markets' currencies to become a viable asset class, worldwide financial institutions must assist emerging countries in the development of their markets, procedures, and expertise.

Special Considerations in Emerging Market Investing

Investors in emerging markets confront several special considerations that differ considerably from the factors facing domestic investors. Among these special emerging market factors are political considerations, regulatory environments, trading and execution procedures, and issues of settlement and custody. Each of these considerations is reviewed by one or several authors.

Political Considerations

Political factors sometimes dominate investment decisions for the investor in emerging markets. Without an accommodating political environment, successful investing is unlikely and may be impossible. John Purcell delves into the plethora of political considerations confronting the emerging market investor and concludes that politics often leads economics in the developing countries. Purcell asserts that the analyst who evaluates and understands the political factors can stay ahead of the market and thus reap commensurately higher returns. Political analysis is also useful in evaluating the important element of sovereign risk of an emerging market investment.

Although the process of analyzing sovereign risk in the developing countries typically does not involve much quantitative data, Purcell argues that it can nevertheless be performed effectively by addressing several key political factors. Specifically, Purcell recommends that the diligent analyst examine a developing nation's political stability, policy coherence, flexibility, adaptability, and political commitment to appropriate economic policies, the strength of opposing political factions, the feedback generated by economic/political policies, and external support for the country's policies. In addressing each of these factors, Purcell concludes that countries experience political cycles as a result of unexpected shocks and crises. He introduces the concept of the "virtuous circle" to clarify how the cycle develops, the multiple phases through which developing countries pass, and the implications of the cycle concept for emerging market investors.

Purcell reminds investors that political analysis must be accompanied by economic analysis. In this connection, the reader is referred to Marc Faber's analysis of the economic cycles in emerging stock markets, discussed later in this overview.

Regulatory Environments

As is the case with political factors, the regulatory environment is a vital consideration to the success of emerging market investing, but it requires complex analysis. Rudolf van der Bijl explains that a serious regulatory effort is generally a precondition to the efficiency, transparency, and investability of a securities market. Moreover, the regulatory environment often dictates how an investor participates in an emerging country's market. To provide an acceptable investment climate, a securities market must perform certain basic functions, which need to be well defined through laws and regulations and through commonly accepted industry practices.

Van der Bijl cautions that fraud, abuse, and systematic risk exist in all markets, and these factors may be especially prominent in emerging markets; thus, the investor should carefully analyze several key regulatory factors before investing in an emerging market. Especially important considerations include how the securities industry sets and enforces its own rules, the role regulators play in economic development, the manner in which the regulatory environment blends into the country's laws and practices, and the sincerity and professionalism of the regulators.

Trading and Execution

Trading in emerging markets assumes a much larger role in the investment process than it does in developed markets. Alexander Peña cautions that the lack of liquidity, inefficiencies, and distrust of foreign investors in many emerging markets place a premium on careful, timely, opportunistic, and realistic trading. He advises that one of the most important investment decisions is the selection of a broker who knows the market: In choosing a broker, the investor must assess the advantages and disadvantages of using local and global brokers and consider confidentiality issues and transaction costs.

Settlement and Custody

Andrew Summers agrees that regulatory considerations must be evaluated. In addition, he focuses attention on settlement and custody issues. These issues may be taken for granted in developed markets, but they can present considerable difficulties in emerging markets. Summers recommends that the investor understand the following five settlement issues before venturing into these equity markets: settlement periods, penalties for failure to settle, delivery versus payment, foreign exchange, and communication barriers.

Summers posits that the key issues with regard to custody are the characteristics of the custodian bank, the extent and quality of the subagent network, and the custodian's foreign exchange capabilities, corporate actions department, and fee structure.

Economic Cycles

Emerging markets experience pronounced economic cycles. Today's explosive market may be tomorrow's economic disappointment, and vice versa. Consequently, to succeed in these volatile markets, an investor must recognize the current economic phase of a country and be able to assess the direction of the economic cycle.

Faber, adding economic analysis to Purcell's political analysis, urges investors to be sensitive to economic cycles in the emerging stock markets. He proposes a multiphase life cycle in which an emerging market moves in phases from obscurity to a high degree of recognition and popularity. Faber contends that early-phase investors often experience a favorable investment climate because fundamentals exceed expectations. In the subsequent phase, however, fundamentals may disappoint expectations, causing securities prices to decline. Consequently, the next phase will be characterized by increasingly inflationary pressures, evaporating liquidity, and deteriorating conditions. Securities prices may then collapse, initiating a period of desperation and disappointment. This sixth and final phase, in Faber's model, will ultimately reverse as the economic life cycle starts over again.

Faber concludes that, although the outlook for emerging economies is positive overall, opportunities are diminishing in countries that rely on exports of industrial products and rising in markets with large resource bases and substantial agricultural opportunities. Most exciting are the opportunities in entrepreneurship in emerging markets, especially in China.

Teresa Goodale echoes Faber's enthusiasm about the potential for economies that are developing free markets. She cites first-hand evidence, gathered during visits in 1992 and 1993 to Eastern Europe and Asia, that Poland, Czechoslovakia, and China now exhibit certain free-enterprise characteristics. Significant obstacles must be overcome, however, before these countries can truly emerge as investable markets.

Trends in Emerging Markets

Bold new trends have appeared in emerging markets. Tata uses an IFC perspective to identify the following three major trends: expansion of the asset class to include debt, real estate, and venture capital; broadening of the investor universe to include foreign institutional ownership; and deepening of the markets. Collectively, these trends indicate that emerging markets will continue to flourish and attract large chunks of foreign capital. These trends are not temporary; indeed, they are likely to grow stronger in the future. These markets may not mature as efficiently as desired, but they are developing and will continue to grow; Tata urges that they be nourished and encouraged.

Asset Allocation in a Portfolio

Asset allocation is at the forefront of the investment process. Effective allocation of resources among different asset classes is generally the most important decision in establishing the overall risk–return profile of a portfolio. The recent recognition of emerging market securities as a separate asset class (or series of asset classes) adds complexity to the choice of asset mix, but it also advances the possibility of raising returns and lowering risks. Given the newness of this asset class(es), an important step in considering emerging market investing is identifying how to construct portfolios of emerging market securities.

The Plan Sponsor's View

Investing in emerging market securities is a relatively new or yet-to-occur phenomenon for most large institutional investors. As a result, viewpoints about how to invest in these markets vary considerably. René Goupillaud uses the experience of ARCO Investment Management Company to illustrate how a plan sponsor might approach emerging markets investing.

Goupillaud confirms that the major reason for investing in emerging markets is the pursuit of superior returns. He believes that emerging markets will offer the best growth opportunities among the various classes of marketable securities. In addition, emerging market investments provide attractive diversification benefits, but Goupillaud warns that these benefits are based on historical relationships, which change over time.

Unlike some other professional investors, Goupillaud regards emerging markets not as a separate asset class but as a segment of international assets. Regardless of classification, he concludes that investing in emerging markets requires commitment and, in agreement with Jimenez, research, which includes as an indispensable element, travel to and understanding of the emerging countries.

Benchmarks for Performance Measurement

Several indexes exist to measure the performance of stocks in emerging markets. Because these indexes vary considerably, selecting the appropriate index is of paramount importance for the investor. Choice of the wrong index can bias a portfolio toward close conformity to the selected index even though a different portfolio might correspond better to the investor's investment policy.

Arjun Divecha, in providing a detailed comparison of five key benchmarks, carefully points out the trade-offs involved in selecting among the indexes. Important factors to evaluate include the countries that are included, the types of country weightings, number of securities, individual security and industry weights, and investability.

Although investable indexes are widely touted as benchmarks, they typically suffer from having so much weight in a few countries that active managers can use them only with difficulty. Divecha recommends the construction of a benchmark for an opportunity set—a subset of the investable set—for a particular investor. The portfolio manager can then be evaluated against a benchmark that accurately reflects the types and conditions of securities that are most likely to be owned in the actual emerging markets portfolio.

Final Note

The authors of these presentations provide investors with valuable insights into the pros and cons and the ins and outs of emerging market investing. Readers seeking further information on these important asset options should note particularly the sources of information given in the presentations of Jimenez and van der Bijl. In addition, an updated bibliography of published discussions of emerging markets is maintained by this author.

Introducing Emerging Markets

Jeremy Paulson-Ellis
Chairman
Genesis Investment Management

> Significant differences exist among emerging markets, but as a group, they share one primary similarity—change, change driven by the rising aspirations of their populations. This characteristic is producing the growth and tremendous opportunities investors in emerging markets are pursuing. Risks accompany the opportunities, but investors can foster success by seeking out economies that have or will soon have political stability, open markets, policies that encourage growth, strong institutional structures, clearly defined investment rules, equitable taxation, market liquidity, and satisfactory intermediaries.

This introduction defines emerging markets, examines the economics and issues that encourage investors to direct a portion of their assets to these markets, discusses the current situation and outlook for these markets, and illustrates the benefits of adding these investments to an international portfolio. In particular, the discussion will look at the concepts underlying the economic statistics and why the opening of their economies and markets to foreign investors should be attractive to national governments. In analyzing what investors should seek from investments in emerging markets, the presentation will discuss the problems of regulation, information flows, and other risk factors.

Neither international investing nor investing in emerging markets is new—particularly for Great Britain. For example, the Foreign and Colonial Investment Trust was established in 1868 and is still going strong. In the latter part of the 19th century, U.K. investment in the United States was substantial, and much of that could be considered investment in emerging markets.

An inkling of the similarity between emerging markets investment in the past and today can be gained from an issue the *Financial Times* published in 1993 to celebrate its centenary. The *Financial Times* marked the occasion by republishing its January 2, 1893, edition. Apart from the usual extensive reporting of the financial markets of the day for 1892, the edition also contained considerable comment on domestic and international economies. Nothing much seems to have changed. Recession was widespread in 1892; one in six of the United Kingdom's cotton spindles was idle. In addition, uncertainty over exchange rates was causing major problems—this time, to the silver rupee, the sole medium of exchange for the cotton trade.

Events in emerging markets were widely covered in this edition. A crisis in Portugal accompanied the collapse of the bond market. The Turkish market had been rigged. Hungary announced its intention to reform its internal administration. The most active foreign stocks were in South America, with such features as the Buenos Aires, Grand Southern, and Central Uruguayan railways. In the best tradition of markets—not solely emerging markets—a full-scale investigation was going on of a scandal among the directors of the Panama Canal Company.

Defining Emerging Markets

The term "emerging markets" is a recent introduction, and it is a convenient way of designating a new asset class to highlight the channeling of investment into the immature stock markets. Definition of the term is a problem, however. If you ask ten people what emerging markets are, you will get ten different answers.

The World Bank definition for a developing country as of 1991 was GNP per capita of less than US$7,910, but a dynamic process governs the definition of an emerging market. The world economy can be thought of as a pyramid, slowly changing, with countries becoming more prosperous and moving up while others come in at the bottom.

A major theme can be found running through any description of emerging markets, however: change. Change may be evolutionary or structural, but underlying the push for development are the rising aspirations of millions of people in the developing world. They want a government that is creating prosperity (defined inevitably, and perhaps unfortunately, by the Western media).

Such development requires massive amounts of capital. In India, for example, a forecast by one minister's advisor recently was that India alone will need some US$10 billion a year in order for the private sector to develop adequately. Thus, governments are attracted to the idea of opening their stock markets and making them accessible to foreign investors.

The kinds of changes going on in the emerging economies are structural changes brought about by development, and political change and reform. Evolutionary changes are being driven by the slowly changing aspirations of people and by demographics.

Change through Development

Development clearly generates above-average growth rates. It stimulates people's aspirations, demands for services, expenditure on the infrastructure, and consumer spending. Construction and financial services are both areas of rapid growth in the emerging economies. A change in consumer attitudes can be clearly seen in many places in the world by the Coke phenomenon: At a certain stage of the economic development cycle, Coca-Cola moves from being a luxury item to a daily necessity.

Political Change and Reform

Governments of emerging economies have been responding to the failure of prior statist and populist economic policies by a disengagement from business. Although they withdraw from much of business, they remain interventionists to a great degree, however, because they believe they can help by intervening. Nevertheless, this disengagement should result in more efficient allocation of resources in the emerging countries and result in enormous opportunities.

Aspirations

In the 1980s, despite all the difficulties and greed in the financial community, two great things happened to the world economy. The first was privatization. Privatization has been epitomized by former British Prime Minister Margaret Thatcher, but the way the British carried out privatization was not necessarily correct. Thatcher sold assets and used the proceeds for current expenditure. However, she also made privatization a household word in many countries, and this process undoubtedly will be followed by other governments. Thatcher has been much talked about and praised in other countries; she is probably held in greater respect outside than inside Britain.

The second great happening in the world was the rise of telecommunications, including its benefits and its faults. Because of satellite television, greater travel, fax, and improving telecommunications in general, a country can no longer be cut off from the outside world. This situation leads to increasing aspirations. The South African government probably rues the day it allowed in the television camera; doing so was the start of the death of apartheid. Telecommunications and the resulting questions that are raised about inhabitants' quality of life are becoming increasingly important in many emerging countries. Telecommunications, therefore, which was a present from the United States, is one of the cornerstones on which these countries will continue to grow: The aspirations of the people in these countries are forcing governments to do a better job than in the past, to allocate resources so that the economy can grow and bring about the growth of wealth for individuals.

Demographic Changes

Demographic changes are altering the pattern of strengths and weaknesses in the world. Let us look at some excellent statistics and forecasts produced by the World Bank and, within these figures, look at the most productive part of a population, in my view—the 25–34 age group, where training ability is at its greatest. The United States and the countries of South Asia will be used as examples.

Based on figures from the World Bank, the United States had a total population of about 250 million in 1990. That figure is expected to rise to 319 million by 2030. In 1990, the 25–34 age group comprised 43.8 million people, or 17.5 percent of the total population. By 2030, this group will actually fall to 38 million, or 11.9 percent.

In 1990, total population in South Asia was 1,182 million, and it is forecast to be 2,162 million by 2030. In 1990, the 25–34 age group accounted for 176 million of this population, or 14.9 percent. By 2030, however, this group is forecast to rise to no less than 379 million, or 17.5 percent of the total population. These data suggest the strengths that will be available in the South Asian countries for productive processes and the number of consumers that will be emerging in these areas.

In 1990, the 70-plus age group in the United States accounted for 20.7 million people, 8.3 percent of the total population. By 2030, this age group will comprise 51.6 million people, or 16.2 percent of the total population.

These contrasting statistics are staggering, and they must be pondered within an environment in which companies will have to consider carefully where to base their manufacturing and how countries are going to develop.

Why Invest in Emerging Markets

The rationale behind investing in emerging markets is an extension of the two basic reasons for any investing outside one's own country: to add value and to reduce overall portfolio risk through diversification. Whether expanding opportunities or reducing risk is the primary motivation is not always clear.

A third factor, a social aspect, may also be a motivating factor for certain international investors. Much of the early investment in Japan in the 1960s from the United Kingdom was sponsored by the Oxford and Cambridge colleges. They were much more ready to accept and develop the intellectual case for investing in Japan than were the more traditionally minded London institutions, such as the pension funds and merchant banks. The social factor may be one reason behind some of the early interest in the former republics that took place after the collapse of the Soviet Union. This motivation is difficult to quantify, and its presence is sensed more in some countries than others.

At the end of the day, however, most institutions have a fiduciary responsibility to their clients or their shareholders, trustees, or governments; thus, they look for ways to produce incremental return on investment in a controlled fashion. For the United States, initial international diversification by U.S. pension funds after the traumas of the early 1970s was driven by a desire to reduce risk; shortly afterward, however, this motivation was overtaken by the realization that the wide world offered many opportunities that were not available in domestic markets.

The overriding motivation pushing institutions toward emerging markets is the desire to add value at the edge of a conventional international equity portfolio. Adding value means doing better than a conventional world index for some period by a reasonable margin. A strong subsidiary factor is, as experience demonstrates, that international investing reduces risk.

Institutions are prepared to invest increasing amounts in emerging markets because they have done extremely well from this type of investment in the past. The best modern example is Japan.

In such markets as that of Japan after World War II, an investor is seeking access to the very high rates of economic growth and corporate profits that typically accompany the takeoff stage of development. In the late 1950s and through the 1960s in Japan, economic growth occurred on a sustained basis at over 11 percent a year. Early investors in the Tokyo market made many times their money, and the controlled way in which Japanese authorities managed the evolution and liberalization of the market served as a model to others, such as South Korea.

Recently, a sizable number of markets have provided excellent returns. **Table 1** shows what returns have been achieved in 15 emerging markets for one, two, and five years as of the end of 1992. The data show that the search for high returns from companies operating in well-managed developing economies or coping profitably with the problems and opportunities in the less well-managed economies is a natural long-term aim, especially for institutions with long-term horizons, such as pension funds or life insurance companies.

Table 1. Emerging Markets Annualized Returns to December 31, 1992
(U.S. dollars)

Country	One Year	Two Years	Five Years
Argentina	−26.2	88.9	46.8
Brazil	2.5	58.5	18.3
Chile	16.5	46.0	35.8
Greece	−27.0	−27.9	−2.0
India	26.2	16.9	16.2
Indonesia	0.2	−25.9	NA
Korea	2.6	−8.8	3.0
Malaysia	28.3	16.4	15.0
Mexico	19.9	54.0	57.9
Pakistan	−13.6	38.5	14.6
Philippines	18.4	35.5	13.3
Portugal	−19.0	−13.0	−14.8
Thailand	42.9	18.3	19.9
Turkey	−45.1	−56.9	−32.9
Venezuela	−42.4	−12.4	19.6
Index benchmarks			
MSCI World[a]	−7.2	3.8	11.0
IFC Composite	0.8	9.6	16.5

Source: IFC and Morgan Stanley Capital International (MSCI).

[a]Representing conventional international portfolio.

Recently, floods of press articles on emerging markets have been describing the flow of funds into open-end mutual funds for investment into emerging markets. Thus, emerging markets have started to become an asset class available to individual investors. Inevitably, this kind of money is more volatile than well-thought-out, institutionally planned money. Therefore, a significant increase in involvement by mutual fund investors could lead to high future levels of volatility in the emerging markets.

The Current Situation

During 1992, many new or additional statistics on the world economies have appeared. Among the most interesting are some long-range forecasts provided by the World Bank. **Table 2** shows the assumptions in the World Bank's scenario for the developed (G–7) countries. One important assumption is the relatively low growth rate for the developed countries. In contrast to this subdued performance predicted for the G–7 countries is the World Bank's forecast (shown in **Figure 1**) for the developing countries. As a group, they are forecast to do nearly twice as well as the developed countries during the remainder of this decade. This forecast is the first area that must be examined.

Table 2. External Conditions Facing Developing Countries
(average annual real percentage change except LIBOR)

	1980–90	1990–95	1995–2000
Real GDP (G–7 countries[a])	2.8	2.5	2.8
Inflation (G–7 countries)	4.5	3.5	3.3
Real LIBOR	5.0	2.8	3.2
Export price of manufactures	3.3	3.3	3.8
Oil	–6.6	–4.4	4.9
Commodities (except oil)	–5.1	–1.0	2.1

Source: World Bank, 1992.

[a]Canada, France, Germany, Italy, Japan, the United Kingdom, and the United States.

The statistics for the various developing areas have major differences, as **Table 3** shows. Note particularly that the figures for rates of growth in real GDP for the Middle East/North Africa show a dramatic resurgence from 0.5 percent per annum for the 1980–90 period to 4.5 percent for 1990 through the year 2000; Latin America's figures go from 1.6 percent to 4.2 percent. Note also how the better performing economies will produce growth at three times the rate of the major economies. The first signs of a resurgence are even visible in Sub-Saharan Africa. These statistics reflect the problems that are still present in Eastern Europe and demonstrate the need for selectivity in emerging market investing.

Remember, however, that government statistics in all emerging markets are subject to some variation from actuality because of the "black" (unofficial) part of the economy, which in some cases can account for as much as 30 percent of GNP. When the head of the statistical office of the Turkish government was asked about the background for some figures being shown, he said, "Well, of course, the statistics are nonsense. They are off by up to 50 percent, but we think they are understatements rather than overstatements."

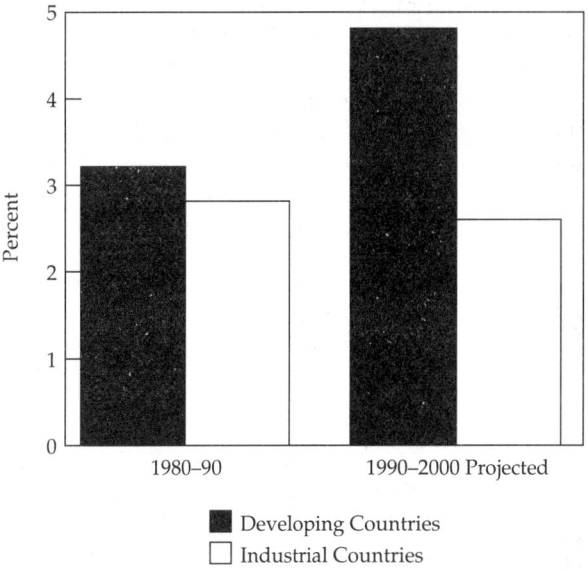

Figure 1. Growth of Real per Capita GDP
(average annual percent change)

Source: World Bank.

Table 3. Real GDP Growth Rates
(average annual percentage change)

Countries	1980–90	1990–2000
G–7 countries	2.8	2.6
Developing countries, of which:	3.2	4.9
East Asia	7.9	7.1
South Asia	5.4	5.0
Middle East/North Africa	0.5	4.5
Latin America	1.6	4.2
Eastern Europe	1.4	1.9
Africa (Sub-Sahara)	2.1	3.5

Source: World Bank estimates.

Nevertheless, the World Bank estimates reveal the general environment and show where companies should be able to prosper. Together with the increased access to stock markets and the desire by authorities to attract investment, these statistics indicate that the climate for emerging market investment during the 1994–2000 period should be as good as ever. Growth does not go in a straight line, however.

In the background to economic growth in the emerging markets, several reasons support continuation of some of the high growth rates that have been achieved:

- low cost, skilled labor—more accurately, a labor force that is eminently trainable;
- cheap land;
- an abundance of underexploited natural resources;
- high savings rates that allow strong investment;
- pro-business policies; although the process of liberalization does not necessarily mean total freedom, it *is* a process of gradually increasing freedom; and
- low tax rates.

Developing countries are experiencing a ground swell leading toward reduced government interference in the economy and, therefore, a greater role for the private sector. Stock markets are increasingly being seen as a useful part of a financial system. The hope is that the strong trend toward privatization will continue to spread among international investors and countries. If banks revert to lending on an uncommercial basis to these countries, however, that critical step could allow governments to go back on their commitments to the opening-up process.

Chile led the way in privatization in the 1980s. When Mexico's privatization program is complete, the companies under government control will be reduced from 1,155 to about 110, which would represent only 5 percent of GDP, compared with 25 percent about 10 years ago.

Although increased domestic accumulation of capital and the development of domestic savings are likely features of the emerging markets for the 1990s, the need for foreign capital to contribute to the privatization process will be acute.

Investing in Emerging Markets

Based on the World Bank definition of a developing country as one with under US$7,910 per capita GNP, the overall universe of emerging markets is, as illustrated in **Figure 2**, 85 percent of the world population, 17 percent of world GDP, and 6 percent of world stock market capitalization. The emerging market universe can be divided into primary and secondary countries as shown in **Table 4**. For investment purposes, the universe can be expanded to include not only those stock markets actually in a developing country but also companies within major stock markets that have a fixed proportion of either sales, profits, or assets in an emerging market. The composition of the universe must be constantly refined.

The definition of emerging markets is changeable, and the markets are mobile. Once a country becomes prosperous, the investor must not stay with it because it will move into the conventional international portfolio. Therefore, investing in emerging markets is about investing in the greatest possible amount of change.

To be successful, investors should look first for reasonable political stability or the promise of it, for open economies, and for economic policies encouraging growth. Strong institutional structures and clearly defined rules for domestic and foreign investment are also important. Discriminatory or penalizing taxation, especially on capital gains, is particularly discouraging to institutional investors.

Figure 2. Profile of the Emerging Markets

World Population

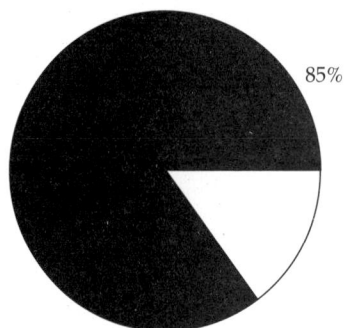

World GDP

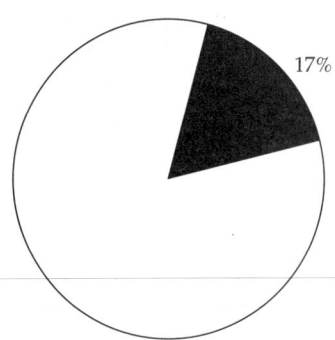

World Stock Market Capitalization

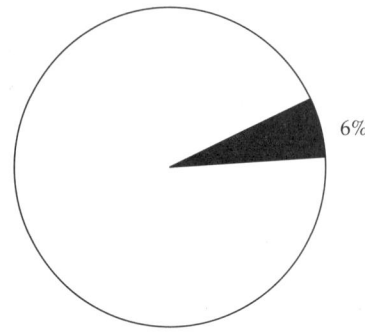

Source: World Bank, 1992.

Table 4. Categorization of Emerging Market Countries

	Primary Focus	Secondary Focus
Asia and Pacific	Bangladesh China India Indonesia Korea Malaysia Pakistan Papua New Guinea Philippines Sri Lanka Thailand Vietnam	Fiji
Europe	Greece Hungary Poland Portugal Turkey	Czech Republic Slovak Republic
Middle East and Africa	Botswana Mauritius Zambia Zimbabwe	Egypt Ivory Coast Jordan Kenya Malawi Morocco Nigeria Swaziland Tunisia
Caribbean and Latin America	Argentina Brazil Chile Ecuador Mexico Venezuela	Costa Rica Jamaica Trinidad and Tobago Bolivia Colombia Peru Uruguay

Source: Genesis Investment Management.

India made some grave mistakes, for example, when it opened up its stock market to nonresident investors. India believed that if it opened its market, everybody would rush in. The authorities did not notice that the demand for capital is massive throughout the developing world and, therefore, the country needed to make itself attractive to investors. India's initial rules contained extraordinarily high capital gains taxes. Nonresident investors, particularly fiduciaries, find it galling to be non-tax-paying entities in their own countries but be required by another country to pay, on the basis of short-term turnover, up to 65 percent of any realized capital gain in taxes. Why would a fiduciary for a non-tax-paying institution go to a country where the short-term capital gains tax is over 50 percent when the benefits could be gained free of tax in other areas of the world? Because of that tax, and a 22-page form that changed four times in the first month and a half, many investors did not want to be bothered with India. The country is now relaxing the rules and has said that it will reduce considerably the rates of tax on realized capital gains that penalize foreign investors.

Investors should look for either a well-established stock market or a new one that has been set up on a workable basis. They also need to find an adequate spread of stocks and reasonable liquidity, although this criterion is often a problem. Liquidity in markets is essential to avoid the takeover of emerging stock markets by flows of hot foreign money. The domestic institutional basis must be developed. The growth of local pension funds, insurance companies, and the like is essential if these countries are to realize their potential in the development of a local capital-raising mechanism.

Another necessity for success in emerging market investing is the development of intermediaries. The local companies need to improve standards of disclosure, and governments have to encourage this process. At present, the potential investor will be able to find little useful information; thus, much research work will need to be undertaken.

Obviously, research must not be the end of the process, however, because the differences in standards and accounting must be reviewed and measured. The importance of this factor was vividly shown to all investment managers by the announcement in New York of the Daimler Benz results on the German and U.S. accounting bases. How Daimler moved from a loss in U.S. terminology of 949 million deutsche marks (DM) to a profit in German terminology of DM168 million is a singular achievement. Researchers once thought getting the figures within 10 percent after six months of work was an accomplishment, and narrowing the differential to 7–8 percent after another six months was magnificent. The Daimler experience showed how difficult the task really is. If this accounting puzzle between two developed countries is difficult, imagine what it is like in emerging markets.

Spending too much effort in trying to refine research, however, may be a waste of time. The analyst must take what the locals publish, interpret it, look at it, and use it.

One of the many criticisms institutions have of emerging markets is the problem of scandals. Scandals do occur in emerging markets, and one of the reasons is that many of the participants in the markets lack understanding of the interrelationships among management, the work force, and the shareholders.

For example, in Indonesia over the years, some transfers of family-owned assets have occurred into publicly listed companies at prices that did not accurately represent value. Also, in the early days of opening up the China market, the backgrounds to the corporate structures were not clearly understood.

A recent feature of emerging markets is the increasingly vociferous activities of some of the investment banks in trying to promote new issues that they can underwrite. Their activities have led to a large number of issues taking place in New York, and in Europe as well, in American Depositary Receipt or Global Depositary Receipt form. Some of these issues appear, in both size and pricing, to be looking too far ahead when the individual companies are considered. Indeed, the investment banks need take account of the size of the local stock market because some match must exist between international development and development in the local stock market. Contribution locally is as important as short-term profitability.

The emerging markets are not very big yet. According to the International Finance Corporation (IFC) statistics for emerging markets, from 1987 to the end of 1992, they grew from $184 billion to about $700 billion. Foreign involvement, however, has increased dramatically. The raw data for historical figures are not available, but according to Micropal, the U.K. data base company, about $30 billion was invested in emerging markets at the end of 1992. Of the total, country, region, and global funds accounted for about $22 billion, separate accounts for $6 billion, and parts of institutional portfolios for the remaining $2 billion.

Regarding the size of some markets, note that as of 1992, the market capitalization of India was US$65 billion, smaller than Wal-Mart Stores. Thailand was US$58 billion, smaller than AT&T. Brazil was US$45 billion, smaller than the Coca-Cola Company. Overall market capitalization and the available float are figures the investor must bear in mind, particularly in light of the excitement about emerging markets that could be generated in the near future.

The likely development of overall market turnover and the role of the foreign investor have only recently been examined. As outlined in the World Bank scenario, more of the developing stock markets can be expected to open to foreigners, the private sector will have a healthy appetite for equity finance, and foreign investors will remain an important factor in the developing countries.

Based on the World Bank definition of emerging markets, **Table 5** shows the markets' total capitalization of approximately US$650 million moving to US$2,500 billion by 1999. The free float should increase, and foreign holdings should increase slightly faster because of the growing emphasis on the area

Table 5. Estimated Emerging Market Capitalization and Foreign Ownership
(dollars in billions; as of December 31)

	1992	1999	Seven-Year Growth Rate
Total	645	2,500	21.4%
Free float (taken as 25%)	161	625	
Foreign holdings	25	130	26.6
Percent of total	3.9	5.6	
Percent of free float	15.6	22.4	

Sources: IFC; Intersec, Ltd.; and Genesis Investment Management estimates.

Note: IFC composite less Taiwan.

by foreign institutions. The domestic markets will develop with the arrival of pension funds and increased investment by pension funds into equities. These sources should match the flow of funds from foreign institutions as equity becomes an increasingly important source of finance.

Adding Emerging Markets to an International Portfolio

The principle of diversification works as well for emerging markets as for mainstream equities. Diversification across a set of emerging markets leads to reasonable stability of returns despite significant volatility in the underlying stock markets. The IFC has done a considerable amount of work on returns from developed and developing markets, and **Table 6** contains a matrix of correlation coefficients for a selection of markets for the five years ending June 1993. Little correlation is evident between emerging and developed markets. Moreover, these correlations have experienced only a slight increase during recent years. Therefore, the investor can construct an emerging market portfolio as an efficient diversification vehicle. Intuitively, one would expect an increasingly integrated world with instant communications to result in increased links between the markets. Such a movement appears to be happening only to a limited degree, however. These correlations are expected to remain efficient because the markets at the top of the pyramid, those that are nearest to graduating, will probably attract the bulk of the short-term money.

Domestic influences are more important than international influences in moving prices most of the time in emerging markets. If these correlations persist, including emerging markets should lead to desirable characteristics for international portfolios. **Figure 3** shows the experience of one portfolio since 1989. The results reflect the mixing of an actively

Table 6. Correlation Coefficient Matrix of IFC Total Return Indexes, Five Years Ending June 1992

	USA	EAFE	BRA	CHI	GRE	KOR	MAL	MEX	POR	THA
USA	1.00									
EAFE	0.44	1.00								
BRA	0.22	0.18	1.00							
CHI	0.09	−0.20	0.21	1.00						
GRE	0.04	0.12	0.21	0.02	1.00					
KOR	0.20	0.39	−0.13	−0.08	−0.20	1.00				
MAL	0.50	0.51	0.16	0.05	−0.01	0.28	1.00			
MEX	0.29	0.15	0.07	0.07	−0.06	0.23	0.33	1.00		
POR	0.32	0.53	0.24	0.07	0.47	0.04	0.22	−0.02	1.00	
THA	0.37	0.21	0.06	0.17	0.18	0.07	0.56	0.18	0.14	1.00

Source: *Quarterly Review of Emerging Stock Markets* (Washington, D.C.: IFC, 1993).

Key:

USA	= United States	KOR	= South Korea
EAFE	= Europe/Asia/Far East Index	MAL	= Malaysia
BRA	= Brazil	MEX	= Mexico
CHI	= Taiwan	POR	= Portugal
GRE	= Greece	THA	= Thailand

managed emerging markets portfolio with a passive index from July 1989 through June 1993, the period during which the fund has been operating. The figure indicates that an investor can reduce risk until 40 percent of the portfolio is in emerging markets.

The longer term statistics produced by BARRA and the IFC show generally the same curve (in fact, somewhat steeper) as shown in Figure 3. One of the primary ingredients in successful investing in emerging markets is the patience to follow a long-term approach. Contrary to much popular mythology, successful emerging markets investment is not a quick fix; throwing money at the latest fashionable country and rotating it will probably lead to disaster and runs the risk of alienating the host country's authorities. Moreover, aggressive foreign investors can create the impression locally that attracting investment is easy and that money will flow in regardless of the quality of information, regulation, foreign exchange, or tax regimes in the country. Such investors also encourage unrealistically high valuations locally, which sucks in a new class of domestic investor whose first experience runs the risk of being extremely painful. This pattern developed in Indonesia and China, where investors were inevitably affected by short-term losses following the initial excitement.

Success requires that the investor search carefully to identify areas and companies that are likely to do well in the long term. Local investors frequently underestimate the attractions of their own stocks and, in these circumstances, it can be highly rewarding to bring to bear experience from elsewhere.

Risk

The risk in emerging markets investing can be broken down into four main categories.

▪ *Political risk.* Will the politicians turn back? This possibility is a real danger. Backsliding in the liberalization process will occur in some countries. The setback is likely to be temporary, however, because the resources for development that citizens are demanding will be available in the future only through the free-enterprise, private sector.

▪ *Absolute risk.* The investor who is heavily in-

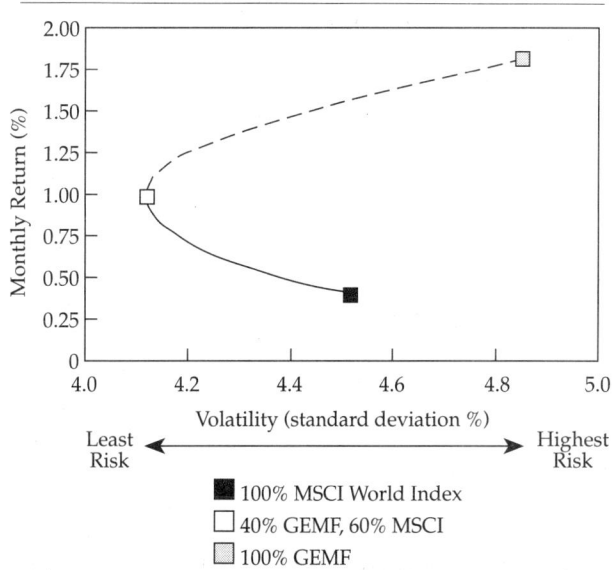

Figure 3. Adding Emerging Markets to an International Portfolio: Added Value and Risk Reduction

■ 100% MSCI World Index
□ 40% GEMF, 60% MSCI
▫ 100% GEMF

Sources: Genesis Investment Management.

Note: GEMF (Genesis Emerging Markets Fund Limited) for July 1989 through June 1993.

volved in emerging markets will occasionally lose money because of misinformation in certain places, but the same is true in developed markets. The investor must be careful and must know the portfolio. There is no substitute for careful work.

■ *Portfolio risk.* Fluctuations will be wide. One reason the overall, global philosophy is appealing is that it eliminates some of the risk in the portfolios.

■ *Business risk.* When managers look back at the end of this decade, if they have not already become involved in emerging markets, will they be among the top performing managers? The risk to the investment manager's career is the risk of *not* being in emerging markets. Staying out of emerging markets will undoubtedly damage the returns achievable in the manager's portfolio.

Overall, the risks exist, but they can be controlled and integrated quite satisfactorily into an institutional-quality portfolio.

Conclusion

Whatever the short-term problems, the aspirations of the millions outside the developed world exist and will need to be satisfied. They wish to enjoy the fruits of economic growth. They have seen what is available and want to taste it and share in it. These aspirations will give rise to opportunities. If investors choose to invest in emerging markets, they will share in the opportunities, and the rewards will be considerable.

Question and Answer Session

Jeremy Paulson-Ellis

Question: How much of the recent market performance among the emerging markets is attributable to the tremendous influx of foreign investor funds into these markets? How would one hedge against the downturn should the individual investors pull out of these markets?

Paulson-Ellis: A real surge in "veneer" investing has occurred in certain emerging markets, but the amount is impossible to quantify. Two types of money are going into emerging markets: the genuinely committed money, which looks at emerging markets as a continuing part of a portfolio, and the money that is being driven by the constant articles in the press. The latter type of money is relatively dangerous because it can turn around, and it could cause considerable problems.

For example, in Mexico, up to 80 percent of turnover in the early part of 1982 was being accounted for by Wall Street investors. Much of that was "recommended money"—that is, money invested to follow the latest hot idea. Mexico was hot one week; then maybe smaller U.S. companies the next; and somewhere else the next week. Protection against that type of money is very difficult. You must look at emerging markets without getting caught up in the fashions.

Another example is China, where at one point in the market-opening process, 18 funds were trying to invest in 15 locally quoted B shares. That situation is dangerous and virtually guarantees losses. Knowledge is the investor's only protection.

Question: In what ways should foreign investors be aware of what the local investors in a market are like, and what are the desirable and undesirable characteristics of local investors?

Paulson-Ellis: One undesirable characteristic is domination of the local investors by foreign money. The flow of hot money in and out of the market may cause disequilibrium and have side effects on the economies. Usually, the effects arise when money is flowing out rather than in.

The channeling of an inward flow of funds can benefit from a certain amount of regulation during an initial period. During that period, the domestic institutions begin to understand how the foreign money is being managed and the aims of the foreign investors. They build up their own structures of pension funds or insurance companies with investment departments and have time to get used to the role of investment into equities. After all, many places have no tradition of institutional equity investment because equity has been owned by individual families, not institutions. As foreigners, visitors, and guests, outside investors should always be cognizant of the state of development of a local market. They should not try to dominate a country, which can bring about the dangerous outflow of funds at some point in the future.

Question: How does China now compare with Japan in the 1950s in terms of its political, legal, and industrial infrastructure as an emerging market?

Paulson-Ellis: China has hardly started. The specialist on China at Genesis Investment Management has said that an enormous amount of work has been done and that change in the freedoms within the economy has been radical. No basic corporate structure yet exists, however, that is as refined as investors would like. The first investment bankers to arrive on the scene in Beijing and Shanghai probably did not bother to define a B share and what the investor would actually own. The bankers were more interested in defining the profit they were going to get at the end of the issue period.

Overall, China has not gone fully down the road of producing procedures and regulations that are satisfactory. Its process compares badly in this respect with Japan, which had a regulatory structure imposed by the United States after World War II, even though the structure was not always followed in some informational areas. In China, there is not yet an understanding of the role of the investor. What is a shareholder? What is the shareholder's role in the development of the economy and of a company? As yet, managers are looking for benefits too much in their own terms rather than as shared with others.

Question: How does Russia fit into the focus list of emerging markets?

Paulson-Ellis: Russia is showing only the first signs of stirring. Russia will be for the next generation of investment managers.

Question: Does the coming of some peace in the Middle East open up the potential for more markets developing there? Is political stability in the Middle East enough to entice you to invest in that part of the world?

Paulson-Ellis: Israel is not an emerging market. It is far too wealthy to be classified as such.

As for the Arab countries, some time will be needed for an overall structure to be put in place. Therefore, more work needs to be done on political stability. In addition, the markets are seldom truly open. At one time in the past, foreign investors could invest in the bond market in Iran (until the government telephoned one day and told everyone to stop). You could also invest in equities, but 90 percent of the equity market was controlled by one brother and 90 percent of the bond market was controlled by another brother.

Question: Given the problems with information flow and the unusual things that go on in these emerging markets, how can an investment manager sitting thousands of miles away (rather than on the ground in the markets) effectively manage a portfolio?

Paulson-Ellis: Where to locate investment management, whether you put it in the market concerned or centrally locate it, is the subject of argument. Some firms believe you must be based everywhere. Communications between the head office and local offices may experience just as many problems, however, as traveling and communicating internally in a central investment management center. If you are following the long-term investment philosophy and trying to assess which economies and which companies have comparative advantages, you will not be following a very active day-to-day policy. Therefore, you can manage away from the markets concerned.

Also, taking an international perspective often allows you to spot trends. Being away from the local market allows you to reflect and make decisions that will add value in the long term. If you sit on top of the local market, you may follow the fashion and be trapped into more rapid turnover than you intended.

Locating management remote from the markets requires a tremendous amount of travel time and expense, however. The managers must spend time in the markets.

Top-Down Investing in Emerging Markets

Lyle H. Davis, CFA
Managing Director
Boston International Advisors, Inc.

> Analysis reported here supports the prescription that investors should be in the emerging markets. Investors need to go further, however, and diversify within those markets.

Emerging markets in the aggregate have interesting characteristics: high investment returns, high volatility, low correlation with other markets, small market capitalizations, limited liquidity, and expensive trading costs. A brief description of each of these characteristics will lay the groundwork for discussion of approaches to composing an emerging markets portfolio.

Characteristics of Emerging Markets

Emerging market returns are attractive. **Table 1** shows the five-year annualized compound rates of return up to July 1993 for the International Finance Corporation (IFC) Global Total Return Composite Index and its component parts. The annualized return on the IFC composite, which is the market-weighted total of 18 emerging countries in the IFC Composite Index, was 11 percent a year during this period. The Morgan Stanley Capital International EAFE Index earned 5.9 percent, and the S&P 500 Index earned 14.6 percent during the same period. As the regional indexes indicate, the Latin American countries, averaging 33.7 percent a year, had the highest returns. The Asian countries averaged only 7.2 percent a year. Argentina produced the best country returns and Indonesia the worst during this period.

These markets exhibit tremendous volatility of returns (risk). Table 1 also shows annualized risk, measured as the standard deviation of monthly returns, for this same five-year period. For example, Argentina's standard deviation was 117 percent; its annualized return was 47 percent.

Despite the volatility of individual countries, these markets offer a huge diversification benefit to portfolios. Most of the inherent risk in these countries can be diversified away by investing in a broad cross-section of the countries. Aggregating the countries together drives volatility down substantially, as evidenced by the relatively low volatility of the IFC Composite Index (22.2 percent standard deviation). The IFC composite's volatility is generally similar to that of the EAFE Index; the U.S. index's volatility is quite a bit lower than either of the other two. The Latin America and Asia regional indexes illustrate that the more diversification, the better; they individually have substantially higher volatility than the IFC Composite Index, with standard deviations of 30.8 percent and 26.2 percent, respectively. Only two countries have a lower volatility than the IFC Composite Index, a fact that also illustrates the power of diversification.

The volatility of returns can be seen quite clearly in **Table 2** in the five individual 12-month periods making up the five-year average shown in Table 1. The annual returns in Argentina, the most volatile country, ranged from –47.0 percent to 260.9 percent. These returns are very end-point specific; that is, the rankings can be much different at different period ends. Some investors may see plenty of opportunity for market timing in these numbers; others will see real risk.

The volatility is illustrated in **Figure 1**, which shows the trailing 12-month total returns, in U.S. dollars, for Argentina, Brazil, Chile, Mexico, and Venezuela. The figure shows that returns can exceed 200 percent. In two instances—one in Argentina and one in Venezuela—returns exceeded 700 percent in one 12-month period. On the downside, in markets where losses are limited to 100 percent, losses of more than 50 percent are not unusual.

Another attractive characteristic of emerging markets is their low correlation of returns with other markets. **Table 3** shows the correlations among the IFC Composite Index, the MSCI EAFE Index, the

Table 1. Comparison of Market Returns and Risks, Five Years Ended June 30, 1993

Market	Annual Return	Annual Risk
IFC Global Total Return Composite Index	11.0%	22.2
Argentina	47.6	117.6
Mexico	42.9	26.7
Chile	42.2	25.9
Colombia	40.3	37.0
Venezuela	26.0	50.6
Pakistan	22.5	28.6
Thailand	19.8	28.0
Brazil	19.6	76.8
Greece	19.0	48.4
Malaysia	15.9	21.2
Turkey	13.3	71.8
Philippines	12.9	32.0
Jordan	12.1	19.4
India	9.5	37.6
Korea	0.6	30.1
Taiwan	–2.2	52.6
Portugal	–3.8	24.3
Indonesia	–16.9	31.4
MSCI EAFE Index	5.9	20.4
S&P 500 Index	14.6	13.2
IFC Latin America regional composite	33.7	30.8
IFC Asia regional composite	7.2	26.2

Source: IFC Emerging Markets Database.

S&P 500 Index, the IFC Latin America regional composite, and the IFC Asia regional composite. The correlation between the IFC Index and the MSCI EAFE and U.S. indexes is about 0.20 percent. Interestingly, the IFC Asia regional composite is highly correlated with the IFC Composite Index but not with the IFC Latin America regional composite.

Table 3 also shows that the countries within emerging market regions are uncorrelated. In Latin America, such neighboring countries as Argentina and Brazil have a negative correlation. The highest correlation in Latin America is the 33 percent between Mexico and Argentina. Statistically, a reasonable conclusion is that the correlations between these countries are totally insignificant. They look like pure noise. There is no "Latin America Effect," at least not one that can be measured.

The correlations between countries in Asia are somewhat higher, particularly between some of the large markets, such as Taiwan, Thailand, and Malaysia. The highest correlation is the 55 percent between Thailand and Malaysia.

The total market value of the countries in the IFC Composite Index was about $850 billion as of June 30, 1993, compared with $6.5 trillion for the EAFE markets, $4 trillion for the U.S. market, and $12 trillion for the world. **Table 4** shows the capitalization of the IFC emerging markets by total market capitalization and by investable capitalization. Emerging markets comprise about 7 percent of the total world market value. The capitalization of the IFC Investable Composite Index (IFCI) is only $238 million. By comparison, the MSCI EAFE Index total value is about $4 trillion, 60 percent of the market value of the countries it represents, and the S&P 500 is about $2.4 trillion, representing almost 60 percent of the total U.S. market.

The country weights are quite different between investable indexes and total-market-value indexes. Mexico, for example, goes from 15 percent of the market value of the IFC Global Composite Index to about 30 percent of the IFC Investable Composite Index market value. In other words, a big difference exists between the gross market values available in the emerging markets and the portion of those markets in which a foreigner can truly invest.

Liquidity in emerging markets is low. **Table 5** shows various measures of liquidity for the countries in the IFC Composite Index. Of these countries, liquidity is concentrated in Taiwan and South Korea, two markets that are still largely closed to foreign investors. The high share of trading in the top ten stocks in many markets suggests that trading is limited and concentrated in a small number of stocks. The trading volume shown in Table 5 represents about 100 percent annual turnover of the value of the markets in aggregate. The shares are trading, but the market values are small in these markets.

The final characteristic of emerging markets is

Table 2. IFC Global Total Return Indexes: Annual Returns as of June 30, 1989–93

Country	1993	1992	1991	1990	1989
Argentina	–24.2%	191.4%	65.7%	–47.0%	260.9%
Brazil	63.8	7.3	66.8	–34.8	27.9
Chile	–9.8	56.5	101.0	40.3	46.1
Colombia	–9.2	243.7	7.5	52.0	6.9
Greece	–27.1	5.2	–46.0	423.6	10.2
India	–30.8	67.2	13.8	5.9	13.0
Indonesia	10.3	–10.6	–41.8	NA	NA
Jordan	48.7	11.6	0.8	20.1	–11.8
Korea	35.8	–21.2	–17.4	–18.9	43.7
Malaysia	27.4	11.4	2.8	23.7	15.8
Mexico	8.3	38.8	63.1	47.4	64.6
Pakistan	–18.2	132.8	30.0	3.1	8.0
Philippines	–8.6	55.2	–11.4	–7.4	57.9
Portugal	–10.2	8.5	–28.1	37.9	–14.8
Taiwan	–10.4	–19.7	9.1	–44.4	103.5
Thailand	30.6	15.9	–19.3	58.4	27.4
Turkey	51.5	–36.2	–59.6	295.5	21.2
Venezuela	–31.4	17.9	234.0	112.0	–44.6

Source: IFC Emerging Markets Database.

NA = not available.

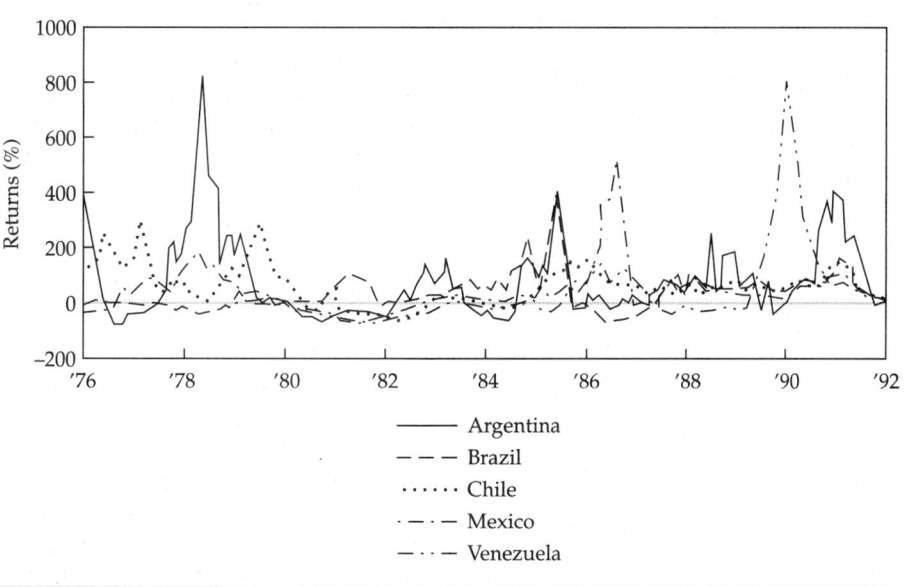

Figure 1. Volatility of Returns: 12-Month Trailing Total Returns in Latin America
(in U.S. dollars)

Source: IFC Emerging Markets Database.

that trading is expensive. **Table 6** shows estimated trading costs in selected emerging markets. As a rule, the minimum cost of trading in these markets is 1.5 percent; it can be much higher and is frequently as high as 5 percent. A typical trade would cost roughly 2.5 percent, or 5 percent for a round trip. Because trading is so expensive, investors must consider carefully how they will earn that cost back.

Table 3. Market Correlations, Five Years Ended June 30, 1993

Regional

	IFC	EAFE	U.S.	LAT	ASIA
IFC	1.00				
EAFE	0.23	1.00			
U.S.	0.19	0.44	1.00		
LAT	0.44	0.16	0.24	1.00	
ASIA	0.96	0.19	0.13	0.20	1.00

IFC Latin America regional composite

	ARG	BRA	CHI	COL	MEX	VEN
ARG	1.00					
BRA	–0.18	1.00				
CHI	–0.02	0.21	1.00			
COL	–0.08	0.15	–0.13	1.00		
MEX	0.33	0.07	0.07	–0.06	1.00	
VEN	0.06	–0.17	–0.20	0.20	–0.11	1.00

IFC Asia regional composite

	IND	IDN	KOR	MAL	PAK	TAI	THA
IND	1.00						
IDN	0.04	1.00					
KOR	–0.16	–0.01	1.00				
MAL	–0.02	0.44	0.28	1.00			
PAK	–0.07	0.07	–0.01	–0.03	1.00		
TAI	–0.15	0.31	0.10	0.22	–0.07	1.00	
THA	0.20	0.35	0.07	0.56	0.07	0.13	1.00

Source: Quarterly Review of Emerging Stock Markets, Second Quarter (Washington, D.C.: IFC, 1993).

Key:
- ARG Argentina
- ASIA IFC Asia regional composite
- BRA Brazil
- CHI Chile
- COL Colombia
- IND India
- IDN Indonesia
- KOR South Korea
- LAT IFC Latin America regional composite
- MAL Malaysia
- MEX Mexico
- PAK Pakistan
- TAI Taiwan
- VEN Venezuela

Portfolio Weighting Approaches

Given the characteristics of emerging markets, the objectives of an emerging markets portfolio is to participate in attractive returns, diversify risk, and minimize trading costs. Various approaches to weighting are available for composing such a portfolio. The primary ones involve capitalization weights, GDP weights, trading weights, equal weights, minimum risk, and forecasted returns.

■ *Capitalization weights.* The assumption behind this approach is that size in some fashion predicts both return and risk. **Figure 2** illustrates the country weights prescribed by two capitalization measures—total market capitalization and IFCI weights (refer to Table 4). The two measures lead to remarkably different weighting schemes. Which of the two approaches is superior is not obvious, but weighting by total capitalization is somewhat misleading for foreign investors because not all markets are fully investable.

■ *GDP weights.* **Figure 3** illustrates GDP weights. This approach assumes that the size of the economies in these countries will have some effect on predicting returns and risks in the markets. Investors have had some success with passive EAFE strat-

Table 4. Total versus Investable Market Capitalizations
(U.S. dollars in billions)

Market	Market Capitalization	Percent[a]	Investable Capitalization	Percent[a]
IFCI[b]	$850.0	7.4%	$238.0	3.6%
Mexico	130.0	15.3	68.4	28.7
Taiwan	122.0	14.4	2.4	1.0
Korea	118.8	14.0	7.5	3.1
Malaysia	118.8	14.0	53.9	22.6
Brazil	76.0	8.9	28.4	11.9
Thailand	62.2	7.3	10.7	4.5
India	59.0	6.9	5.9	2.5
Chile	34.7	4.1	4.7	2.0
Argentina	27.0	3.2	13.4	5.6
Turkey	22.9	2.7	15.1	6.4
Indonesia	17.1	2.0	5.4	2.3
Philippines	16.6	2.0	5.4	2.2
Portugal	10.4	1.2	4.0	1.7
Greece	9.4	1.1	4.8	2.0
Pakistan	7.1	0.8	1.5	0.6
Venezuela	7.1	0.8	2.4	1.0
Colombia	5.3	0.6	3.5	1.5
Jordan	5.2	0.6	0.8	0.3
EAFE[b]	6,394.0	56.0	3,858.0[c]	59.0
United States[b]	4,184.0	36.6	2,444.0[c]	37.4
World[b]	11,428.0	100.0	6,540.0	100.0

Sources: Quarterly Review of Emerging Stock Markets, Second Quarter (Washington, D.C.: IFC, 1993), and *Emerging Markets Factbook 1993* (Washington, D.C.: IFC Emerging Markets Database).

[a]Individual country markets are percentage of IFCI; all others are percentage of world market.
[b]Dollar figures are rounded.
[c]Investable capitalizations for the EAFE and the United States represent the market values of the MSCI EAFE Index and the S&P 500 Index, respectively. For the other countries, investable capitalization represents the IFCI.

egies using GDP weights; one advantage this weighting offers is that it moderates the exposure to Japan that would result from a capitalization-weighting approach. In the case of emerging markets, Brazil

Figure 2. Capitalization Weights

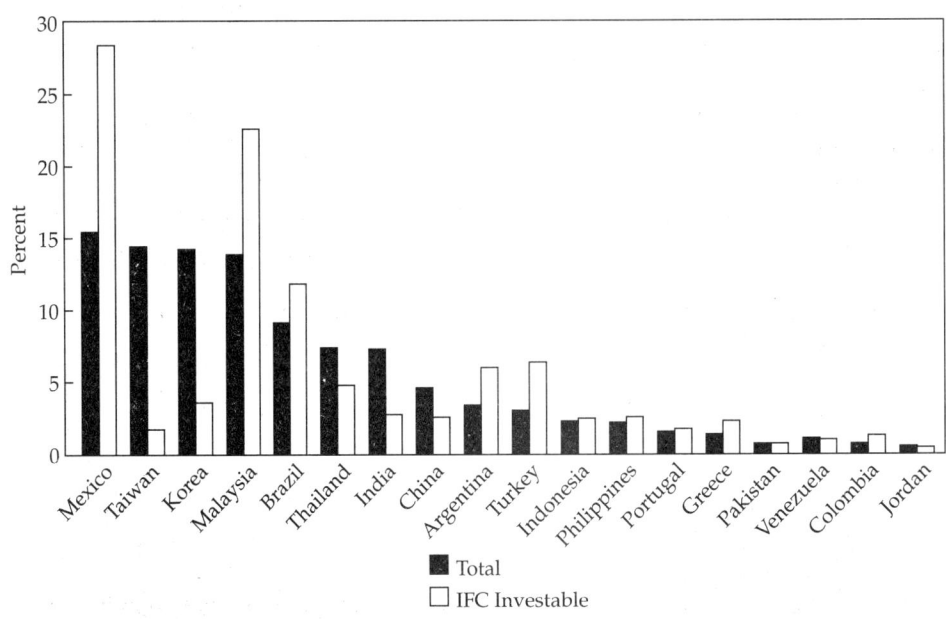

Source: IFC Emerging Markets Database.

Figure 3. GDP Weights, 1991

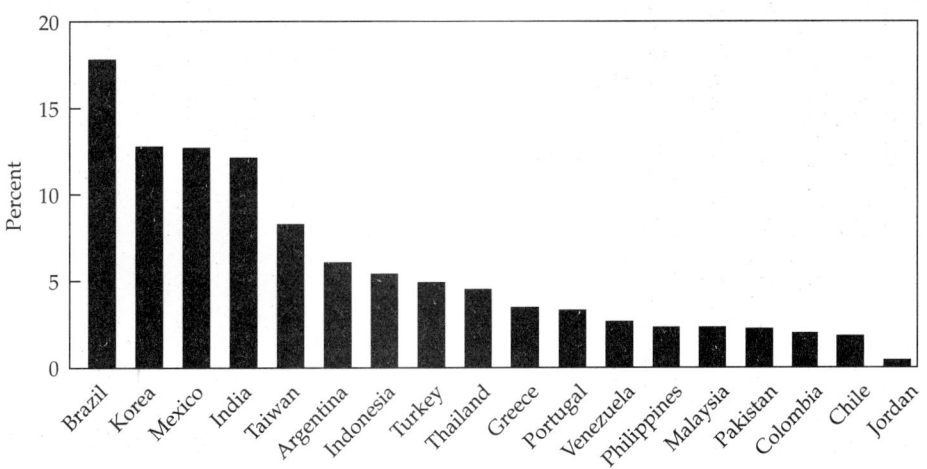

Source: IFC Emerging Markets Factbook, 1993.

Figure 4. Trading Weights

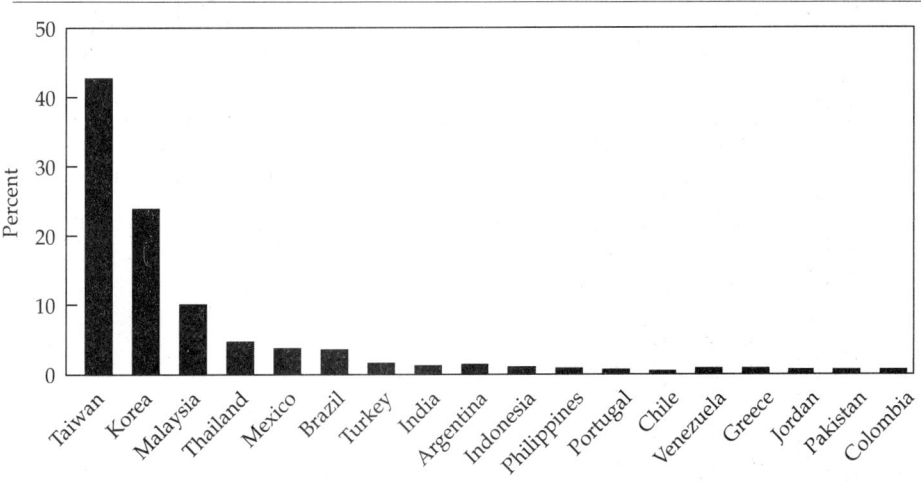

Source: Quarterly Review of Emerging Stock Markets, Second Quarter (Washington, D.C.: IFC, 1993).

had the largest economy in 1991 based on dollars of GDP, followed by Korea, Mexico, India, Taiwan, Argentina, and so forth. Following the GDP-weighting approach would prescribe investing 17–18 percent in Brazil and on down to less than 1 percent participation in the small countries. The approach would result in beneficial diversification but would also provide fairly high concentration.

■ *Trading weights.* An alternative is allocation by trading weights (refer to Table 5); that is, weight each country by its share of total trading in the emerging markets. The rationale is that liquidity is correlated with returns. The allocation to emerging market countries by trading weights is illustrated in **Figure 4**. This allocation, because it is essentially based on relative liquidity of markets, is concentrated heavily in Taiwan. This strategy is thus not viable for most foreign investors because their participation in Taiwan's market is restricted.

■ *Equal weights.* The ultimate diversification is achieved by applying equal weights to emerging country markets. **Figure 5** shows two versions—one using pure equal weights and one using size-adjusted equal weights. The pure approach assigns about 6 percent to each of the 17 countries in the IFC Index. (Indonesia is absent from certain figures because five years of data are not available for it.) The alternative is to give a large allocation to the five largest countries—Brazil, Mexico, Malaysia, Argentina, Thailand, and Turkey—and a smaller allocation to the 11 small remaining markets.

■ *Minimum risk.* Investment may also be allocated through a model that generates the minimum-risk (minimum-variance) portfolio. This approach

Table 5. Liquidity in Emerging Markets: Value Traded

Country	First Half 1993 (Millions of U.S. Dollars)	Second-Quarter Daily Average	Share of Trading in Top Ten Stocks
Taiwan	$184,845	$1,083	23%
Korea	107,558	874	13
Malaysia	45,462	545	13
Thailand	24,094	161	34
Mexico	18,897	151	51
Brazil	17,639	177	53
Turkey	7,284	82	37
India	6,969	61	40
Argentina	4,878	33	73
Indonesia	3,202	23	40
Philippines	2,143	17	49
Portugal	1,800	16	36
Chile	1,173	9	61
Venezuela	864	10	90
Greece	859	5	51
Jordan	845	9	48
Pakistan	505	5	57
Colombia	262	3	66

Source: Quarterly Review of Emerging Stock Markets, Second Quarter (Washington, D.C.: IFC, 1993).

Table 6. Estimated Trading Costs in Selected Emerging Markets

Market	Commissions and Taxes	Impact	Total
Latin America			
Argentina	0.9%	1.5%	2.4%
Brazil	1.1	1.5	2.6
Chile	1.5	1.5	3.0
Mexico	0.5	1.5	2.0
Venezuela	1.1	1.5	2.6
Europe			
Greece	0.9	1.5	2.4
Portugal	0.8	1.5	2.3
Turkey	0.9	1.5	2.4
Asia			
Indonesia	1.0	1.5	2.5
Malaysia	0.6	1.5	2.1
Philippines	1.7	1.5	3.2
Thailand	1.0	1.5	2.5

Source: Boston International Advisors.

assumes that return correlations will remain stable over time. **Figure 6** shows weights for the minimum risk portfolio for the 17 emerging markets. The theory is that the opportunity for returns is equal in each of these markets, and therefore, the goal is to minimize risk. The information in Table 2 and Table 3 is used by an optimizer to prescribe (in this case, using the BARRA emerging markets model) a portfolio. Some minimum and maximum parameters must also be stated; otherwise, the optimizer will simply pick the lowest risk market. In this case, as shown in Figure 6, the optimizer came up with the largest weight in Mexico, then Malaysia and Chile. These markets were given a weight of 10 percent each, which was the maximum allowed the optimizer.

■ *Forecasted returns.* This approach allocates investments based on forecasted returns, on a risk-ad-

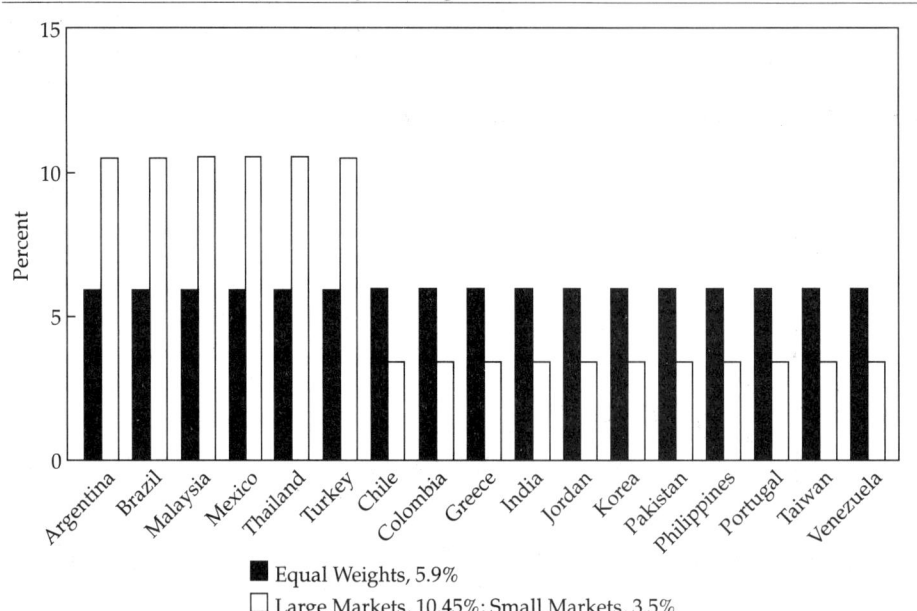

Figure 5. Pure and Adjusted Equal Weights: 17 Countries of IFCI

■ Equal Weights, 5.9%
☐ Large Markets, 10.45%; Small Markets, 3.5%

Source: Boston International Advisors.

Note: Five years of data not available for Indonesia.

Figure 6. Minimum-Risk Portfolio: Optimized Minimum Variance

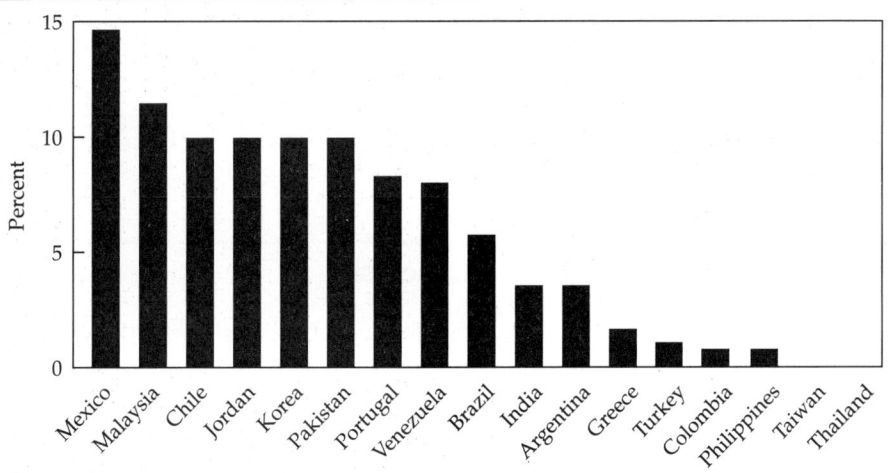

Source: Boston International Advisors.
Note: Five years of data not available for Indonesia.

justed basis, as shown in **Figure 7**. Using historical returns instead of forecasted returns, the optimizer would generate a portfolio similar to the minimum-risk portfolio shown in Figure 6.

Table 7 compares the return and risk for the five years ended June 1993 for each of the weighting schemes and the IFC Composite Index. If market weights based on full market capitalizations for the whole period had been used, five-year returns would have been about 9.8 percent with a 19.2 percent standard deviation. These results are not very different from those of the weighting by IFCI capitalization (return of 15 percent and standard deviation of about 19 percent), which is to be expected. That the weighting by investable capitalization produces higher returns is probably an accident. The results for GDP weights are also remarkably similar to the results of the capitalization-weighting approaches.

The use of trading weights produces a terrible return because of Taiwan and Korea; these country markets had poor returns and the biggest weights over the five-year period. This approach also destroys diversification because of the concentration in those two markets.

The two equal-weighting strategies are interesting because they produce similar returns to GDP and market-capitalization weighting, in the 20 percent range, but with considerably lower risk. This approach provides the many benefits of diversification by broadening exposure to different markets.

Using an optimizer really drives down risks. Returns are similar to returns for the two equal-

Figure 7. Forecasted Return with Optimized Risk

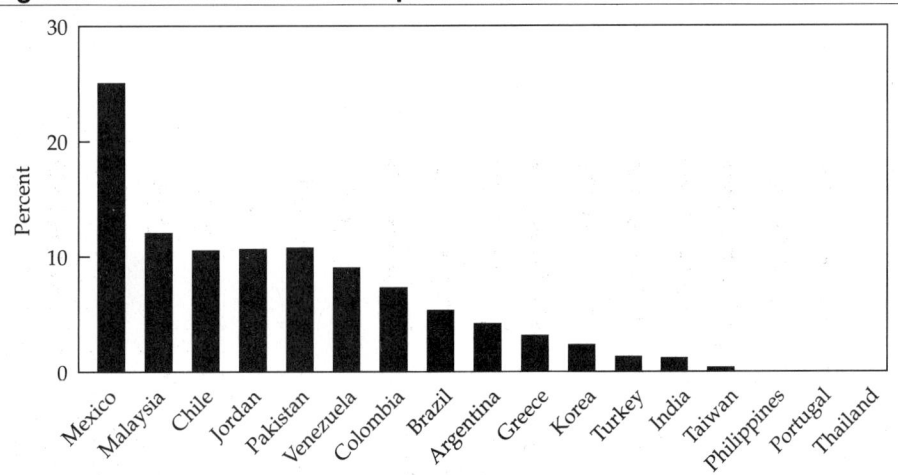

Source: Boston International Advisors.
Note: Five years of data not available for Indonesia.

Table 7. Risk and Return Results for Portfolio Weighting Approaches

Approach	Return	Risk
Market-capitalization weights	9.8	19.2
IFCI weights	15.0	19.9
GDP weights	18.8	22.1
Trading weights	6.3	30.7
Equal weights, pure	20.0	13.4
Equal weights, adjusted	22.8	16.4
Minimum risk	21.7	10.5
Forecasted returns	29.1	12.2
IFC composite	11.0	22.2

Sources: Boston International Advisors and IFC Emerging Markets Database.

Note: Simulated returns; five years ending June 30, 1993.

weighting strategies at about half the risk exposure. The use of the historical returns and risks in Table 1 can create a portfolio with superior return without adding much risk beyond the minimum-risk portfolio. The results in Table 7 are looking backward, however, so nobody is in reality going to achieve returns with low risk like those shown.

Conclusion

Two conclusions stand out. One is: Be invested in the emerging markets. They are and will continue to be attractive. The second is: Diversify, diversify, diversify. High concentration in these markets brings with it an enormous amount of risk.

Question and Answer Session

Lyle H. Davis, CFA

Question: Indexing is used by those who believe that active management cannot add incremental value in an efficient market, but emerging markets are clearly inefficient, and transaction costs are high. Why would anyone want to use an indexed emerging markets fund?

Davis: Indexing can be considered an alternative in these markets for two reasons. One of the implications of inefficiency across markets is that an investor can move between markets efficiently. The data I showed suggest that such a move is difficult, however, because the window of opportunity is usually short, narrow, and crowded in terms of trading, plus it is expensive. Aggressive market timing in these markets is a heroic undertaking.

A fundamentally more important reason for indexing is that many large investors want to experience the return benefits that emerging markets as an asset class are likely to provide. Not many are interested in investing in Argentina or any other country by itself. They are interested in emerging markets because the countries tend to have rapid growth rates, rapid development of their financial markets, and rapidly developing and broad investment opportunities. Investors want to participate in those opportunities with as low a risk as possible. Indexing is one reliable and low-cost way, but not the only way, to do that.

Question: How do you manage foreign exchange risk in your country asset allocation models?

Davis: We don't. Currency risk goes with the territory. All of the returns I showed are dollar-based returns. Managing exchange rate risk or currency risk in these markets is almost impossible. Even if you want to try, the currencies have no real forward markets. And the cost of currency hedging would be excessive. You must reconcile yourself to the fact that, in these countries and markets, you are taking the currency risk; that is part of the deal and cannot be avoided.

Question: If the transactions are so expensive, does that cost have a meaningful impact on an active trader over a long period?

Davis: If you are an active trader, cost has a meaningful impact on performance. If, for example, you are going to pay 5 percent round-trip costs and turn over 100 percent of your portfolio, you have a huge cost you must earn back—much larger than in any other market—before you are even with your transaction costs.

This fact argues that these markets are inefficient, in the sense of the market mechanisms being inefficient. It does not say anything about the pricing mechanism per se—that is, the valuation mechanism—but it argues that you should take a passive approach, or at least invest for the very long term and be very confident in the stocks you choose. If you have to trade stock often, you are quickly going to be behind the eight ball.

Question: Wouldn't a passive investor have to do a lot of rebalancing of the portfolio to meet the indexes?

Davis: If you are truly a passive investor and can put together a good index portfolio, you should not have any turnover cost at all, theoretically, merely the initial cost to buy.

Question: To what extent could a major redemption from the mutual funds that are now heavily invested in emerging markets disrupt the lack of correlation of returns that emerging market investors are enjoying?

Davis: If $30 billion has gone into emerging markets from various foreign sources and the total value of those markets is $800 billion, the redemption would have to be tremendous to affect them all simultaneously.

Question: A pronounced trend in the Latin American market is increasing exports among the countries. Will this trend increase intermarket correlations?

Davis: I expect the market correlations to increase in time as the markets become a part of the world financial market. Trade flows, however, do not appear to be good predictors of market correlations.

Question: Are the returns from your portfolio weighting approaches adjusted for transaction costs? What are the rebalancing frequencies?

Davis: The portfolio approaches shown are meant to be examples of different weighting schemes. The results shown are simple buy-

and-hold returns for five years with no rebalancing, except for the equal-weighting strategies, which were rebalanced annually. Trading costs were considered in the optimized strategies but were not included in the returns.

Question: Are the commissions shown in the trading costs in Table 6 local commissions only? If so, do you ever use U.S. firms for trading? Why or why not?

Davis: The commissions shown are the local commissions and taxes. These costs will generally be the same whether a local or U.S. broker is used. We often use U.S. brokers for simplicity and convenience in relation to time zones when trading in several markets simultaneously.

Question: Aren't the bid–offer spreads (market impacts) much lower in the large emerging markets (at 0.5 percent) than shown in Table 6?

Davis: The 1.5 percent market impact shown is Boston International Advisors' rule-of-thumb estimate for the cost of trading. The realized cost may be lower or higher depending on the market at the time of trading and the securities traded.

Question: Considering its much lower transaction/turnover costs, wouldn't a market-capitalization-weighted index portfolio significantly outperform other strategies?

Davis: No, turnover in the other strategies is moderate, and differences in returns are not offset by transaction costs.

Bottom-Up Investing in Emerging Markets

Shaw B. Wagener, CFA
Vice President
Capital International, Inc.

> Stock pickers can be particularly effective in emerging markets because the markets are less efficient than developed markets and are relatively uncorrelated with other markets, because company performance can vary from market performance, and because research on individual companies and cross-border comparisons can provide a significant advantage in emerging market investing. The greatest opportunities often lie in companies that provide infrastructure, such as telecommunications companies. To be successful, stock pickers in emerging markets must be growth managers and must concentrate on absolute valuation, management quality, and country environment.

This presentation first discusses what a bottom-up portfolio manager does and how that relates to the top-down approach to investing in emerging markets, which focuses on country allocation based on macroeconomic factors. Second, the broad factors that make a bottom-up approach effective in managing emerging market portfolios are outlined. How stock picking can be adapted to emerging markets is also discussed; stock picking in emerging markets is slightly different from what is done in developed markets. Finally, the bottom-up approach is applied to three companies in emerging markets.

Advantages of Bottom-Up Investing in Emerging Markets

By focusing on the fundamental characteristics of various companies and comparing them with the valuations they carry in their capital markets, a stock picker tries to assemble a portfolio that will provide superior returns for a given level of risk. Being a good stock picker requires plenty of top-down knowledge, but stock pickers use this knowledge to pick companies, not countries. Rather than assigning arbitrary values to traditional top-down considerations like interest rates, the political environment, and other macroeconomic data, a bottom-up portfolio manager looks at a company's valuation and compares that with the outlook for the company based on its operating environment. Assigning probabilities to the various macro outcomes leads to an investment conclusion. The combination of decisions on individual companies determines the country allocations.

Several factors make bottom-up investing effective in emerging markets:

- Emerging markets are less efficient than developed markets.
- Emerging markets are relatively uncorrelated with each other and are usually relatively volatile as individual markets.
- Risk in emerging markets is a combination of several factors, including lack of information, low liquidity, and macroeconomic volatility.
- Independent research of companies adds value to the investment process in such an environment (quantitative screens are not enough). Differences in accounting standards can be adjusted. Meetings with managers and plant visits allow the investment manager to store up impressions of competitiveness, corporate culture, and ability to adapt to a changing environment's hidden assets and liabilities.
- Stock selection matters in emerging markets. For example, Thailand had a relatively good 1992 in its broad index; the market went up roughly 30 percent in dollars, but Thai bank stocks doubled. In Brazil, even the large-capitalization companies, which compose the majority

of the Brazilian stock index, showed significant differences in returns. Among the four major companies, Petrobras, Brazil's major oil company, was up 250 percent in dollar terms for the nine months ending September 1993, while Vale, another major large-cap firm, was up only 30 percent.

Differences between Developed and Emerging Markets

Bottom-up investing approaches used in the developed markets must be adapted for use in emerging markets, primarily because of differences in the markets. One big difference is that the developing markets lack catalysts for asset revaluation. Investment bankers may be able to go in and find real values in the future, but at this moment, that catalyst is missing. The real value in emerging markets is finding growth; the developing countries are growing at two to three times the rate of the developed countries. Therefore, almost all emerging market managers are growth managers. In developed market investing, stock pickers can be either value or growth managers.

Another contrast with developed markets is that the strongest growth stories in emerging markets are often in what would be mature businesses in developed markets, such as cement, utilities, and telecommunications. The reason is the need for infrastructure in these countries. These industries grow at higher rates than the countries' already high rates (in comparison with developed countries) of GDP growth.

Unlike developed markets, the focus in emerging markets should be on absolute valuation rather than relative values. The markets swing dramatically from undervalued to overvalued, so buying a stock that is cheap relative to its own market is dangerous in this environment, particularly when the market is overvalued.

In emerging markets, growth estimates take in a wider range of possible macroeconomic events than they do in developed countries. Nominal interest rates generally move in a broader range, as do economic growth rates and inflation rates. Growth rates of companies are also affected by the quality of management, which has a greater impact on productivity and profitability in emerging countries than in most developed markets.

Finally, cross-border comparisons of similar businesses can uncover excellent values in emerging markets. This aspect can lead to bottom-up managers making investment decisions that are contrary to the decisions top-down managers would make. For a demonstration of this feature, let us look at one industry that would be in both a top-down and bottom-up portfolio—the telecommunications industry.

Applying Stock Picking in Emerging Markets

Virtually every country has a telecommunications company, which makes this industry a good one to illustrate the basics of stock picking in emerging countries. First, consider the general environments in Southeast Asia and Latin America during the past several years. Since 1990, Southeast Asia has been more politically stable than Latin America and has had stronger economic growth, now being spurred on by decreased nominal interest rates in the Southeast Asian countries. Moreover, Latin America has lower and more fragile growth prospects. Although widely in place in Latin America, democracy has not necessarily meant political stability. Political stability is particularly worrisome in large-market-capitalization countries like Brazil.

The telecommunications business is a classic for fundamental investors. The factors affecting this business are clear, and how telecommunication companies make money is easy to understand. In addition, bottom-up managers can look at valuation in a myriad of ways, so this industry is perfect for stock picking. **Table 1** contains valuations for the telecommunications companies in Malaysia, Chile, and Brazil.

Table 1. Comparative Telecommunications Valuations

Characteristic	Telekom (Malaysia)	CTC (Chile)	Telebras (Brazil)
Access lines (millions)	2.1	1.2	10.6
Estimated growth (3 years)	14%	10%	12%
Revenue/line	$690	$590	$822
Employees/10,000 lines	141	64	84
Cash flow/line	$366	$257	$329
Price to estimated 1993 cash earnings	16.8	12.0	2.5
Aggregate value/access lines	$6,211	$3,464	$1,075

Source: Merrill Lynch.

Note: Prices as of August 30, 1993.

The first four lines in Table 1 give a sense of each company and how it operates. For example, the extent of access lines gives an idea of size. Telebras is five times the size of Telekom and almost ten times the size of CTC. The projections for the real earnings growth rates for three years are based on many environmental factors, such as regulatory structure and political environment. In general, the figures are the result of analyzing what kind of growth rates companies operating in Brazil, Malaysia, and Chile—given the macro situations in those countries—can expect to achieve.

Number of employees per 10,000 lines quantitatively measures the qualitative characteristics of management. Obviously, the company with the fewest employees per line is achieving better employee productivity than its competitors. The cash flow per line, ratio of price to estimated 1993 cash earnings, and aggregate value per number of access lines are also useful valuation parameters.

Most stock pickers would want to own a little of CTC, which seems reasonably valued, and a lot of Telebras, which is clearly the cheapest stock of the three. One might argue about the cash flow per line and the way it is generated, but by any consideration, Telebras is the cheapest stock. In fact, one could argue that it is a better operator than Telekom, the most expensive stock. Stock pickers would probably not touch Telekom.

CTC is an excellent operator. Chile has generally been considered the "most Asian" of the Latin American countries by top-down folks and most people who have observed the country; that is, it has the best political stability and the highest growth rates of the Latin American countries.

By picking specific telecommunications stocks, the stock picker has ended up by making a country allocation. Although the specific stocks were picked one at a time, suddenly the stock picker has a great deal of exposure to Brazil and some exposure to Chile. This is in contrast to what a top-down investor would be likely to do. Considering political stability, interest rates, and economic growth rates, a top-down investor would conclude that Southeast Asia is more attractive for investing than Latin America.

Conclusion

The characteristics of developing markets create an excellent environment for bottom-up investment managers to add return within a specified level of risk in emerging market portfolios. A stock picker must consider a number of top-down factors when assigning projected growth rates to individual companies. By focusing on absolute value of a company rather than its relative value to the home market, an investor can take advantage of the lack of correlation among emerging markets. The approach to bottom-up investing in emerging markets is essentially the same as in developed markets, but the type of industries one finds attractive and the range of possible outcomes is greater in emerging markets. Because emerging markets are more volatile than developed markets, they generate opportunities to take advantage of stock prices at variance with the fundamental values of the companies. That opportunity is a dream come true for stock pickers.

Question and Answer Session
Shaw B. Wagener, CFA

Question: How do you respond to the statement that 80 percent of returns are explained by country allocation rather than stock selection? When and how should one decide between top-down or bottom-up analysis?

Wagener: A bottom-up approach should contain a little of a country-down approach, and vice versa. The statement that 80 percent of returns come from country selection relates directly to the point that a bottom-up stock picker is a country selector. I would not be surprised to find a high correlation between the largest stocks in the stock market and how they perform relative to the stock market. Lyle Davis demonstrated that these markets are very concentrated.[1] The large companies usually dominate the performance of the individual markets in which they trade. So, to say that a country selection determines stock market returns is putting the cart before the horse. The stock markets themselves are so concentrated in a few companies that if you bought, for example, the four companies that make up most of the market capitalization in Brazil for bottom-up reasons, you would end up with a country allocation in Brazil. If the stocks move, then in fact, country returns are determining stock returns, but the stock picker's country allocation is achieved one stock at a time.

Question: Have you had the situation in which a pension consultant, for example, comes to you with an attribution analysis and says, "You did a great job on your country allocation, but you did a lousy job on your stock selection?" If so, how do you handle the situation? Do you explain that you are doing *only* stock selection?

Wagener: That situation happens often. No one believes a stock picker sits around and just buys and sells companies. If you say the returns are the result of a country-allocation process, you are explaining it backwards. You are looking at the result rather than the process.

Question: Given the 1,000 percent inflation rate in Brazil, how was the appropriate discount rate on the cash earnings multiple for Telebras determined?

Wagener: The difficulty of ascertaining what the real rate is in a country like Brazil is one thing that has bothered me a lot about the top-down approach. The interest rates, or what generated those rates, that were driving stock prices in Brazil four years ago were significantly different from today's. So the fixed-income instrument that generates the real rate of return for an investor has changed in Brazil, and it changes quite often in most emerging markets. When it comes to ascertaining the actual growth rate or discount rate based on some real rate within the market, the answer comes back to the accounting issue: Most items are accounted for in U.S. dollars. If you account for changes on the company level in dollars, you are asking: What is the real cost of borrowing for this company in dollars? In time, a rational relationship will develop between real rates and P/Es, and the cost for the stock will be at some premium relative to a U.S. company. It will not be a huge premium, however, as the market seems to indicate.

Question: Which index does Capital International use for the emerging markets?

Wagener: At the beginning of emerging markets investing, clients thought of everything in terms of real returns, an absolute number. Today, most of our clients want to have results related to a benchmark. Our emerging market growth fund thus recently decided on a combination of the International Finance Corporation Investable Index and the MSCI Emerging Markets Free Index, a 50/50 benchmark, under the theory that each index has advantages and disadvantages but that they are both generally going in the right direction. We do not intend to manage the fund any differently, regardless of the benchmark.

---

[1] Please see Mr. Davis's discussion, pages 19–26.

Valuation Techniques for Emerging Market Securities

Donald M. Krueger, CFA
Vice President
Templeton Investment Counsel, Inc.[1]

> The long-term investor in emerging markets faces difficulties because of currency and political uncertainty and a lack of company information. Choosing the correct valuation measures and basing company valuations on forecasts are particularly important. In making down-to-earth forecasts, the analyst's most valuable tool is conscientiously applied common sense.

Investors use various approaches to valuing securities and forming portfolios. Templeton Investment Counsel uses a bottom-up, value-oriented, long-term, commonsense approach to the investment process, with few differences between the ways emerging markets and developed markets are handled. This presentation discusses the benefits and problems with long-term investing in emerging markets and highlights the key aspects of a bottom-up approach to emerging market investing.

Long-Term Investing in Emerging Markets

Emerging markets are somewhat different from the developed markets. For one thing, long-term investors have historically received greater returns from emerging markets than from developed markets.

Long-term investors in an emerging market can take advantage of certain opportunities because they do not compete head-to-head with local investors. Local investors in these markets invest differently from global investors. Local investors often use the market like a casino, betting on stocks apparently without regard to value. At times, local activity in the emerging market will be liquidity driven, while at other times, it will be theme driven.

For many years, the Japanese market was very much like an emerging market in this respect. Rumors might arise, for example, that had short-term implications for the price but were inconsistent with the expected long-term returns forecast. With that environment, the Japanese market created opportunities for value-oriented investors.

A long-term investor in emerging markets can capitalize on the wisdom and experience gained from watching countries and companies over long periods of time. For example, the automobile stocks in Malaysia recently were bid down because of pessimism over a drop in car registrations. To Templeton, however, the drop looked like merely a cyclical trough caused by government policy to tighten the purchase requirements. The country's real GDP growth was intact at 7–8 percent a year for the next five years. We expected the government to relent about purchase requirements, and auto registrations would pick up. Indeed, there would be pent-up demand for autos; as consumption, wealth, and per capita income increased, people would buy cars. That type of scenario was attractive to us because experience shows that auto sales do well over time in countries and economies experiencing real growth, despite short-term cycles.

Long-term investors will look through any trough of a cycle back to a normalized part of the cycle. The fortunes of some company may appear bleak, and the stock may be selling at a very low price-to-book-value ratio (P/BV), but the long-term investor may be able to make something of the stock. For example, some of the banks around the world are selling at quite low P/BVs because they have had terrible problems with their provisions. They made bad loans and had to write them off. Adequate provisioning is expected to take two or three years. If the basic integrity of the balance sheet is sound,

---

[1] Mr. Krueger is currently with Soros Fund Management Company, Inc.

however, and the banks do not have to raise large amounts of equity, then by about 1998, provisioning will be down to "normal" levels. The banks will be able to earn reasonable rates of return.

Another advantage to long-term investing in emerging markets is avoiding the high transaction costs of emerging markets investing by trading infrequently. A good return after transaction costs in these markets is hard to achieve if a portfolio is turned over rapidly; in some cases, the round-trip transaction costs, including market impact, are 10 percent—5 percent to get in, and 5 percent to get out.

Finally, the companies in emerging markets often want long-term shareholders—if they are going to have foreign shareholders at all—so they welcome the long-term investor. Top management welcomes visits from investors with a record of a long-term approach to the process, and managers are often more frank than they are with short-term investors about the challenges, as well as the opportunities, facing their companies.

Problems with Investing in Emerging Markets

Investing in emerging markets is not without problems. Indeed, major problems revolve around the quantity and quality of information about the markets and the companies in the markets, currency uncertainties, political instability, and misleading value measures.

Information

The biggest problem is probably the lack of reliable information. Highly developed markets—such as the Australian, Hong Kong, U.K., or U.S. markets—are overbrokered, and investors are deluged with information. In any portfolio manager's office, the investor will find piles of information, most of which is not read. Developed markets are also followed by seasoned analysts who are able to provide additional information. Furthermore, information is readily available from companies.

The investor in emerging markets is operating with significantly less information. In these markets, most analysts do not understand what a bottom-up, value-oriented investor is seeking. The analysts seem to think in terms of 90 days, not five years. Moreover, most of the analysts are inexperienced; the average analyst's age in some of these emerging market countries seems to be 23 years, and many do not know what a stock is until they are hired by the local brokerage firm. A fiduciary with millions of dollars to invest cannot rely on what these analysts are recommending. The information content is not there. In addition, company managers in developing countries often do not understand long-term investors' needs and interests.

Obtaining quality data from emerging markets is a challenge. As hard as we try, Templeton's data on emerging markets are not as clean as the data of U.S. firms. Because of the data problems, the analysts dealing with emerging markets must be extremely careful with their analyses and decisions.

A related problem concerns balance sheets. Many local brokerage firms do not provide balance sheet information; they concentrate on profit-and-loss statements. Templeton, however, considers the strength of the balance sheet to be the single most important set of data to use when determining whether to include a company in our portfolios.

The stronger the balance sheet, the better, because emerging market companies are acting in volatile environments and can sink quickly if they do not have strong balance sheets. If they are in danger of sinking, the signs may not become apparent until too late without an accurate balance sheet.

As companies deteriorate, they may try various tactics to stay afloat that may injure investors. For example, they may do rights offerings, and existing investors' equity positions could become seriously diluted. Although these companies may not go out of business, the large amounts of equity they have issued are at the expense of their shareholders.

To assess the strength of a company's balance sheet, Templeton compares earnings volatility with balance sheet leverage. High earnings volatility combined with high leverage is considered risky; low earnings volatility with low leverage is considered conservative. Generally, our rule is to accept combinations of high volatility and low leverage and of low volatility and high leverage in companies. This rule is a commonsense approach to making an investment decision. A company with high operating leverage *and* a highly leveraged balance sheet brings with it serious levels of risk. If revenues decline significantly, the company could be out of business. On the other hand, if a company has a stable revenue base, the investor may be willing to live with a highly leveraged balance sheet.

Currencies

Currencies are another challenge. No one knows how to predict what currencies will be doing five years from now. This ignorance is particularly troublesome in emerging markets because hedging in the currency markets is impossible. Templeton's general assessment is that, if a company does not have any foreign sources of revenue and if it and the country where it is located have a lot of foreign debt on the balance sheets, in time, the company will see its local currency depreciate. We avoid that company.

Politics

Political unrest can be another characteristic of emerging markets. Analysts need to be able to determine whether a political problem will have short-term or long-term consequences in the equity market. For example, a few years ago, riots occurred in Thailand about the way the government was elected; the same military cabinet that had been thrown out was being put back in. Despite the unrest, Templeton determined that what was happening in Thailand was most likely a short-term incident that was not going to be a major disaster for our five-year earnings' estimates. Therefore, when short-term investors pushed the stocks down dramatically in one week, we bought aggressively. A few weeks later, local investors had forgotten about the protests and drove the price of stocks up. Using a long-term investment philosophy, we were able to take advantage of the short-term moves.

Misuse of Earnings Ratios

People are often tempted to buy emerging market stocks on the basis of low price-to-cash-earnings ratios while ignoring the earnings numbers. This approach may not always work, as was the case in Japan in the late 1980s when the steel companies were aggressively adding capacity. Because of increasing amounts of depreciation, earnings were declining. Although these stocks may have looked attractive to some investors, the truth of the matter was that the region was adding too much capacity for these companies to make steel competitively and earn a reasonable return on capital.

Investors should not invest blindly according to conventional wisdom. Those buying on a cash-to-earnings basis must be careful to ask *why* the company is selling at such a low ratio of price to cash earnings. Generally, there is an explanation. For example, perhaps much of the incremental capacity in a capital-intensive company should not be added because it will not be able to produce a reasonable return on investment.

Not only in Japan, but in the other developed markets and the emerging markets, the days of being able to raise money at negative rates are over. In many Japanese companies, capital spending has declined sharply in the 1990s. To reflect that decline, depreciation will also be declining during the next several years. Price-to-cash-earnings ratios will be increasing because depreciation will be declining. If everything else remains the same, the P/Es of these companies will probably decline because of the lower depreciation charges on the Japanese companies' profit-and-loss statements.

The lessons of Japan can be applied to many emerging markets. For example, Siam Cement was recently a great favorite of foreign and local investors. The company was very profitable, and it was selling at a low price-to-cash-earnings ratio. The investors were not considering the excess cement capacity being built up in Thailand, however. Suddenly, the company could no longer achieve a satisfactory rate of return. When Siam Cement's real situation became evident, its profitability and stock price collapsed.

Misuse of Book Values

The definition of book value is another problem area in emerging market investing. Analysts must know how each company measures book value because no standard exists. As in developed countries, some countries use historical assets and some revalue their assets. Investors should be particularly careful in analyzing companies that revalue assets.

Just because a stock is cheap on the basis of price to book value does not mean it is attractive; it may deserve that price. Japan's steel industry, for example, is selling at a low P/BV, but that book value may not be worth much. The industry will probably continue to have write-offs. Investors should pay up for book value only if the long-term returns on that book appear solid.

Bottom-Up Valuation Approach

Templeton's investment process for the emerging markets has three stages: country-entry analysis, country/company scanning, and intensive company analysis.

Country-Entry Analysis

Prior to entering a country, Templeton searches for good data sources, analyzes the accounting characteristics of the country, examines existing custodial facilities, and studies the settlement procedures.

■ *Data sources.* Finding good data is difficult. Information cannot be found simply by hooking up to an electronic data base such as Compuserve, Compustat, or Lotus One Source. Analysts must find the sources on their own. A significant problem is that many investment banks and brokerage firms *think* they have information, but it is generally not good, clean information.

■ *Accounting characteristics.* To understand the accounting characteristics of a country, Templeton managers meet with both local accounting firms and international auditing firms doing business in that country. We also meet with chief financial officers from various companies to see how they view the world. Often, we must develop our own accounting standards to make data comparable among countries.

■ *Custodial facilities.* Many of the emerging markets Templeton has entered did not, when we first evaluated the countries, have custodial facilities that met our needs. We found corruption, scandals, counterfeit securities, and activities done under the table, none of which is appropriate for clients' portfolios. Prior to entering a country, we make sure we are comfortable with all custodial and subcustodial relationships.

■ *Settlement procedures.* Settlement procedures must make sense and be "doable." In some countries, the process may look good, but in reality, it does not work as planned. In Poland, for example, what was supposed to be a three- to four-day settlement period turned into seven days, just for documents to go from one end of a building to another. Investors must make sure the settlement systems are working for them.

Country/Company Scanning

The second phase of the investment process involves scanning Templeton's data base on emerging markets for countries and companies that are attractive on the basis of our value criteria. The emerging markets data base includes up to ten years of historical and adjusted financial data and a five-year forward earnings estimate for each of 4,000 companies in about 30 countries around the world. The list of companies and countries is constantly changing as we explore new opportunities.

The earnings estimate is probably the most important piece of information in the data base from an investor's perspective. The five-year earnings estimate represents what we think a company will be doing in the future.

Not all countries are easy to analyze. In China, for example, we have had trouble getting historical data. The Chinese companies emerging from the Communist quagmire have few financial records that make sense. Potential investors in these companies need information to analyze before making investment decisions. Indeed, as fiduciaries, investment managers have the responsibility to gather whatever data they can in order to make investment judgments.

Intensive Company Analysis

Intensive company analysis is the third and most difficult stage of the investment process. It requires studying historical accounts; visiting companies; evaluating managers and ownership structures; making adjustments for currency, inflation, and corporate actions; and using common sense to calculate relative value measures. Tracking down and verifying the information is very important; so the people who do this analysis spend a lot of time on the road.

Obviously, Templeton's managers cannot follow closely all of the companies in the data base. Instead, we use selected relative valuation criteria to screen the data base for about 1,000 attractive companies. Only about 200 of the 1,000 are actually purchased for the emerging markets portfolio, and in any particular year, we sell the most expensive 20 percent of the portfolio to make room for the more attractive stocks that have recently been identified. The process is fairly dynamic, creating a turnover of about 20 percent a year.

Valuation Example

The following example illustrates how various valuation criteria can be used to evaluate alternative stocks. **Table 1** presents several basic valuation measures for three companies in the same industry. This approach is independent of any country, but for simplicity, countries can be assigned: Say, Company A is in Hong Kong, Company B is in Australia, and Company C is in Japan.

Many investors use P/Es to compare companies. From that perspective, Company A is selling at 15 times current earnings, Company B is selling at 20 times earnings, and Company C is selling at 3 times earnings. Looking at P/Es based on current earnings is not appropriate in emerging markets, however, because growth rates and discount rates can vary widely. Using *future* earnings forecasted on the basis of research and common sense is the more appropriate approach. For this example, using the present value of the earnings five years in the future leads to P/Es of 12.5 for Company A, 19 for Company B, and 30 for Company C.

The analysis is now quite simple. Based on relative five-year P/Es, Company C is not a great value right now. As bottom-up, fundamental, long-term, value-oriented investors, we would have difficulty making a case to invest in "Japan" at 30 times earnings, particularly when we could buy a "Hong Kong" company at 12.5 times earnings.

For some reason, many people also use the overnight debt rate to discount equities, which is also not appropriate. For a five-year investment horizon, the five-year debt rate should be used.

Final Comment

The way to be successful in emerging markets is to

Table 1. Valuation Example

	Company A	Company B	Company C
Assumptions			
Five-year earnings growth rate	15%	10%	7%
Five-year cost of debt	8	7	5
Risk premium	3	2	2
Current values			
Price (P)	$1,500	$2,000	$3,000
Earnings per share (EPS)	100	100	100
P/EPS	15.0×	20.0×	30.0×
Five-year values			
Year-five EPS (EPS$_5$)	$201	$161	$140
Present value of EPS$_5$ [PV(EPS$_5$)]	120	105	100
Price/PV(EPS$_5$)	12.5×	19.0×	30.0×

Source: Donald M. Krueger.

use common sense and use it more conscientiously than you would in more familiar markets. Investing in emerging markets is more difficult than investing in developed markets, so common sense is even more important in the emerging markets. Even though the information you have about the market and company may not be as good as the information you have in other markets, you can still apply common sense. You can still apply the insights and wisdom you have accumulated from following other markets and industries in other parts of the world. And you can do it successfully.

Question and Answer Session
Donald M. Krueger, CFA

Question: Against what type of benchmark does Templeton evaluate its portfolios' performance, and how volatile are the portfolios relative to the benchmark?

Krueger: We use the standard benchmarks used for portfolios of the emerging markets—the EAFE, International Finance Corporation, or MSCI Emerging Markets indexes.

Volatility is usually relatively low because we tend to buy stocks that are cheap on a P/E and P/BV basis. Our holdings have relatively high dividend yields. When markets collapse, our holdings tend to collapse a little less. When the strategy is working correctly, the holdings are undervalued stocks that everybody else avoided at some point in the stocks' cycles. We try to pick them up at that point in the cycles, so they also tend to appreciate reasonably well. Our volatility is thus on the low end of the scale.

Question: How do you determine a long-term discount rate, particularly for countries like Brazil or Mexico with wild inflation rates?

Krueger: The oversimplifying assumption we use is that those wild rates will not last. Over a long period, the cost of capital might go up and it might go down, but eventually, all rates will gravitate to some normalized, worldwide cost-of-capital level adjusted for normal long-term inflation. Currently, the long-term cost of capital is somewhat lower than it might have been in, say, 1982, which we take into account.

Question: How much range do you find in equity risk premiums among the different companies you evaluate?

Krueger: We like to be conservative. For example, everybody is saying the international banks in Asia will experience asset growth of 15 percent a year. Maybe they are right, but we will be more conservative; not many businesses grow at 15 percent a year for five years. We might use a growth rate of 12 percent a year to compute the risk premium in such a case.

We do not quantify the risk premium per se on a company-by-company basis. We build it into our five-year earnings forecasts. It is built into the assumptions.

Question: What gives Templeton the ability to predict five-year earnings with enough confidence to use them as a primary investment criterion?

Krueger: Our approach has a long history of working. We recognize that we are not going to get the predictions down to the second decimal place. We may occasionally be way off, but when we make these earnings predictions, we are asking basic questions about these companies, questions that everybody should be asking.

For example, we ask: Is this particular company capable of growing at twice GNP or one-half GNP? Does this company have enough pricing power that it will be able to raise prices during the next five years? Or is the competitive situation changing in such a way that it will have to lower prices?

What about margins? Is this a capital-intensive industry, so the company will have to do a lot of capital spending? If so, its income statement will see an increase in depreciation, which tends to narrow margins. Is the company in a field that is experiencing much technological change? Does it have some advantages the other competitors do not have? If so, margins may be able to widen somewhat.

What will happen to labor rates? What is likely to happen to tax rates? How about the number of shares outstanding? In order to finance its growth, will this company need to issue a great deal of capital in the next several years? How is it likely to do that?

In short, we try to build into our model what we think is likely to happen during the five-year period by using a commonsense approach. At the end of the process, we come up with a number that we are willing to use as one of the tools to help in the investment decision. The five-year estimate is an important tool, but only one of the tools we use to determine that 20 percent of the cheapest companies in the universe in which we want to invest.

Question: How many companies does a typical Templeton analyst cover in how many different countries? For example, of the 1,000 companies in the data base, how many would you or any other analyst follow?

Krueger: Every portfolio manager at Templeton is an analyst, which may be somewhat different from other organizations. We are a research-driven organization and spend more of our time on research than on portfolio management. Except for the Hong Kong-based emerging markets team, the primary responsibility is an industry responsibility, and a secondary responsibility is a country responsibility.

As an analyst, I typically follow about five countries and one major industry. My industry responsibility is all the many international banks, both in the emerging and developed markets, that we have in our portfolios. As for countries, I am responsible for our holdings in China, Taiwan, the Philippines, Thailand, Israel, and South Africa and for monitoring what is happening in those countries.

The average analyst follows about 70 companies. The analyst is responsible for maintaining earnings estimates, for knowing what is going on, and for the investment decision. Much of our compensation is based on the performance of the stocks we recommend.

Question: What are the limitations/restrictions on short sales in different emerging markets?

Krueger: Short sales are generally not permitted, but sometimes shares can be borrowed offshore, away from the control of regulators.

The Research Challenge: Analyzing the Numbers

Gary S. Schieneman
Vice President and Director of Latin American Research
Smith New Court

> As emerging markets develop, stock picking and fundamental analysis become increasingly important. Understanding the accounting is key to this analysis.

In general, emerging markets in the early phases of development are evaluated more by macroeconomic information than by fundamentals. For example, the macroeconomic news coming out of Argentina has been very positive, which has led to a recent upsurge of foreign investors returning to that country and others in Latin America.

The P/E multiples summarized in **Table 1** reflect this macroeconomic influence. The high Argentina multiple is not supported by fundamentals. While profits have increased in Argentina, companies continue to be plagued with high labor costs and outdated technology. The International Finance Corporation (IFC) multiple used in Table 1 is high, in part, because of the number of loss companies included in the index.

Brazil is the opposite in macroeconomic-versus-fundamental characteristics. The Brazilian market has produced terrible macroeconomic news. Inflation is increasing at stratospheric levels, and the government does not seem able to govern. Although Brazil has an efficient and competitive private sector, its poor macroeconomic and political developments receive the major attention.

Multiples in emerging markets can vary considerably from one source to another. A common practice is to exclude companies that show losses or minimal profits, which biases the multiples downward. Earnings multiples in Brazil are affected by whether some rather significant extraordinary tax gains are included in the earnings number; the IFC includes the tax gains in reported figures; Smith New Court believes they should be excluded.

We believe Brazil is in reality more expensive than it appears to be from these numbers. The private sector is valued, on average, at double the multiples at which the state-owned companies such as Telebras, the telecommunication monopoly, trade. Telebras composes about 40 percent of the Brazilian stock exchange.

The Importance of Financial Reporting

In the final analysis, one invests in companies, not countries. Deciding which stocks to own requires fundamental analysis, and particularly in Latin America, fundamental analysis requires understanding the financial reporting model being used.

Financial reporting in most emerging markets follows one of two basic accounting models—the U.K. model or the U.S. model. The choice of accounting model usually follows the flow of capital. U.K. capital predominated in Asia, while Latin America was a U.S.-capital sphere of influence. So, U.K.-oriented models are generally found in Southeast Asia (exceptions are the Philippines and Indonesia), in India, and in Africa, and primarily U.S.-oriented models are found in Latin America. Because of these orientations, accounting differences among the countries of Latin America and among many of the countries of Southeast Asia are not nearly as great as many people think. There are fewer differences within these regions than among the supposedly more sophisticated countries of Europe.

Inflation Accounting

When inflation such as that summarized in **Table 2** is experienced, unadjusted historical-cost information is not meaningful. Dealing with moderate inflation may be more difficult than dealing with the high inflation of Brazil. In the Brazilian high-inflation environment, everything is indexed. The

Table 1. Latin American Fundamentals: IFC Investable Index as of September 3, 1993

Country	Price to Earnings	Price to Book Value
Argentina	23.3	1.75
Brazil	11.3	0.66
Chile	16.3	1.73
Mexico	14.2	2.01

Source: IFC.

challenge is to make sure the index is appropriate and is currently applied. From an operating perspective, the major penalty from hyperinflation is the difficulty, if not impossibility, of long-term planning. Collecting receivables is far more critical than capital budgeting. In moderate-inflation environments, where things are not indexed and cost increases cannot automatically be passed on, managing a business is a tougher challenge.

Table 2. Inflation in Latin America

Country	1989	1990	1991	1992
Argentina	4,924%	1,344%	84%	18%
Brazil	1,783	1,477	480	1,158
Chile	21	27	19	13
Mexico	20	30	19	12
Peru	2,775	7,650	139	56

Source: Smith New Court.

The most important factor affecting accounting information in emerging markets, particularly in Latin America, is inflation. The objective of inflation accounting is to express financial statements in terms of a currency with constant purchasing power. The first step in this process is to classify balance sheet accounts into monetary and nonmonetary items. Monetary items are items that are expressed in terms of a fixed amount of money, such as cash, receivables, accounts payable, and long-term debt (if it is not indexed). Monetary items are not adjusted on the balance sheet, but the effect of inflation on these items—a purchasing power (monetary) gain or loss—is measured and reported as part of net income.

Nonmonetary items are assets or liabilities whose values change as a result of inflation. They include fixed assets, inventory, indexed receivables and liabilities, and investments. Nonmonetary items are adjusted for inflation with an offsetting increase to shareholders' equity.

The income statement and comparative financial statements are also adjusted for inflation. The objective is to express all data in currency with purchasing power as of the latest balance sheet date (that is, constant currency). The income statement adjustment is generally made monthly by applying an index representing the effect of cumulative inflation on the transactions reported during the month. All prior-period comparative data (balance sheet, income statement, cash flow, etc.) are also restated for cumulative inflation through the balance sheet date. The result is that all comparisons are in real terms.

Monetary Gains

The potential significance of monetary gains is shown in **Table 3**. Cemex, Mexico's largest cement company, reported monetary gains for the three-year period of 1990 through 1992 that ranged from 186 percent of operating income to a "low" of 35 percent. In 1990, most of what Cemex reported as net income resulted from borrowing money and reporting a big inflation gain. If inflation accounting had not been used, Cemex would probably have reported a net loss in 1990. The quality of Cemex's earnings improved as inflation fell: By 1992, monetary gains were only 35 percent of Cemex's operating income.

Table 3. Cemex: Monetary Gain
(millions of constant 1992 pesos)

Item	1990	1991	1992
Operating income	781	1,452	1,689
Net interest income (expense)	–953	–151	40
Foreign exchange loss	–330	–151	–69
Monetary gain	1,452	731	591
Net financial income	169	429	562
Monetary gain/ operating income	185.9%	50.3%	35.0%

Source: Cemex annual reports.

Table 4 shows the inflation (monetary) gain for YPF, Argentina's major integrated petroleum company. Most of YPF's earnings in 1991 could be simplistically considered a monetary gain, but in 1992, little monetary gain occurred. One reason is that Argentina, unlike other countries, uses the wholesale price index rather than the consumer price index for inflation accounting purposes. Wholesale inflation was virtually nil in Argentina during 1992, so infla-

Table 4. YPF: Inflation Gain or Loss
(millions of pesos)

Item	1991	1992
Operating income	266	529
Inflation gain	236	2
Other, net	91	–76
Restructuring and other	–338	–196
Net income	255	259

Source: YPF annual report.

tion gain was nil. Although earnings in both years were the same, their quality was far higher in 1992.

In addition to inflating income, monetary gains also, in my opinion, distort cash flow. Information provided by Latin American companies includes monetary gains as part of cash flow, but you cannot pay your bills with monetary gains; you need real cash.

Nonmonetary Items

Adjusting nonmonetary items for inflation introduces a new basis of accounting when replacement or reproduction cost (i.e., current cost) is used. In Argentina, for example, a technical revaluation of financial statements that represents the excess of replacement costs over general inflation is undertaken annually. This valuation, which applies primarily to fixed assets, can be significant. Comercial de la Plata, an Argentine holding company with significant interests in energy, construction, and public services, reported a technical revaluation comprising 22 percent of shareholders' equity at the end of 1992.

Although many would argue (and I agree) that current cost is a better basis of valuing fixed assets than historical cost, this practice is not permitted in the United States and many other countries. The result is that, when inflation accounting is used, traditional valuation measures, such as price to book value (P/BV), are not comparable with those in countries that use historical-cost accounting. P/BV figures in the United States would be much lower than they are, for example, if U.S. companies carried fixed assets at current cost.

Table 5 shows how significant current-cost accounting adjustments were for Soquimich, a Chilean nitrate producer. Fixed assets were revalued in Chile in the late 1980s. As a result of this revaluation, Soquimich's earnings were reduced 70 percent in 1991 and 38 percent in 1992 because of depreciation on revaluation. This information was disclosed in a reconciliation to U.S. generally accepted accounting principles (GAAP) contained in Soquimich's recent prospectus for an American Depositary Receipt offering in the United States. (You may be interested to note that the second largest accounting difference applies to futures/forward exchange accounting.)

Constant Currency versus a U.S.-Dollar Perspective

Mexico adopted inflation accounting in the 1980s when the country was experiencing relatively high inflation. So far in 1993, inflation is about 9 percent a year. Inflation accounting would not be permissible in the United States with such a rate, but it con-

Table 5. Soquimich: U.S.–Chilean GAAP Reconciliation
(thousands of U.S. dollars)

Item	1991	1992
Net income, Chilean GAAP	4,123	17,130
Subsidiaries with negative equity	1,802	−85
Price level/monetary correction	2,432	310
Depreciation on revaluation	12,388	11,111
Accrued vacation pay	−641	−453
Deferred taxes	−707	−2,360
Futures/forward exchange	−2,310	3,100
Net income, U.S. GAAP	17,087	28,753

Source: Soquimich prospectus.

tinues to be followed in Mexico. Remember that inflation accounting affects comparative results to the extent that only real changes are reported (that is, a company must earn the inflation rate in order to stand still). With a 9 percent rate of inflation, the rest of the world would use nominal changes to measure performance. The result would be 9 percent greater than what is reported. So, Mexican companies are penalized when compared with their international peers.

Table 6 shows the effect of this difference on the first-half 1993 results for Telmex, Mexico's telephone company. Telmex's earnings changes are far more impressive on a nominal or U.S.-dollar basis than in the constant pesos used for Mexican reporting purposes.

Table 6. Telmex: Comparative Performance, First Half 1993 versus First Half 1992
(percent change)

Item	In Constant Pesos	In Nominal Pesos and Dollars[a]
Revenues	7.5%	18.1%
Operating income	6.4	16.9
Net income	3.6	13.9

Source: Telmex.

[a]Because the peso exchange rate was about the same at June 30, 1993, as it was at June 30, 1992, the U.S.-dollar comparative results are essentially the same as nominal-peso results.

Brazilian Issues

A major issue in Brazil is the index used for inflation accounting purposes. **Table 7** summarizes percentage changes in the index used for inflation accounting (the monetary correction index), the consumer price index (CPI), and currency devaluations for the 1989–92 period.

The difference between monetary correction and devaluation is important because, unlike the rest of Latin America, a dollar perspective rather than a

Table 7. Brazilian Indexes
(percent change)

Year	Monetary Correction	Inflation (CPI)	Devaluation
1989	1,464%	1,783%	1,401%
1990	845	1,477	1,397
1991	480	480	528
1992	1,158	1,158	1,045

Source: Smith New Court.

local-currency perspective is used for most facets of Brazilian business. In a dollar perspective, earnings for 1989 and 1992 would be higher than in a cruzeiro perspective. The reverse would be the case for 1990 and 1991; in those years, Brazilian companies looked much better in cruzeiros. The reason in 1990 is that the index for inflation accounting was about half the rate of inflation. In my opinion, the 1990 results were totally misleading because of this difference.

The 1990 index problem resulted in an understatement of fixed assets and equity in balance sheets and an overstatement of profits. Law 8200, enacted in 1991, adopted the CPI for inflation accounting, and a one-time adjustment to equity corrected the prior year. A tax on resulting monetary gains (which are taxable in Brazil) was deferred for four years. It is this tax that is discounted if paid early and has generated huge extraordinary gains for a number of companies. Telebras, for example, reported a US$690 million gain from such discounting in 1993.

Mexican Foreign-Debt Translation

Cemex (refer to Table 3) has roughly $3 billion in dollar debt on its balance sheet. Its latest borrowings were to pay for the acquisition of its Spanish cement subsidiaries. Because the peso has been so strong, the debt should result in a minimal exchange loss of about 90 million nominal pesos (NP). Under Mexican inflation accounting, Cemex translates the dollar debt into pesos and then computes a monetary gain on the translated dollar debt. If an inflation rate of 9 percent is assumed, the 1993 monetary gain from borrowing in dollars will be roughly 845 million pesos, or US$240 million—about 40 percent of the company's earnings. From a financial reporting viewpoint, the borrowing and the acquisitions appear to have been cost free because of inflation accounting.

Other Accounting Differences

Accounting differences other than inflation accounting in Latin America are generally not significant. Deferred taxes, leases, contingencies, and earnings per share are some of the more recurring differences.

Conclusion

Many analysts believe that the way to handle accounting differences is to convert financial information to U.S. GAAP. The conversion may not always be correct, however, and it may not always be feasible, because not everything will be known. For example, without Soquimich's registration statement, in which the differences in the accounting for futures contracts (in Table 5) were disclosed, the analyst would not know the difference existed—much less be able to convert the figures to U.S. GAAP.

More important than restating is understanding the differences in accounting approaches. Understanding the differences will provide important insights into the quality of earnings and allow the investor to make a more informed investment decision.

Question and Answer Session

Gary S. Schieneman

Question: What is hyperinflation?

Schieneman: By accounting standards, *high* inflation is defined as cumulative inflation for a three-year period of 100 percent. A cumulative higher rate is hyperinflation.

The current hyperinflation area is Brazil. In the summer of 1993, inflation was 30 percent a month, and analysts thought that was the magic level that would trigger hyperinflation. Now, in the fall, the inflation rate is 35 percent a month.

Question: When monetary gains are subtracted from earnings, shouldn't interest rate expense, which also has a large inflationary component, be subtracted?

Schieneman: The theoretical justification for the monetary gain is that it is an offset to high nominal interest rates. The problem I see, from a cash flow perspective, is that monetary gain is not the source for paying this high interest. The source is maintaining prices at a level sufficient to recover costs, including interest.

Most first-line companies in Latin America do not borrow locally. To borrow locally and pay a real rate of interest of, say, 25–30 percent is suicidal. Top companies borrow abroad, which is one reason the monetary gain creates so much income. These companies are not paying interest rates at anything near the inflation-adjusted interest rate.

Question: Is net income a good valuation measure relative to cash flow or cash earnings?

Schieneman: I believe cash flow is superior to net income. Net income is a statistic; it should be treated as a statistic and nothing else, then it can be used correctly in evaluating companies. Unfortunately, net income is so ingrained in valuation that we use it for a purpose for which it was never intended. Net income is subject to accountants' decisions about what to include and exclude. It is a difficult statistic to use unless you understand how the number was calculated.

Question: In practice, are internationally traded stocks valued on the basis of U.S. GAAP results or local GAAP results?

Schieneman: Generally, on local GAAP results.

Question: If the biggest portion of total return in emerging market investing is driven by the country bet, why invest in companies rather than countries?

Schieneman: Companies are important because, at some point, fundamentals do kick in. If no fundamentals are supporting the country bet, that bet strikes me as pretty poor.

The Research Challenge

Josephine S. Jimenez, CFA
Managing Director
Montgomery Emerging Markets Fund

> Information for company valuation in emerging markets must be gathered from various published sources, participants in the local markets, and most importantly, country and company visits. Analysts will have to build their own data bases, but once the data are complete, they can use sophisticated optimization models to value and compare investment opportunities.

If Graham and Dodd were analysts today, they would find intriguing values in emerging markets. In their book, *Security Analysis*, Graham and Dodd defined undervalued companies on the basis of net quick liquidation value, which is specified as current assets minus total debt as a percentage of market capitalization.[1] A company with a high ratio is an "acquisition candidate," according to the authors, and in some emerging markets, ratios as high as 60 percent can be found. Therefore, emerging market investing is of great interest.

Three important aspects of the research in emerging markets are discussed in this presentation: where to obtain information, what is involved in analyzing companies and markets, and how value is defined in emerging markets. Two companies that have attractive characteristics as investments are then used to illustrate the valuation techniques described.

Where to Get Information

One of the great challenges of investing in emerging markets is to accumulate data and then make sense of what has been accumulated.

Public Sources

The International Finance Corporation (IFC) and the International Monetary Fund (IMF) are excellent sources of information for stock market aggregates.

The IMF publishes two books that are very useful to analysts in furthering an understanding of the macroeconomics of each country. These books, *International Monetary Statistics* and *International Trade Statistics*, detail exports and imports by country and export destinations for each country. This type of information is important for analysts who are developing a top-down approach. It can be used to forecast the outlook for inflation, for example, or for real GDP growth.

In addition to publications, a number of software products provide valuable data. PC Globe, released by PC Globe of Tempe, Arizona, for example, is a software program that presents the demographics for 222 countries. Gender and age distributions are valuable information for emerging market analysts. On average, 52 percent of the population in these markets are under age 19, which has major implications for the type of industries that will grow the fastest in the economies.

The commodities pages of newspapers are another useful source of information. Changes in food prices are a particularly revealing statistic. Food prices were up substantially in fall 1993 as compared with the previous fall, in part because of the floods in the U.S. Midwest. Pork bellies were up about 55 percent, broilers up about 18 percent, and wheat up about 21 percent. Emerging markets often benefit from rising commodity prices. The significant increase in wheat prices, for example, is a positive development for Argentina. Increases in commodity prices also suggest, however, that inflation will be on the rise in many of these countries. Food items represent as much as 45 percent of the consumer price indexes in some emerging markets.

---

[1] First published as *Security Analysis: Principles and Technique*, by B. Graham and D. Dodd (New York: McGraw-Hill, 1934); currently available as *Graham and Dodd's Security Analysis*, by Sidney Cottle, Roger F. Murray, and Frank E. Block, 5th edition (New York: McGraw-Hill, 1988).

Other interesting statistics are the significant weaknesses in the prices of basic metals, such as aluminum and copper. That information is valuable for analysts looking at the soft drinks, telecommunications, and home appliance industries because aluminum is used as a packaging material and copper as an electrical conductor.

Local Market Participants

Local brokerage firms are an excellent source of information. The local research team can provide information on how each market operates and details of the accounting principles and local valuation parameters.

Valuation parameters observed by local investors in emerging markets are not always the same as those used in the U.S. market. Some markets, for example, are driven by absolute book values. In those countries, domestic investors think a stock is cheap when it trades below book value. For example, domestic investors in South Korea expect shares to trade above 5,000 won per share, which is the par value of all companies in Korea. Not knowing this attitude can hinder U.S. investors' trading strategies.

Travel

The most interesting and profitable challenge in obtaining data is conducting original fundamental research. It involves visiting companies in emerging market countries, meeting with managers, and visiting the plants. For company and country research in emerging markets, judgment is important, and time spent in the countries is the best way to form judgments. In company visits, analysts can learn about underlying production processes and make assessments of the quality of labor relations and so forth. In addition to visiting companies, analysts should talk with suppliers, talk with customers, spend time at supermarkets and department stores, and analyze relative prices. Much can be learned by examining such commonly available information as, for example, the price of lettuce in Warsaw compared with the price in Budapest.

Analyzing Companies and Markets

In researching companies, the goal is to find the one that will provide the home run. Some investors analyze emerging markets on the basis of bottom-up stock picking, some analyze on the basis of top-down analysis, and others use a combination of both approaches.

For analysis purposes, the data on companies in emerging markets are not difficult to obtain. In most countries, companies publish annual statements, and in some cases, quarterly statements. Differences in accounting principles, however, make comparing financial ratios across borders difficult.

Most U.S. analysts take for granted that data bases of historical data will be available for making comparisons, but in emerging market countries, these data bases must be built. Some of the countries do not bother to accumulate historical data because they know their countries have changed or because a country has experienced major economic shocks. Historical data nevertheless need to be collected; despite the possible changes, historical figures allow the analyst to assess how a company performed at a specific time in the country's history and within the specific circumstances of that time. For example, when inflation in Argentina reached a peak of 20,000 percent for the 12 months ended March 1990, the correct investment strategy at that time would have been to emphasize companies with high cash balances because real interest rates had been high. Finding such companies is more efficiently accomplished if a data base of companies has been built. The most helpful company data base is one with at least five years of historical financial information. The historical data base is not sufficient for making earnings forecasts, however; the information gleaned from company visits is an important input. In addition, because inflation can be high in many of these countries, when evaluating the stock price at any point, the analyst should adjust earnings estimates to remove the impact of expected inflation that has not yet taken place. Not making the adjustment could artificially lower a P/E estimate because the denominator will be higher than the "real" earnings.

The same modern portfolio theory (MPT) that is used for developed markets can also be used to determine asset allocations in developing markets, where each country is considered an asset class. The goal in MPT portfolio optimization is to determine the combination of country exposures that will generate the highest risk-adjusted return.

Optimization models require expected returns, standard deviations, and a correlation matrix. Regression models can be applied to predict the expected returns in each country. Input factors such as closing prices of the local index, real GDP growth, interest rates, growth in the money supply, and inflation can be used in the regression model.

Expected returns should be estimated net of capital gains and dividend withholding taxes and net of transaction costs, because these factors tend to vary by country. For example, Venezuela imposes a 20 percent withholding tax. Transaction costs (including brokerage commissions, estimated bid–ask spreads, and other fees, such as stamp duties) range from 0.75 percent in Israel to 3.85 percent in India.

Understanding where the numbers come from is important. For example, analysts following Latin America should investigate whether the profits are stemming primarily from positive "net monetary corrections," which arise when fixed assets are greater than shareholders' equity. Obviously, companies that have a high fixed-asset intensity and high debt levels benefit from this adjustment. Thus, before concluding that a stock is attractive on the basis of low P/Es relative to its industry and the local market, an analyst should examine the earnings composition. Net monetary correction is a noncash source of profits and is, therefore, a negative entry in the cash flow statement.

For emerging markets, the qualitative issues—for example, demographics, domestic fiscal and monetary policies, regional and global trends, and the international competitiveness of each country in specific industries—are important considerations when selecting the industries in which to invest. The world is becoming smaller; import barriers are being removed, and export subsidies reduced or removed. These changes have significant effects on companies' operating margins. The objective in industry selection is to position the fund strategically in the most attractive sectors of the economy, those that are likely to grow the fastest.

Accounting principles vary considerably by country, so standardizing the numbers is critical. Without standardization, comparisons of companies across country borders are extremely difficult. One approach to standardization is to reclassify the reported accounts disclosed by these companies into U.S. generally accepted accounting principles or some other standard measure of accounting, such as average price in U.S. dollars per unit sold or sales per employee. Once reclassified, the operating margins, for example, can be expressed in one currency.

Other statistics that can be used to assess the underlying value of a company include such data as the market value of the inventories. Some countries with high inflation carry inventories based on historical costs, as did Brazil when the Legislacao Societaria method of accounting was observed prior to 1993. In these systems, companies that tend to have a high number of days to sell inventory tend to possess "hidden values" in periods of rising inflation. The amount involved can be substantial. When I visited the production plant of Marcopolo, a bus manufacturing company in Brazil, in 1989, the company had a market capitalization of $13 million, but during my visit, buses in the parking lot ready for shipment were worth three times the market capitalization of the firm. That circumstance was a great clue to value, and in addition, the company was highly profitable, had low debt, and was investing to expand capacity.

In making investment decisions, an expectation of the stock's trading range is particularly important. An analyst should establish a fair trading range for each stock. One method to estimate this range bases it on relative P/E. The historical valuation relative to the local market is a useful starting point. Adjustments should then be made based on changes in the underlying earnings momentum and financial quality of the firm.

Value in Emerging Markets

Finding value in emerging markets requires analysis and judgment. To illustrate these concepts, the following discussion will use two companies that have potential as attractive investments.

Nikas, a company in Greece that manufactures sausages, is an example of a bet on the underlying expansion potential of a company. Nikas has an excellent product line commanding 20 percent of the Greek sausage market. The company will double its capacity by year-end 1993. According to its 1992 balance sheet, Nikas's net fixed assets are $15 million. Its net quick liquidation value is $13 million, which is equal to 25 percent of the market capitalization of the firm. The company can fund its expansion program through internally generated funds, but the stock is trading at a discount to the market. This company thus has great potential, particularly once European economic growth accelerates and more tourists can afford to travel to Greece.

The second example illustrates hidden value in an East European country. FTE Universal is a Polish company that has been losing money since 1989 but is the only listed export company in the country. No broker wanted to visit this company, but I asked for a visit because *The Financial Times* was filled with news that Western Europe was considering inviting the East European countries to become members of the European Community; I wanted to find export-oriented companies. In Poland, I discovered that, although Universal was losing money, it owned a huge building that had an appraised value of $18 million but was carried on the books at only $2 million. The total market capitalization of the company was only $11 million.

Question and Answer Session

Josephine Jimenez, CFA

Question: Why do emerging markets lend themselves to sophisticated optimization techniques?

Jimenez: The markets are so inefficient in comparison with developed markets that optimization techniques can be used to take advantage of market inefficiencies and to control risk. For instance, the historical standard deviations of returns for both Argentina and Brazil are in excess of 100 percent. A portfolio-optimization program can actually control the risk element and design a portfolio that can deliver the highest risk-adjusted return.

Question: What is the optimal mix of top-down and bottom-up approaches to asset allocation in emerging markets?

Jimenez: The two are equally important. Using quantitative asset allocation models provides considerable rewards in these inefficient markets.

Question: How much time do you spend traveling?

Jimenez: When I travel to a country, I visit three to five companies a day unless I am visiting a plant. My travel duration is a minimum of two weeks and a maximum of six weeks. I generally visit three to six countries in a six-week period, usually on the same continent. Traveling around the same continent allows me to see what is happening at that time and make comparisons among countries.

Question: How much of the returns achieved by Montgomery Emerging Markets Fund can be ascribed to stock selection and how much to country allocation?

Jimenez: Montgomery has not yet finished its portfolio attribution program, but the preliminary results indicate that the quantitative output of the asset allocation model has consistently beat an index strategy. Furthermore, our "target portfolio," which reflects our judgment on the quantitative output, has actually performed better than the quantitative target. Our stock-picking performance has also been good; the performance in most countries has been better than the local index.

Question: Are you satisfied with the existing benchmark indexes such as the IFC index?

Jimenez: The number of countries represented in the existing published indexes is limited. Because Montgomery has investments in 24 countries, we have country exposures that are not in any of the indexes. We built our own index to include all those countries.

Question: In Montgomery's mean–variance optimizer, how do you overcome instability of historical cross-country correlations?

Jimenez: We use a trailing 60-month correlation matrix.

Question: Do any published sources exist for investors' expected returns (or market risk premiums) in emerging market countries?

Jimenez: No, but these expected returns can be derived, which Montgomery has done, through independent study.

Question: If the market structure is not enough to forecast earnings for each company, what should analysts do—use local research?

Jimenez: The analysts need to obtain a copy of the country's accounting principles from a local accounting firm and then sharpen their pencils.

Question: Excluding Mexico, which emerging market countries are expected to have the safest political climates for the next five years?

Jimenez: The coming year, 1994, will be a major election year in many emerging markets, which means the possibility of new governments coming into power. I do not expect more major political shake-ups, however, than those that have transpired in the past few years. Political turmoil will generally involve such phenomena as corruption scandals and labor protests as workers demand more social and economic benefits.

Building and Administering Country Funds

David H. Gill
Director
Morgan Stanley Emerging Markets Fund, Inc.

> Quality is the most important facet of a new country fund, and quality is achieved primarily through the sponsorship and structure of the fund. For the ongoing management of the fund, the primary role of maintaining quality belongs to the board of directors. The board must take responsibility for controlling the fund's costs and volatility in net asset value, for the fund's performance, and for its governance.

This presentation briefly summarizes the reasons for investing in emerging market funds and discusses important aspects of setting up, administering, and monitoring such funds. Throughout the discussion, the issue of corporate governance will be of particular importance. Fund managers, investment bankers, custodians, administrators—anyone involved in mutual funds, including emerging market and country funds—are reminded that making careless mistakes, lack of appropriate due diligence, has definite consequences.

What needs to be remembered is that a mutual fund, country fund, or any collective investment vehicle is supposed to be an efficient means of helping other people make investments. Therefore, the investment manager must invest in a correct and efficient way; the goal is not simply to get superior investment results, but to get them at the lowest possible cost. If that goal is not achieved, the manager will lose customers.

The Pros and Cons of Investing in Country Funds

The emerging markets continue to outperform the mature markets by a wide margin, with decreasing volatility as a group. Since January 1990, the International Finance Corporation (IFC) Global Investable Total Returns Index has increased over 65 percent, much more than comparable world indexes. The emerging markets' share of world market capitalization has also increased, from 5 percent to more than 7 percent between year-end 1990 and 1993. Moreover, the real GDP growth rate for developing countries continues to outpace that of the developed countries by about 2 percent, and according to the International Monetary Fund (IMF), the difference is likely to increase to near 3 percent.

The emerging markets' stocks remain cheap by most measures when compared with those in the mature markets. The prospective average P/E multiple for emerging markets is about 5 percentage points lower than the multiple for other markets. Furthermore, the numbers behind these ratios, because of improved standards enforced by local securities and exchange commissions and accounting bodies, are increasingly accurate and comparable to those from the developed markets.

Finally, as purchasing power parity (PPP) becomes increasingly used as a measure of economic size and growth, the allocations by institutional investors to emerging markets should increase. Various approaches to weighting are possible—market-capitalization weighting, GDP weighting, and so forth. The next approach could be PPP-weighted GDP. A report by the IMF pointed out that, if PPP is taken into account (which also means taking into account the underground, "black," economy), the so-called developing countries' share of world GDP is not 17 percent but almost twice that figure.

Investment managers still tend to use market capitalization weightings more than GDP weightings in determining country allocations, because market capitalization reflects what can be bought. The use of market capitalization probably explains why most professional investors target about a 7 percent share for emerging markets in their portfolios. Weighting by GDP would increase that share to 15 percent. Weighting by GDP should increase as developing countries reduce restrictions on foreign portfolio investment, bring withholding taxes into line, and encourage their companies to list abroad and issue American Depositary Receipts (ADRs) and Global Depositary Receipts (GDRs). Increased allocations will increase liquidity and reduce volatility.

If one does invest on a GDP weighting basis, using the PPP GDP can improve portfolio results—at least theoretically. If one cannot buy the stocks, however, one cannot get up to the kind of weighting that makes the most economic sense and maximizes profit potential. For that purpose, investors need to note Jay Tata's comments about the other means of investing early in emerging markets—venture capital, private investing, real estate, and so forth.[1]

For example, the first fund in Vietnam, launched in about 1991, had no stocks. The portfolio was close to 100 percent real estate. Such a fund might be considered a real estate fund rather than a country fund, but the point is how to make money investing in emerging markets and in country funds of emerging markets; the instrument does not matter much so long as the investment has the expectation of an above-average rate of return and the investor truly understands the risks. (In the case of real estate, that risk is the total lack of liquidity.) Balancing potential return and risk is part of the due diligence process.

Because of the appeal of emerging markets investing, the number of emerging market funds has grown from fewer than 100 in 1990 to more than 200 in 1994, and their market capitalization has grown from US$7.5 billion to nearly US$50 billion. Direct participation, especially through ADRs and GDRs, may increasingly be the most profitable way to invest in emerging markets, but for all but the largest investors, regional or global emerging market funds are the most efficient entry vehicles. Having an ERISA-qualified manager to hold responsible for results offers some comfort. Moreover, fees paid to fiduciaries probably total no more than the fees necessary to pay banks and local brokers for processing foreign exchange transactions and custodial arrangements. Most markets now have negotiated commission rates; they can be as low as 0.2 percent for institutions, although they are still 1 percent to 2 percent for small customers.

Country funds are appealing in comparison with direct participation also because of the rising interest in niche markets within the established emerging markets, in the "pre-emerging" markets of the former socialist countries, and in the exotic markets of small countries. In these markets, specialized management of the investing is of crucial importance. Examples of niches are such sectors as utilities or telecommunications and venture capital (private investing). Venture-capital funds are being formed in Latin America and Eastern Europe. Most small countries are still either reluctant to accept foreign investors except through a fund or have complicated rules that are best handled by a specialist.

Establishing Country Funds[2]

Country funds have existed since the end of the 19th century. Various country funds may have bells and whistles and different approaches, but all successful country funds have to meet the same basic requirements: high-quality sponsorship, appropriate structure, and proper governance. New funds that are incorporated in jurisdictions with high-quality regulatory and sensible tax environments, that are well sponsored, and that have sensible policies, strategies, and structures are more successful than their competitors in raising money and maintaining strong secondary markets.

Quality

"Doing it right" is very important, not simply in the sense of achieving good returns. Setting the highest standards gives the best results. Funds that are considered first class tend to trade at higher prices than other funds for the same country with similar policies and investment performance. Therefore, high-quality funds will have an advantage; they will sell at either a higher premium or at a lower discount than the immediate competition, the similar funds for that country. If you are the manager of a fund for Country X, and you are competing with ten other Country X funds with similar policies, and your fund is in the secondary market at a 20 percent discount from net asset value (NAV) while the best fund is at a 30 percent premium, you are going to get a few questions from your investors and directors, and if your shareholders are unpleasant, you may get written questions from their lawyers.

Table 1 shows different discounts and premiums of similar funds as of August 1990, and not much has changed since that time. An approximately 30 percent spread still exists between what are obviously perceived to be the worst and best quality funds. For example, the London-listed Chile fund now trades at a 30 percent discount, and the one in New York trades at a slight premium. An article in *The Financial Times* more than a year ago mentioned some embarrassment in London about the U.K. Chile

---

[1] See Mr. Tata's presentation, pages 125–26.

[2] This and the following section draw on David B. Gill, "How to Set Up a Country Fund," Chapter 6 in *Investing in Emerging Securities Markets* (London: Euromoney Publications, 1990: pp. 29–38).

Table 1. Selected Emerging Markets Closed-End Country Funds

						As of 31 August, 1990	
Fund	Market Listing	Date of First Offering	Gross Initial Size (US$millions)	Offering Price per Share[a]	Market Price per Share	Premium/Discount to NAV (%)	Total Market Value[b] (US$millions)
Regional funds							
EMGF	Luxembourg	May 86	$383.21	$20.75	$30.98	—	$591.16
Templeton E.M. Fund	AMEX	Feb 87	115.00	10.00	14.38	-5.80%	165.31
EMIF	Luxembourg	Feb 88	117.81	10.28	14.92	—	170.98
Asian Development Equity Fund	Luxembourg	Jan 88	100.00	10.00	15.90	—	159.00
Chile							
Chile Fund	NYSE	Oct 89	80.50	15.00	14.38	-10.70	77.15
Five Arrows Chile Fund	London	Feb 90	75.00	10.00	6.50	-34.60	48.75
India							
India Fund	London	Jul 86	127.80	1.70	4.16	-9.40	312.00
India Growth Fund	NYSE	Aug 88	60.10	12.00	15.50	-12.00	77.65
Indonesia							
Jakarta Fund	London	Aug 89	21.00	10.50	17.50	-14.50	35.00
Nomura Jakarta Fund	Hong Kong	Sep 89	30.00	10.00	10.67	—	32.01
Indonesia Fund	NYSE	Mar 90	60.00	15.00	12.75	-7.10	51.00
Korea (South)							
Korea Fund	NYSE	Aug 84	150.00	10.88	16.63	49.60	358.37
Korea Growth Trust	Hong Kong	Mar 85	31.50	10.50	30.50	-0.90	91.50
Korea International Trust	Luxembourg	Nov 81	27.25	10.48	40.50	-3.10	105.30
Korea Trust	Luxembourg	Nov 81	26.03	14.87	48.50	0.20	84.88
Korea Europe Fund	London	Mar 87	116.13	4.04	4.70	11.10	134.94
Malaysia							
Malaysia Fund	NYSE	May 87	96.60	12.00	14.25	4.50	114.71
Malaysia Growth Fund	Luxembourg	Apr 89	45.25	10.00	10.75	—	48.64
Malacca Fund	London	Jan 89	36.40	10.40	14.50	-9.70	50.75
Mexico							
Mexico Fund	NYSE	Jun 81	147.31	7.47	13.63	-6.20	272.38
Portugal							
Portugal Fund	London	Aug 87	42.32	10.58	6.63	7.70	26.50
Portugal Fund	NYSE	Nov 89	69.00	15.00	10.88	-16.20	50.02
Thailand							
Bangkok Fund	London	Aug 85	44.17	17.72	69.00	-8.40	172.50
Thai Fund	NYSE	Feb 88	114.96	12.00	18.50	-5.60	177.23
Thailand Fund	London	Dec 86	31.14	10.38	38.87	—	116.61
Thai Prime Fund	Singapore	Sep 88	155.00	10.00	17.00	-3.60	263.50
Thai International Fund	London	Nov 88	80.03	10.67	17.50	2.70	131.25

Source: IFC Emerging Markets Database.

[a] Offering price per share reflects weighted-average price of initial and subsequent offering prices.
[b] Figures in the "Total Market Value" column do not reflect rates of return because they do not take into account dividends paid.

funds, one of which got down to about a 40 percent discount at a time when the NYSE equivalent was at a premium. The managers of the U.K. Chile fund were in deep trouble and had to go through several maneuvers to reduce that discount—redeem stock and many other strange things. Although the maneuvers moved the discount up a bit, the spread is still about the same now as it was.

Sponsorship is a most important contributor to the quality of a fund. Sponsors can be the government of the country, an organization like the IFC, an investment manager, or an investment bank. All of them have different objectives, and some objectives are better for quality than others. The better the quality of the institutions involved in sponsoring the fund, the better the fund appears, and the better it usually turns out to be down the road when listed and traded in the secondary market. One of the most unlikely country funds ever established (next to Vietnam) is the Mauritius Fund. Mauritius is an attractive little island in the Indian Ocean with a good economy, but it is practically unknown and was, a while ago, not investor friendly. It would not have a country fund without the quality of the sponsors (Crown Agents, a U.K. entity with a 160-year record of doing business in small countries) and their ability to attract other investors, who give the sponsors the benefit of the doubt.

Structure

The next contributor to quality is structure, in both the broad and the narrow senses. Where is the fund incorporated? Is it in a satisfactory regulatory environment? Is the tax environment satisfactory?

One of the key elements in establishing a country fund that will keep your investors happy is to keep the fiduciaries out of court. Fortunately, not much has gone wrong in the U.S. market in the past five years or so, so the discussion is mostly precautionary at present. Conflict of interest is a major concern in country funds, and in mutual funds in general. The old European approach, which may be growing in the United States, is the poorest extreme of fund administration. In the European approach, the separation of functions can be characterized as follows: One financial conglomerate is the sponsor, the underwriter, the investment manager, the custodian, the administrator, and the broker. Such a fund is not perceived to be high quality because it has so much potential conflict of interest. This structure is another reason the London-listed closed-end country funds sell at a 30 percent average discount to NAV relative to the equivalent NYSE-listed funds. A degree of independence among underwriters, investment managers, and custodians reassures shareholders that conflicts of interest are largely minimized. A single financial supermarket may be applying the appropriate rules, but the shareholder has more confidence if the custodian is not owned by the same manager and the underwriter is not directly related.

For example, in one fund in which the underwriter was affiliated with the investment manager, the underwriter's trading department accidentally made a substantial profit trading in the fund shares shortly after issuance when the shares were still restricted on the usual conflict-of-interest basis. Through due diligence, the underwriter eventually determined the firm had broken through its "Chinese Walls" and advised its investment manager affiliate. The investment manager came to the fund's board of directors, confessed all, and said the investment bank would give the fund back all of the profits it made; that is the law. In addition, the board had to arrange for independent legal counsel to make certain the settlement was fair in the views of all concerned. This repair work cost a lot of money—not to the fund, which probably made money because it got all of the profits, and not to the shareholders because directors insurance covers such situations. The legal steps were expensive, time-consuming, and painful.

More important than corporate governance in influencing spreads between funds' net asset values and secondary market prices is liquidity, as evidenced by the continuing disadvantages of London-listed funds vis-a vis their New York counterparts. A recent report by Lipper Analytical Services highlights this factor; Lipper reported that all ten of the emerging market funds with the highest discounts were incorporated under U.K. or Netherlands law and all but one of the ten funds with the highest premiums were U.S. incorporated and NYSE listed. Since 1990, an interesting evolution has been going on in the regulatory environments of the United States and the United Kingdom, the two countries where most funds are listed. Whereas in London, regulations enforced by the Securities Investment Board (SIB, the equivalent to the SEC) continue to tighten, London Stock Exchange standards appear to have relaxed. For example, at least 200 investors used to be required for a London listing (compared with the 2,000 required by the NYSE), but listing in London now requires many fewer than 200 if the investors are large institutions managing numerous individual portfolios. This change has done nothing good for liquidity.

Managing and Monitoring Funds

Governance is concerned with how investment performance compares with established benchmarks and with maintaining the quality of the fund, in the sense of the structure and ethical standards, the fiduciaries' contract arrangements, and standards of reporting to shareholders. Management of corporate governance is becoming increasingly important. All kinds of entities have recently been established to promote shareholders' rights, and in the industrial sector, independent members of the boards of companies have caused or forced shake-ups of management. The same general concern applies to everyone working in the overall administrative and investment aspects of fund management. Fiduciaries must do what they say they are going to do and be able to document it.

As with any other company or organization, the board of directors or board of advisors is responsible for the fund's corporate governance. The board approves the initial structure and manages/monitors the fund on behalf of the shareholders. The board is responsible for the costs of establishing the fund (for the efforts made by the sponsors to make sure that start-up, legal, prospectus, and underwriting costs are reasonable and justifiable) and for the quality of the contracts with the fiduciaries. All of this information is contained in the prospectus, which the board approves. Being on the board of a country fund is no different from being on the board of IBM except that, instead of overseeing internal managers running the company, country fund boards are overseeing external fiduciaries, investment managers, custodians, and so forth. In the eyes of the SEC, the SIB in London, and the law, the board of directors is responsible for what happens.

In the United States, the SEC requires that the majority of a fund's board be "disinterested" or "independent" individuals—that is, not associated with any of the fiduciaries or officers of the fund. An essential function of the board is the periodic review of all fiduciaries' contracts and auditors' appointments and fees; these contracts must then be approved at the shareholders' annual meeting.

In practice, no such thing as a 100 percent independent director exists. At the beginning of the fund's life, directors are nominated by the sponsors of the fund, investment managers, underwriters, and so forth. To that extent, therefore, they are friends of management. Of course, directors of high repute named in the prospectus indirectly help sell the initial public offerings. A fund sponsor would be foolish not to have in mind a list of potential independent directors who are competent in the appropriate subjects, intelligent, and experienced. Moreover, the managers know that such directors, once elected, will behave responsibly in the interests of all shareholders.

The result of these legal and commonsense factors is that 99 percent of U.S. independent directors take the job seriously, which is not always the case in other types of companies and with funds incorporated outside the United States.

In the United States, the procedure for approving the prospectus is fairly simple: When the fund creators sign off on the prospectus, that is the end of their responsibility. The process in the United Kingdom, which in the past had a reputation for being somewhat casual in its securities laws, changed with the Financial Services Act in 1986. Now, the rules are stricter than they are in the United States. For example, directors of U.K. funds must fill out a form answering about 600 questions on the accuracy of everything in their prospectus and provide information on the sources of the information. For one fund, one of the questions asked if we could assure that the national seal for this country was really the national seal.

The board of directors should not, however, try to micromanage what the investment managers or the custodians are doing in the actual operation of the fund. Any shareholder who thought the directors were micromanaging would be justified in selling immediately, because directors are not day-to-day managers and they should stay out of it. If directors are not happy with management, they should fire the managers and replace them.

So far, the directors' monitoring function has been described primarily as making sure the fund is complying with regulations and its own policies and procedures and making sure its numbers are accurate. The main objective, of course, is for the board to assure the ongoing performance and governance of the fund—to measure results in terms of costs and performance and to make sure the results are satisfactory.

Since 1990, the number of funds for the same country with similar objectives has become sufficient enough to make possible meaningful performance comparisons. This approach is a great improvement over having to use a country or regional index as a benchmark. In addition, the local exchanges are using improved technologies, and funds understand the indexes prepared by local exchanges better than they did in the past. Further improvements are still needed, however. For instance, in Mexico, Telmex still represents 30 percent of the local index, so that index has little value in measuring funds with strict diversification requirements. The IFC investable indexes provide a valuable guide. Nevertheless, some funds, in their advertising, compare their performance with an index that makes them look good but has no relevance.

Cost performance measurement has also been helped by the increased number of comparable funds now operating. What is now evident is that single-country funds of more than $100 million in assets should have total operating costs (excluding brokerage commissions) not exceeding 1.7 percent. Costs can be as low as 1.2 percent. Many investment managers now place voluntary caps of 2 percent on total operating expenses, with overage deducted directly from their management fees. **Table 2** and **Table 3** illustrate the costs of various aspects of operating funds—manager fees, custodial fees, and so forth. These tables show the kinds of information directors review and give an idea of the cost differences among the United States, the United Kingdom, and other European jurisdictions. These cost figures, again, help explain why the London-based funds sell at either lower premiums or higher discounts. In theory, high operating costs could result in strong investment performance; if the fees are higher than average, more due diligence and hard work is probably going on, more staff is working on behalf of fiduciaries, and thus results are probably better. In practice, there is little correlation between costs and performance; in fact, some of the best performing funds have below-average cost ratios.

Although performance and the monitoring of operating costs consume most of their time, directors must also pay close attention to volatility of the fund's NAV and share price, and to portfolio turnover and brokerage costs, all of which affect performance and quality. For example, if turnover and commission rates are high (over 50 percent and 1 percent annually, respectively), NAV is reduced 1 percent annually. The questions, then, are: Considering the market impact costs, does short-term trading in illiquid markets add value, and is "best execution" being obtained?

The role of audit committees in country funds is taken more seriously now than it was five years ago. The SEC requires audit committees for all registered funds, and the NYSE requires them for all listed companies, but previously, an audit committee met once or twice a year with the auditors, agreed to the audit plan and the auditor's fees, and had a private discussion without management to make sure the managers were not doing things that might be slightly coercive as far as the auditors were concerned. (Major issues in many countries have been managers putting pressure on auditors to report more favorably than they might otherwise and managers hiding information.) The savings & loan scan-

Table 2. Emerging Market Funds' Operating Cost Ratios: Selected Non-U.S. Closed-End Funds
(percent of fund assets)

	Advisory and Administration	Custodian	Auditors	Legal	Directors and Other Expenses	Total Excluding NA and Taxes	Estimated Total Excluding Taxes[a]
Baring Chrysalis Fund, Ltd. (FYE 12/31/91)	0.81%	0.27%	0.01%	NA	0.17%	1.26%	1.27%
Beta Global Emerging Markets Investment Trust (FYE 12/31/91)	2.45	NA	0.05	NA	0.94	3.44	3.72
Emerging Markets Strategic Fund (FYE 12/31/91)	1.77	0.30	NA	NA	0.28	2.35	2.36
Fleming Emerging Markets Investment Trust (FYE 6/30/92)	1.35	NA	0.03	NA	0.43	1.80	2.08
Genesis Emerging Markets Fund (FYE 6/30/92)	1.20	0.29	0.02	NA	0.74	2.31	2.32
New Frontiers Development Trust (FYE 9/30/92)	1.51	NA	0.03	NA	0.74	2.31	2.59
Templeton Emerging Markets Investment Trust (FYE 4/30/92)	2.32	NA	0.02	NA	0.01	2.35	2.63

Source: Data provided by Lipper Analytical Services.

FYE = fiscal year end.

NA = not available.

[a]Where custodial and legal expense figures were not available, they were assumed in each case to be, respectively, 0.27 percent and 0.01 percent.

Table 3. Emerging Market Funds' Operating Cost Ratios: Selected U.S. SEC-Registered Closed-End Funds

Fund	Average Risk Assets ($millions)	Administrative/ Advisory	Transfer Agent	Custodian	Legal	Audit	Directors	Shareholder Reporting	Misc.	Total Expenses before Taxes
Emerging Markets Growth Fund	1,138.6	0.820%	0.000%	0.241%	0.011%	0.001%	0.009%	0.000%	0.031%	1.11%
Morgan Stanley Emerging Markets Fund	175.8	1.383	0.074	0.366	0.034	0.033	0.048	0.001	0.083	2.02
Templeton Emerging Markets	232.7	1.400	0.009	0.284	0.010	0.018	0.011	0.130	0.045	1.91
Latin American Investment Fund	88.1	1.501	0.039	0.281	0.159	0.036	0.025	0.085	0.195	2.31
Scudder New Asia Fund	107.1	1.129	0.019	0.261	0.049	0.050	0.076	0.060	0.144	1.79
Scudder New Europe Fund	150.6	1.243	0.001	0.221	0.028	0.038	0.077	0.047	0.107	1.76
Indonesia Fund	43.1	1.175	0.069	0.214	0.200	0.055	0.048	0.058	0.172	1.99
Korea Fund	252.2	1.050	0.012	0.200	0.075	0.028	0.046	0.025	0.076	1.51
Malaysia Fund	111.5	1.129	0.100	0.275	0.034	0.028	0.100	0.001	0.049	1.72
Thai Fund	176.2	1.058	0.049	0.104	0.013	0.018	0.072	0.001	0.063	1.37

Source: Data provided by Lipper Analytical Services.

dal, however, highlighted the problems caused by a lack of any requirements for the functions of audit committees. With no requirements and no one responsible for making sure the auditors and managers had a correct relationship, pulling the wool over the auditors' eyes was not difficult. Had the savings & loans been required to have functioning audit committees, half the disasters would never have occurred because the managers would have been caught much earlier.

Conclusion and the Future

The ultimate responsibility of the board is to make sure that the country fund's investment return is reasonable relative to what was promised in the prospectus and relative to reasonable investor expectations. Is the fund properly run? Is the administration set up so that the investment manager can do a good job and the costs are not unreasonable?

Emerging market funds will continue to expand—despite predictions a few years ago that investing in emerging markets would shift to ADRs and so forth. Innovation and niche funds will continue. Those in the business of promoting funds who do not find niche markets, either specialized funds in big countries or funds in new countries, will lose opportunities.

The pressure on fiduciaries to reduce costs is much higher today than it was in 1990; therefore, sponsors of funds and investment managers that cannot get their costs down close to the U.S. fund level run the risk of losing business. Costs and fees are expected to go down, however, as competition and the number and size of equity funds increase and as local markets become increasingly professional.

Registration in the United States with the SEC and listing on the NYSE remain the best paths to establishing a first-class fund. Even foreign professional investors view the advantages of these paths as outweighing the disadvantage to them of accepting a foreign jurisdiction.

Private placement funds will continue to attract a large following as institutions remain wary of having to mark to market the listed funds that fall to discounts. Large institutions will commit $25 million or more to these private funds, but not to listed funds.

The current challenge for investment bankers, managers, and investors is deciding when pre-emerging and exotic markets, such as China and the countries in Eastern Europe, are about to become respectable and when the old ones have graduated to mature status. Who would have imagined in 1990 that close to 30 China funds would exist today? But substantial return opportunities await those early birds who entered China through the venture-capital types of funds. And who would have thought the embryonic Polish market would become acceptable so quickly, with stock tripling during 1992?

Question and Answer Session

David H. Gill

Question: I have found that London investors are much better informed about closed-end funds than American investors and have better sponsors. Could the apparent discount differential be a coincidence? Have you tracked it over time?

Gill: I have tracked it over time, and closed-end funds have a long history of trading at massive discounts in the U.K. market. London managers and investors are more aware of the discount situation than U.S. managers because the Londoners have had the biggest problems. For example, a bunch of vulture funds were set up in the United Kingdom specifically to buy out closed-end funds, such as the Chile country funds that I mentioned. The vulture funds were to take control of these funds at discounts and liquidate them. It was an easy way to make money.

Question: Why would a potential shareholder want to subscribe to a closed-end fund in the United Kingdom knowing that the fund is likely to go to a significant discount in the near future?

Gill: The buyers of the initial public offerings are hard to understand. A number of U.S. funds have bought into these listed U.K. funds in the after market, however, for much the same reason as the U.K. vulture funds—to take advantage of the deep discounts on the principal. That kind of activity is the best way to put more money into a particular foreign market. For example, the various U.S.-listed India funds have bought the U.K.-listed India funds at 30–40 percent discounts rather than put more money directly in India because of the restrictions on repatriating capital. That strategy turned out to be remarkably successful in the past couple of years. When the Indian market took its big hit, declining some 50 percent, these London fund discounts decreased to 2–10 percent, so the U.S. funds suffered less than they would have if they had invested directly. If, for example, the Indian market went down 25 percent during the investor's period, and the fund that was bought at a 35 percent discount improved merely to a 15 percent discount, the U.S. fund's NAV lost hardly any value in India in comparison with the potential 25 percent loss. The arithmetic is simple: Assume the market is 100 and the investor buys the fund at a 35 percent discount, or 65. The market drops to 75. The fund discount drops to 15 percent. Therefore, the fund shares are worth 75 minus 15 percent, or 63.75.

Question: In the United Kingdom, as has happened in the United States, have any corporate-raider type groups gone after a closed-end mutual fund that is trading at a sharp discount? Do you think these types of activities will result in a narrowing or the actual evaporation of the discount?

Gill: In the United Kingdom, raids occur not so much with emerging market country funds as with other funds. Raiders are sometimes surprised, however, as in the case of an investor in the Mexico Fund, Inc., on the NYSE several years ago who did not read the prospectus before investing in the fund in order to take it over and liquidate it. The prospectus stated that the underlying contracts with the Mexican government meant it could *not* be liquidated under any circumstances for ten years. This poor guy spent tens of millions of dollars before he spent the time to read the contract.

Question: Do differences in exchange rate expectations affect closed-end fund prices relative to net asset values? Could this effect explain some of the spread between the U.K.-traded and U.S.-traded Chile funds?

Gill: As to the first part of the question, yes, any expectation of change in the future affects current prices of the fund shares as much as it does the underlying portfolio. But, no, it should not affect the difference in discounts (or premiums) between London- and NYSE-listed funds, because the market expectations for exchange rate changes would be assumed to affect Chilean stocks the same way. In other words, the only circumstances that would result in a change in the spread would be if numerous shareholders in the London-listed fund who were not shareholders in the NYSE-listed fund had very different foreign exchange expectations from the NYSE shareholders. That circumstance is not impossible, but it's highly unlikely.

Managing Emerging Market Fixed-Income Portfolios

Marc Wenhammar
Head of Fixed Income
Latin American Securities

> The debt markets in the developing countries are vigorous and offer a wide range of instruments. The surge of Eurobond issues signifies a desirable return of the developing countries to the international capital markets. Important steps in managing a global portfolio that includes emerging market debt are knowing the investor's goals and, because of the markets' volatility, how actively to trade, achieving sufficient diversification to eliminate systematic risk, prior research to allow speedy moves in the market, and close contacts with the secondary and new-issue markets.

Investing in the fixed-income instruments of emerging markets is rapidly expanding. Debt instruments in the emerging markets are attractive for several reasons, including:

- *High returns.* Even after the recent rally in fixed-income securities, returns to emerging market debt are still high. One reason is that, because some of these countries have defaulted on their debt in the past, investors are wary of their debt instruments and the countries must pay a premium for access to the capital markets.
- *Asset class.* Emerging market fixed-income instruments are becoming a separate asset class with low correlation with other asset groups. The size of the fixed-income market, variety of instruments available, the returns, and number of players in the market—all indicate that the fixed-income debt of emerging markets can play a distinct role in investors' portfolios.
- *Improving creditworthiness and prospects for sustainable growth.* Overall, these countries have attractive futures, but not all countries are equally attractive. Investors must exercise choice and invest carefully. These countries are in different stages of reform.

This presentation will describe the size and composition of the fixed-income market in developing countries and discuss important concerns in the management of fixed-income instruments within a portfolio.

Market Characteristics

The size of the emerging markets' debt market is estimated to be almost $400 billion. The exact size varies, however, depending on one's definition of instruments and what one considers part of the accessible debt market. **Figure 1** shows the range of instruments composing the market. Some people include as part of the market private placements, bank loans, and domestic debt that is accessible to foreign investors based on registration requirements, liquidity, and so forth. Because as much as half of the total debt market is *not* accessible or liquid, investors should think in terms of a $200 billion market.

This market is growing. In 1988, the only investment instruments were bank loans and domestic debt that was awkward to play; Brady bonds did not yet exist. Today, Brady plans are in place in a number of markets, and Brady bonds are increasing. Eurobond issuance is also increasing. Looking forward, investors can expect more Brady plans to bring more bonds to the market. The opening of local markets will continue to provide expanding opportunities.

Latin America currently dominates the fixed-income market in the emerging countries; most of the existing debt and a significant part of the new debt is from Latin America. The geographical scope of the market is expanding, however, in Africa, Eastern Europe, and Asia.

Most emerging market debt is not rated invest-

Figure 1. Market Size

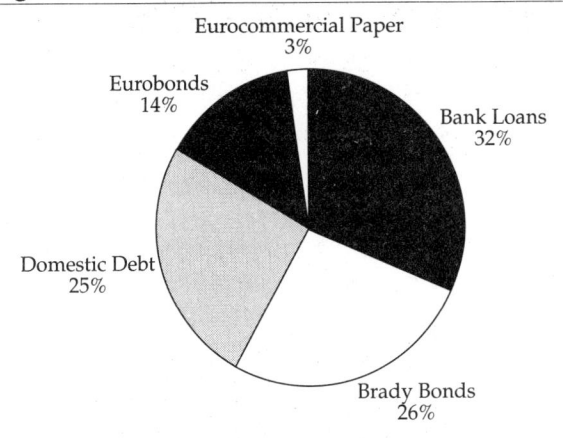

- Eurocommercial Paper 3%
- Eurobonds 14%
- Bank Loans 32%
- Domestic Debt 25%
- Brady Bonds 26%

Source: Latin American Securities.

ment grade. **Table 1** compares debt ratings by Moody's and Standard & Poor's for a sample of markets. In Latin America, most people consider only Chile to be investment grade, but Colombia is rated investment grade by Standard & Poor's. Other countries rated investment grade by at least one rating agency are the Czech Republic, Turkey, and Indonesia. The remainder aspire to receiving an investment grade rating; it is important to the emerging countries because it opens the market to a large pool of investors who are limited to investment grade or better investments.

A rating agency's perspective may not be current, because the agencies rely on several years of history for each rating. By the time an agency publishes a new rating, the time may have passed at which one could capture a move in bond prices resulting from improved creditworthiness. Some countries, in fact, display "investment grade anticipation" moves. For example, Mexico is expected to receive investment grade rating soon, even without the North American Trade Agreement (NAFTA) if Mexico proceeds carefully to continue reforms. Part of that expectation is already in the price, but not all of it.

A variety of fixed-income instruments exist in the emerging markets. These instruments can be classified under several headings: sovereign bank loans, Brady and pre-Brady bonds, Eurobonds, Eurocommercial paper, and domestic debt (instruments or paper that trade locally inside the markets and are generally denominated in local currency). The Brady bonds restructure the old debt of countries that meet the requirements of the Brady plan. Eurobonds offer access to international capital markets for the new debt.

Brady Bonds

The Brady plan allows countries to transform nonperforming debt into debt that performs, giving some principal back to the lenders and alleviating some of the borrowers' debt burdens. Thus, Brady bonds, which are bearer bonds, are sovereign debt packaged as long bonds, generally with collateral. Participation in a Brady plan and issuing Brady bonds requires a seal of approval from the International Monetary Fund and other multilateral agencies. To qualify for Brady bonds, a country must be undertaking basic and drastic reforms in the areas of budget deficits, tax receipts, and inflation controls.

When collateralized, Brady bonds are a mixture of U.S. Treasury securities and developing country risk. These bonds typically carry a 12- to 18-month interest rate guarantee.

Figure 2 shows the share of Brady bonds by emerging market countries. Mexico was the first to issue Brady bonds, which it did in 1989, followed by Venezuela, Costa Rica, Uruguay, Nigeria, the Philippines, and Argentina. In late 1993, Mexico, Venezu-

Table 1. Emerging Market Debt Ratings by Country

Country	Moody's	S&P
Turkey	Baa3	BBB
Chile	NR	BBB
Czech Republic	Baa3	NR
Indonesia	NR	BBB–
Colombia	Ba1	BBB–
Venezuela	Ba1	BB
Hungary	Ba1	BB+
Mexico	Ba2	BB+
India	Ba2	BB+
Philippines	Ba3	NR
Argentina	B1	NR
Brazil	B2	NR
Investment grade	Baa3	BBB–

Source: Latin American Securities.

NR = not rated.

Figure 2. Brady Bonds by Country

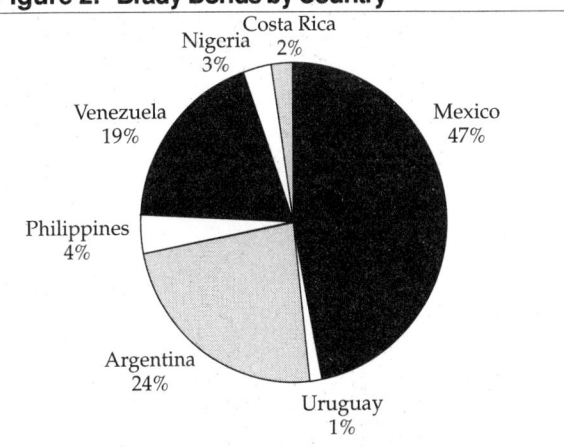

- Costa Rica 2%
- Nigeria 3%
- Venezuela 19%
- Mexico 47%
- Philippines 4%
- Argentina 24%
- Uruguay 1%

Source: Latin American Securities.

ela, and Argentina dominated the market, but Brazil was expected to represent about 30 percent of the market if it qualified to issue Brady bonds.

Brady bonds come in various types; different bonds were issued to accommodate the preferences of different lenders for interest rate levels, and the level of debt forgiveness granted in the rescheduling negotiations. Some are traded and some are not. The bonds are easier to clear and to reschedule than the original loans, and they usually trade at a premium to the loans.

Brady bonds come with different options, which complicates the investment analysis. Typically, the terms vary by country, but the structures are similar. As Brady plans increase, the options become more complicated. Some people are concerned at the moment about Brazilian Brady bonds because of the complexity of options the bonds are likely to have; the question is whether investors will know how to value and trade these bonds.

Enhancements to Brady bonds can vary. For example, the principal might be collateralized, and the interest can be guaranteed for a certain period; some bonds have attached warrants linked to the price of oil.

Examples of Brady bond variations, and the acronyms by which they are known for convenience, are as follows: par bonds (PARs), discount bonds (DISCs), front-loaded interest-reduction bonds (FLIRBs), new-money bonds (NMBs), debt-conversion bonds (DCBs), and past-due interest bonds (PDIs). PARs and DISCs are the most frequent types of Brady bond.

■ *Par bonds*. PARs are exchanged dollar for dollar and carry a coupon rate below that of the market. Typically, the rates are fixed, although Argentina recently issued step-up par bonds, and maturities are 25–30 years with a "bullet" payment at maturity. (In a bullet, unlike an amortizing bond, all principal is paid at maturity.) Principal is collateralized by U.S. Treasury zero-coupon bonds, and interest has an 18-month rolling guarantee (escrow account).

■ *Discount bonds*. DISCs are exchanged at a discount to the face amount, with a market-rate coupon. The rates are typically LIBOR + 13/16 percent. Maturities are 25–30 years with a bullet payment at maturity. The size of the discount depends on the level of forgiveness. Some DISCs are collateralized for principal and carry interest guarantees. Costa Rica, for example, has interest guarantee, but the principal is not collateralized.

■ *Front-loaded interest-reduction bonds*. FLIRBs are fixed-coupon bonds for which the interest rates are stepped up to higher levels for a certain number of years and then the FLIRBs turn into floating-rate bonds. Collateral is not required on the principal, but the interest payments are guaranteed during the period of fixed rates. When the bond becomes a floater, the guarantee is removed. These bonds typically amortize for a ten-year average life.

These bonds are not easy to value. For example, the Venezuela FLIRBs started with a coupon of 5 percent in 1990, stepped up to 6 percent in 1992, will step up to 7 percent in 1994, then in 1995 will go to LIBOR + 7/8 percent until maturity in 2007.

■ *New-money bonds and debt-conversion bonds*. NMBs and DCBs are floating-rate bonds, typically at LIBOR + 7/8 percent, that amortize for a 10–15 year average life. These bonds have no collateral or guarantees. Because they have no collateral, they represent pure country risk; thus, they tend to be more volatile than other types of bonds and react more to what is going on in the country at any moment.

■ *Past-due interest bonds*. PDIs are issued to pay for the interest on interest. Countries have dealt with their nonperforming debt in different ways. In Argentina, the debt traded in one of two ways—with accrued interest, and without accrued interest. Argentina recently issued some PDIs called FRBs (floating-rate bonds).

In anticipation of issuing Brady bonds, Brazil has handled its nonperforming debt in different ways. First, Brazil issued "interest due and unpaid" bonds (IDUs) to deal with the problem of accrued interest. Currently, IDUs are carrying a high coupon (at 8.75 percent). At the end of 1993, they will become floaters paying LIBOR + 13/16 percent. What will happen to the market value of those bonds at that point is not known.

Brazil also offered what is the equivalent of forward contracts on the forthcoming Brady bonds, when and if they are issued. Investors pay for these bonds only upon delivery, not now. The drop-dead date was November 30, after which the deal was off. Because of delays in negotiations, the deadline has been extended to the end of February 1994.

Brady bonds are valued in terms of cash flow yield. Some people also calculate the "stripped yield," which reflects the pure sovereign risk. The stripped yield may be useful for analytical purposes, but it is not sufficient to those who invest in order to receive principal and interest.

Investors must also consider the risks associated with these bonds. Despite the collateral and the guarantees, default risk, which is primarily sovereign risk, remains. In the case of the Nigerian Brady bonds, for example, both the principal and the interest are collateralized, but uncertainties over interest payment have increased, raising the odds for nonpayment at the next interest-payment date. Because of the collateral, the investors forgo interest until the bonds mature; they then get their U.S. Treasuries back. Political and macroeconomic analysis is very important in assessing this default risk.

The biggest risk in Brady bonds is market risk. Essentially, Brady bonds are bonds with 30-year maturities and strong links to U.S. Treasuries; therefore, U.S. interest rate changes are a significant risk for the investor. In fact, an important part of the recent rally in emerging market fixed-income instruments can be linked to declining interest rates in the U.S. market. Of course, another part of the rally relates to the significant inflow of money into these markets. The investor who is thinking of taking on money market or short-term exposure should keep in mind that Brady bonds are longer term instruments, not at all money-market-type investments.

Brady-to-Be Bonds

Most emerging markets are lining up to issue Brady plan debt. Two countries, Brazil and the Dominican Republic, are in the final stages of implementing Brady plans, and a number of other countries are in line for Brady plans by 1995, including Poland, Ecuador, Panama, and Peru. Following them, Bulgaria, Honduras, the Ivory Coast, Russia, Nicaragua, Cuba, North Korea, and Vietnam are likely Brady plan countries. In combination, these countries represent more than US$80 billion in debt.

Values for the existing debt of these countries depend on each country's situation. For Brady-to-be instruments, speculation on news of debt restructurings and the time horizons for completing Brady-type plans drive prices. Obviously, strong medium-term economic fundamentals are positive for prices, as are short time horizons. Clearly also, the investment analysis should include sound fundamental research, scenarios on debt-restructuring terms, debt–equity-swap potential, analysis of liquidity in the market, and an assessment of the likelihood that the country will complete the Brady plan.

The countries nearest to final Brady plans will obviously be the easiest to value. An investor can value the outstanding loans of Brazil, Poland, Ecuador, Peru, and Panama, for example, by assuming a certain level of debt forgiveness and applying a discount rate that reflects completion risk (of the Brady exchange) and medium-term prospects. The values for countries such as Cuba, Nicaragua, Vietnam, and North Korea will be much more speculative. The upside in these cases will initially come from debt–equity swaps (projects, privatizations) increasing the demand for that debt paper and sporadic direct debt buy-backs from the countries themselves.

Brady-to-be instruments are not easy to trade or settle. The spreads are wide; spreads between bid and offer vary between 1 and 2 percentage points, while Brady bonds have spreads of less than a quarter of a point. Also, liquidity is thin, and rumors still play a disproportionate role in the market.

Relationships are very important to successful trading in these markets. Therefore, investors need to know the other parties. It is in the best interest of counterparties for the investor to do more than one trade with them, because the markets contain so few traders.

Investors have several options for buying the instruments of Brady-to-be country bonds, some of which are warrants, special-purpose vehicles, and structured products.

Eurobonds

Emerging market Eurobonds represent the return of the developing countries, especially in Latin America, to the international capital markets. The new issues launched in the Euromarket (generally denominated in U.S. dollars and trading outside their countries of origin) have multiplied in the 1990s, as **Figure 3** shows. Latin America represents 75 to 80 percent of the nearly US$20 billion of new debt issued in 1993.

Figure 3. Eurobonds: The New Debt

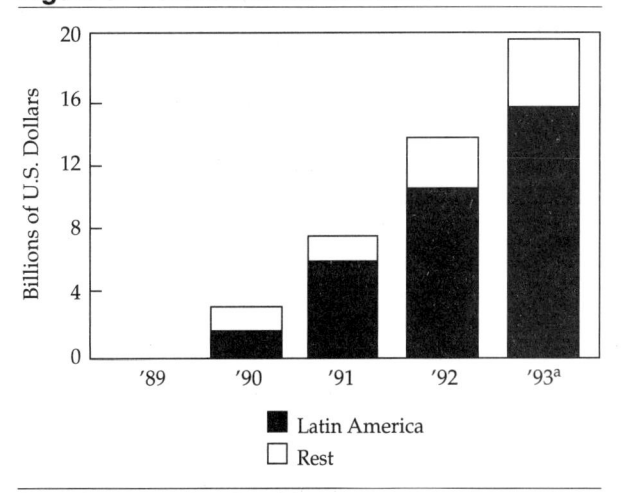

Source: Latin American Securities.
[a]Projected.

Eurobonds provide access to international capital markets for countries and companies trying to raise new capital. Eurobonds are typically less volatile than Brady and Brady-to-be bonds, and they offer an attractive yield.

Eurobonds are used to provide financing to countries that are in the midst of economic reforms and cannot generate the financing internally. Typically, the money is used to fund increases in productive capacity, infrastructure, and privatizations. In the past, governments of developing countries would tap outside markets for capital and redistribute it internally according to political agendas. Now, these governments are turning over financing, as well as companies, to the private sector.

Since the return of the developing countries to international markets, their sovereign Eurobonds have been providing relatively high yields. **Figure 4** shows the yields for four Latin American countries; all these countries' Eurobonds are yielding more than U.S. Treasuries. The bond yields reflect specific country risk, with Brazil yielding the highest and Mexico the lowest, but country risk is not the only determinant of yield: Although Venezuela, for example, is still rated better than Mexico, Mexico provides a lower yield.

Figure 4. Eurobond Yields in Latin America versus the U.S. Treasury Bond Yield as of September 1993

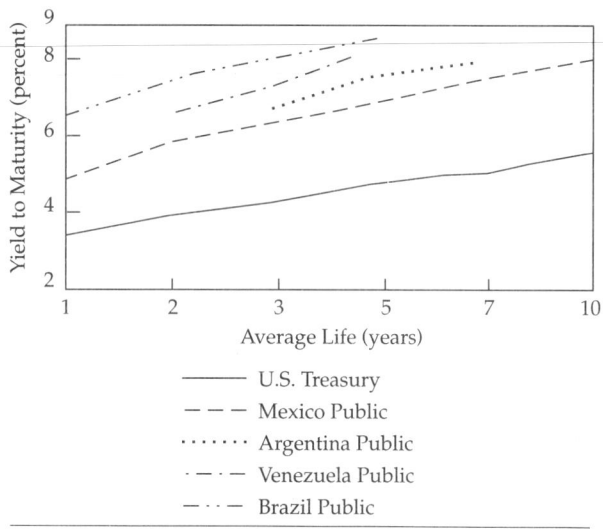

Source: Latin American Securities.

Chile is not included in this set because it has not been an active issue. Chile's debt currently yields about 200 basis points more than U.S. Treasuries, which would place it below Mexico on Figure 4.

Emerging market issuers are generally willing to pay the premium over U.S. Treasuries to secure Eurobond financing for several reasons. The first is that sufficient local financing is not available in most countries. Second, Eurobond financing is less expensive than most local financing options. One reason is that most countries are experiencing high real interest rates as a result of their local stabilization policies, which complement the budget-restrictions part of economic reforms. Third, the rates of return on these types of investments are much higher than they would be in more developed countries. Finally, the credit history of these countries is poor; they are happy that anyone is willing to lend them capital.

The market for new-debt Eurobonds is not yet efficient, however. Investors must analyze potential issues carefully, and selectivity is essential because the region is under-researched and the premiums paid reflect no quality differentiation.

Most new-debt Eurobonds have three- to ten-year maturities, which reflects the fact that these countries are in the early stages of their restructuring and most lenders are not yet willing to lend for long horizons. Most maturity dates are 1998 because the majority of these instruments are five-year bonds. The challenge for many of these countries is to extend the maturity.

Deal sizes range from US$40 million to US$1 billion. The early issues were in the range of US$40 million to US$50 million. An important buying source then was offshore accounts held out of their countries of origin by emerging markets' nationals (flight capital). These investors knew what the debt was worth and were comfortable buying it. Clearly, new investors have now entered the market; the flight-of-capital accounts would not be able to absorb the recent large issues. The size of the issue obviously affects the liquidity of the market for new-debt Eurobond issues.

Corporate Eurobonds are mainly used to finance companies' expansion activities. To date, corporate issuance has outpaced sovereign issuance. **Figure 5** shows the distribution of corporate Eurobonds among emerging Latin American countries. Mexico has issued the largest volume, 42 percent of the market. Most Brazilian corporate bonds represent bank

Figure 5. Issue Volume of Corporate Eurobonds, 1989 to Mid-1993

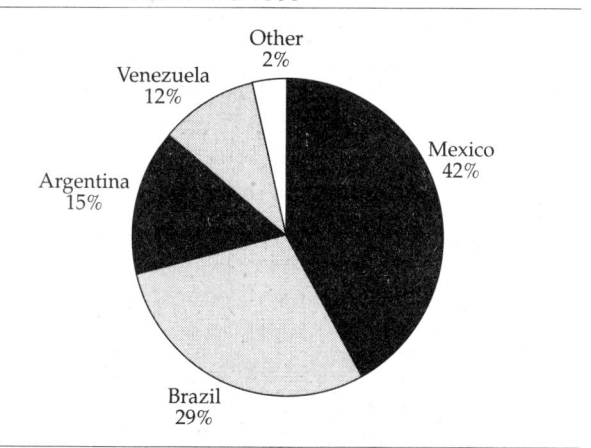

Source: Latin American Securities.

issues. Generally, the bank is borrowing the money internationally and then lending it internally. So far, few Brazilian corporate Eurobonds have come to the market.

Corporate Eurobonds pay a country premium plus a company premium. The premiums for the best companies approach their country's premium; those for the worst are much higher. The ranking of countries by spread is similar: The smallest spreads are found for Mexican companies (250–400 basis points), and the largest for Brazilian companies (350–550 basis points). These spreads are not constant, however, so analysts should pay attention to the quality of the companies and the relative pricing among the markets.

Eurobond investments require significant microeconomic research into the companies. A lot of the valuation techniques are similar to those used to value high-yield bonds, but the investor also needs to assess the capacity of the company to react to rapid and deep structural changes. Because of the companies' unique operating environments, an investor needs to value each company premium. The survival strategy in a hyperinflation environment, for example, may not work in a normal inflation environment. One company might decide to forgo cost efficiency to acquire needed infrastructure. Another company might have to adjust to the loss of monopoly protection. Cash balances are particularly important for these companies.

Analysts should also pay attention to macroeconomic developments. The ramifications of NAFTA for Mexico, for example, are important considerations for Mexican Eurobonds.

Investors should trade carefully in all the corporate bond markets. Secondary markets are inefficient and have mispricings. Spreads change on the basis of rumors, as was the case not long ago with the Telecom Argentina bond. In that case, the spread narrowed from about 400 basis points to 300 basis points because of a rumor that Argentina was going to issue a five-year bond with a spread of 250–300 basis points. The bond was issued, and the spreads on Telecom and other Argentine issues dropped to 300 basis points and even less. Going into the secondary market requires a critical mass in terms of amount of investment and research capacity; it also requires active monitoring of the issues and knowledge of the operators in the marketplace.

In the past, some issues traded better than others in the primary markets. Lately, demand has been higher than supply, so new issues have been trading up. In soft markets, investors have to be aware of what is trading and what is not. The market today, late 1993, is soft. It is nervous, which is normal after the rally that has been taking place in 1993.

Eurocommercial Paper

Eurocommercial paper denominated in dollars is another way of playing the short-term emerging markets. Eurocommercial paper is very flexible for short-term liquidity management, with yields between 4.5 and 7.5 percent. Currently, about $7 billion is outstanding, but this paper does not trade much. Most investors hold the instruments to maturity. Diversity is increasing among issuers as companies issue Eurocommercial paper to test the market. By and large, research on these companies is available. Three-month investments in Eurocommercial paper entail some risk but not nearly as much as five-year notes.

Documentation is still deficient in the market, and investors should study the issuing information carefully to know what they are buying. Reading the fine print pays off.

Local Instruments

Local instruments are U.S. Treasury or foreign treasury bills of short-term maturity, such as 90, 180, or 360 days, in the local markets. The return to a foreign investor is the sum of the return in local currency and the changes in the exchange rate. These instruments have both currency risk and market risk. In Argentina, for example, local rates are not high in real terms, so investing in short-term local instruments involves taking on market and currency exposure not present in longer term bonds.

Although the currency risk in these instruments can be hedged, doing so completely negates the return. A three-month bet on the currency is preferable.

Managing a Portfolio

Emerging market instruments are varied enough to suit many different investment needs. The first step is to set an investment brief. Is the investor looking for income or total return? For instance, in Latin America, equities do not generate income, so if you want yield, you have to invest in fixed-income instruments. Equities provide possible capital gains for an investor oriented toward total return.

Portfolios can be structured to focus on one type of instrument, such as corporate Eurobonds, to invest globally, or to focus on one geographical segment. Generally, diversification by country alone is not sufficient, however, because the portfolio will retain significant systematic risk. The risk is similar to holding a portfolio of single-maturity bonds: If the price goes down on one, it goes down for the whole portfolio.

Investors can either trade actively or buy and hold to maturity. Whether the philosophy is trade or hold needs to be well specified at the outset. These markets are volatile, and investors need to specify how to deal with this volatility. Of course, the middle road is to have a core that guarantees a steady and predictable income and enhance that core by playing around with some arbitraging opportunities.

Managing the portfolio requires a good macro- and microeconomic framework. This knowledge will allow the portfolio managers to operate within short time intervals, reacting quickly to the way the market has moved. Good research involves tapping both international and local sources. Some local research is excellent, but not all of it is of such quality. Local research tends to underestimate the effects of money flows and can lack a global perspective. International research, on the other hand, tends to underestimate the dynamics of change in a country. Managing the portfolio also requires close contact with the secondary market and an active monitoring of new-issue activity.

Question and Answer Session

Marc Wenhammar

Question: What circumstances would make the emerging fixed-income markets crash?

Wenhammar: These markets could be brought down if U.S. dollar interest rates were to double in the next year. Even if short-term rates went up, these markets would get squeezed in the short term. Another potential cause of softness in the market, if issuers continue to supply new instruments, is oversupply.

Question: Some U.S. managers of high-yield portfolios are enhancing returns by adding Brady bonds to their portfolios. Do you think Brady bonds are appropriate for those kinds of portfolios?

Wenhammar: The answer depends on the brief. Brady bonds represent 30-year maturities in high-risk areas. Personally, I am cautious with Brady bonds, so I maintain a diversified exposure. Sometimes the volatility is induced by big investors changing their positions; at other times, it is induced by fundamental changes in the market.

Question: Why invest in emerging market debt when emerging market equities are available?

Wenhammar: Several reasons: Equities have low dividend yields, so you have to turn to debt if you require income rather than capital gains; also, the two assets are not correlated, which allows diversification.

Question: How does the volatility of Latin American bonds as an asset class compare with the volatility of Latin American equities?

Wenhammar: Although the statistical history is too short for fair comparisons (longer term series for bonds are, of course, not available), a one-year comparison would show bonds with an annualized volatility of 8 percent and equities with above 15 percent.

Question: Please elaborate on liquidity. To what extent can Brady bonds and other instruments be traded, and what are transaction costs?

Wenhammar: Brady bonds are the most liquid of the bonds (routine trades of US$2 million plus, bid–offer spreads of 25 basis points), followed by Eurobonds, of which the bigger issues (above US$100 million) are the more liquid, with trades of US$1 million plus and a 50-basis-point spread. Smaller issues are less liquid.

In addition to the bid–offer spreads, trading costs include Euroclear/Cedel costs.

Question: Does it matter who the underwriter is in Eurobond markets and who the escrow agent is for the Treasury backing the Brady bonds?

Wenhammar: No, the underwriter and escrow agent really don't matter. Probably more than a half-dozen underwriters are capable of dealing in the Euromoney markets; they can do the underwriting and contribute support when the markets get soft, which provides a two-way price and a reasonable spread.

One typically chooses as the escrow agent the firm that did the Brady deal. For example, in Argentina, Citibank was the agent, so Citibank could be the escrow agent. Then again, the escrow agent only provides a custodial function, and who performs that function does not matter much.

Question: Will the recent move in the Polish elections away from privatization have any impact on or derail any Brady plans in the works?

Wenhammar: It will not derail the plan, but some delays in getting the Brady plan implemented could occur.

Question: When investing in local short-term debt instruments, do you evaluate the risk of nonconvertibility of the foreign currency (at maturity) in addition to the other forms of risk you mentioned?

Wenhammar: Yes, Latin American Securities incorporates this risk in the analysis, in what I would call a binary way: If we have any reason to think the risk could materialize at maturity, we do not invest; if we do not see that likelihood at all, we invest.

Emerging Markets from a European Perspective

Patrick O'Brien
Director
Swiss Bank Corporation

> The popularity of emerging markets' fixed-income instruments, particularly Eurobonds, has grown dramatically since 1990. Latin America has become a favorite of European fixed-income investors, and signs are that Japanese interest in Latin American bonds is increasing. European and Far Eastern institutional interest is expected to reduce the cost of funds for emerging market borrowers in all markets.

Because emerging markets account for a substantial proportion of the countries of the world, investors have numerous opportunities to make emerging market investments. Some of the developing countries are driven by debt, and others are driven by equity. For example, South America is driven by debt because no interbank market or syndicated loan facilities are available there, but that deficiency has never been a problem in Southeast Asia. China is an equity-driven market; a syndicated loan facility has been available to Chinese borrowers for years. Which mode South Africa will follow remains to be seen. South Africa will probably have a combination of debt and equity. No reason now exists that banks should not again lend freely to South Africa.

This presentation will discuss two aspects of the development of emerging markets, both from the European perspective—the creditworthiness of the countries, and the development of investor interest in emerging market fixed-income instruments in European currencies.

Creditworthiness in Emerging Markets

The ascent to investment grade is not always smooth for emerging countries, and ratings do not always match economic reforms or political realities. For example, European opinion is that the terrorist situation in Colombia prevents that country from achieving a rating higher than the BBB it has been awarded by the rating agencies.

Figure 1 illustrates the ascent to investment grade and indicates at which points various emerging markets are. When a country is at a particular stage, one can predict where that debt ought to trade. The critical stages in the progression are the completion of a Brady plan or final restructuring, successfully passing through the period of deepening economic reform, and achieving balanced growth. Investors should look for consistency between credit ratings and economic reality. One-off opportunistic investments should be avoided.

Creditworthiness is not always on the increase in a developing country, or even constant from one year to the next. **Table 1** shows credit ratings for various developed and emerging markets in 1992 and the change in ratings for those markets since 1991. In 1992, seven of the eight developed markets experienced deteriorating credit ratings, and the eighth did not change (Germany remains flat). Yugoslavia's credit rating has obviously deteriorated. Most of the other countries, however, are showing improved credit ratings, particularly countries in Latin America; Argentina showed the best improvement.

To a fixed-income investor, Latin America looks good. The region has had consistent growth since 1989, and this growth is expected to continue. In fact, the growth rates in Latin America are higher than average for the developing nations as a whole. Even inflation seems to be under control in Latin America, with the exception of Brazil. Argentina's 1993 year-on-year inflation expectation is only 8.5 percent, similar to Mexico's. This control of inflation illustrates the new fiscal responsibility prevalent in emerging markets. The expectation of growth in developing countries remains significantly higher than expecta-

Figure 1. The Ascent to Investment Grade

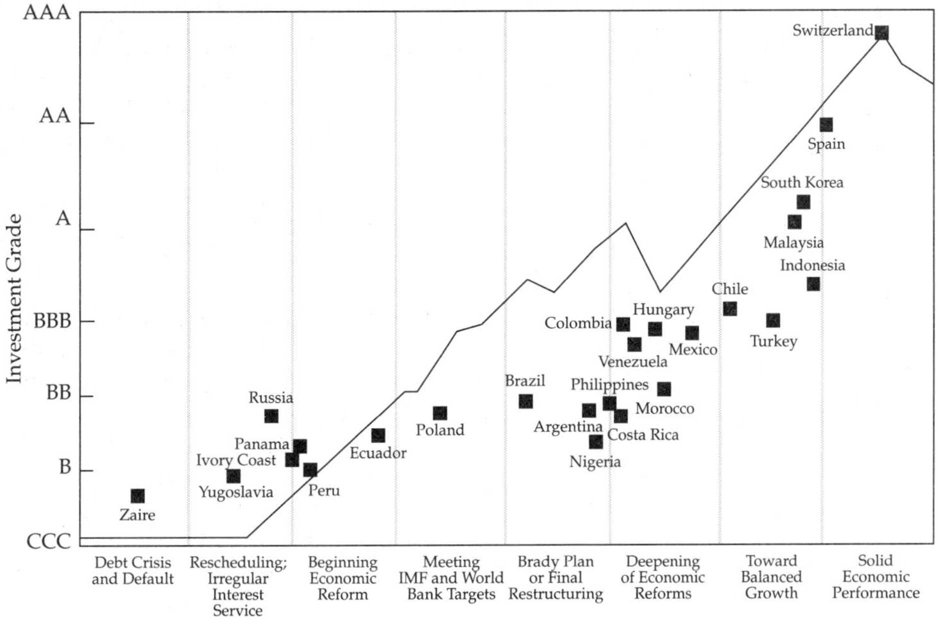

[Figure showing investment grade ratings (CCC to AAA) plotted against economic development stages from "Debt Crisis and Default" through "Rescheduling; Irregular Interest Service," "Beginning Economic Reform," "Meeting IMF and World Bank Targets," "Brady Plan or Final Restructuring," "Deepening of Economic Reforms," "Toward Balanced Growth," to "Solid Economic Performance." Countries plotted include Zaire (CCC), Yugoslavia, Ivory Coast, Panama, Peru (B), Russia, Ecuador, Poland (BB), Brazil, Argentina, Philippines, Nigeria, Costa Rica, Morocco, Venezuela, Colombia, Mexico, Hungary, Turkey (BBB), Chile, Indonesia, Malaysia (A), South Korea, Spain (AA), and Switzerland (AAA).]

Source: Swiss Bank Corp.

tions for countries in the Organization for Economic Cooperation and Development.

Growth of Fixed-Income Markets

The emerging markets' fixed-income instruments have grown tremendously in popularity since 1990. The market took off, in part, to fill voids in the fixed-income markets of the developed countries. In the United States, interest rates declined significantly between 1990 and 1993. At the same time, spreads between AAA- and BBB-rated instruments halved. The combination of these events created a window for a high-yield product. Emerging market Eurobonds filled the void.

The issuance of Eurobonds from Latin American countries rose dramatically between 1990 and the beginning of 1993. In 1990, only a handful of issues were launched, totaling less than US$2 billion, and they were chiefly from Mexican sovereign agencies. As of September 1993, the issues numbered about 120, with a volume close to US$14 billion. These Latin American Eurobonds represent about 7 percent of all Euromarket issues and about 9 percent of all Eurocommercial paper issued.

In volume of Latin American Eurobond issues, Mexico, with about US$12 billion issued from 1990 to 1993, dominates. The highest portion of issues were in U.S. dollars, which makes sense in light of the dramatic decline in U.S. interest rates.

The profile of issuers changed considerably during the 1990–93 period. A substantial rise in issues by privately owned banks and private corporations is alarming. Relatively thinly capitalized entities are tapping the international capital markets, and many investors are not fully aware of what they are buying.

European Interest in South American Bonds

South America experienced a large flight of capital, estimated to be between $100 billion and $400 billion, in the 1980s. Swiss Bank Corporation's estimate for the amount is close to US$200 billion. About 35 percent of this money went to Europe, 25 percent to New York, 20 percent to Miami, and 20 percent to Texas and the West Coast of the United States. Some of this money provided the initial impetus for the revival of the Latin American bond market.

European interest in emerging markets can be divided into three phases. During 1990 and 1991, private money dominated, buying almost 75 percent of Latin American issues sold into Europe. During 1991, institutional investors began to play an increasing role, and in the third phase, 1993, institutions represent more than half of the market.

Asset allocations by fund managers in most European countries differ from those typically made in the United States. In most European countries, a typical portfolio will comprise 80 percent fixed-income instruments and 20 percent equity. The fixed-income component of most portfolios will comprise government bonds and top-quality corporate bonds. No below-investment-grade bond market exists; neither a high-yield corporate bond market nor a junk

Table 1. Changing Credit Ratings in the Developed and Developing World

Country	Institutional Investor 1992 Credit Rating	Percentage Change from 1991
Developed markets		
Switzerland	91.8	−0.6
Japan	90.8	−0.8
Germany	89.0	0.0
United States	87.1	−1.0
France	85.7	−1.6
United Kingdom	84.6	−0.2
Canada	81.6	−1.3
Italy	76.1	−3.8
Asia		
India	37.5	−2.3
Philippines	25.2	2.9
Vietnam	16.9	1.2
Africa		
South Africa	39.8	7.6
Morocco	30.1	6.4
Algeria	28.9	−15.7
Nigeria	19.6	0.5
Ivory Coast	16.5	−4.1
Eastern Europe		
Hungary	42.3	3.4
Poland	24.7	0.8
Bulgaria	19.8	−10.6
Yugoslavia	12.5	−48.9
Latin America		
Chile	45.9	11.7
Mexico	42.6	10.1
Venezuela	39.0	5.1
Colombia	37.2	1.6
Brazil	27.1	2.3
Argentina	26.2	29.7
Costa Rica	23.8	5.8
Ecuador	20.4	3.0
Panama	18.2	6.4
Dominican Republic	17.1	0.6
Peru	13.3	0.6
Nicaragua	7.9	11.3

Source: Swiss Bank Corp.

bond market has ever existed in Europe. Investors buy liquid instruments and speculate through the currency markets.

The past three years have been difficult for European portfolio managers; declining fixed-income yields and extremely volatile currency markets have made the traditional approach to fixed-income fund management more difficult than in the past. Since 1990, interest rates have declined in all the major markets. In the search for higher yields, emerging market debt looks attractive.

The sharp decline in European interest rates during 1993 and the relative stability of currency exchange rates after the 1992 Exchange Rate Mechanism crisis produced a surge in nondollar issuance of Latin American bonds between 1990 and fall 1993. From a borrower's perspective, access to the nondollar market allows these countries to diversify their funding sources and reduce their reliance on a single (U.S. dollar) market. To date, almost 1.3 billion German marks of Latin American bonds have been issued. Mexican state entities have issued bonds in British pounds, Canadian dollars, German marks, Italian lira, Swiss francs, Austrian schillings, and Canadian dollars.

The impact of Japan on emerging market issues cannot be ignored. In February 1993, Mexico issued its first Samurai (Japanese yen bond) since 1978. The aggressive interest of Japanese investors in emerging market paper may well distort levels that borrowers achieve in these markets. In September 1993, significant private placements had been made into Japan some 20–30 basis points tighter than is available elsewhere.

Conclusion

Although the U.S.-dollar market has dominated issues from Latin America in the past, circumstances in Europe and the Far East are rapidly changing that situation. In today's environment of lower interest rates, European institutional interest is certain to increase—a factor that should reduce the cost of funds for emerging market borrowers. Most institutional U.S.-dollar investors are not aware of the depth of fixed-income interest within the various European markets. Although these developments in Europe may not directly affect those U.S. investors, they will certainly have an impact on the cost of funds to borrowers. Once the swap market for these borrowers deepens, yields in all currencies will decline.

Investing in Emerging Market Currencies

Francisco Portillejo
Director, Capital Markets and Treasury, Latin America Foreign Exchange Coverage
Swiss Bank Corporation

> Investors' primary considerations when investing in emerging market currencies should be risk and the characteristics of the counterparty. To reduce the risks of currency investing, sophisticated financial institutions can and should assist emerging markets in developing their markets, particularly in introducing derivative products.

In addition to investing in emerging market equity and fixed-income instruments, investors should consider emerging market currencies. Indeed, currencies are an important part of all international investing, and emerging market currencies should not be ignored by institutional investors. In this presentation, Latin American currencies will be used to illustrate the key factors an investor should keep in mind when investing in emerging market currencies.

Currency Risk Factors

The key risk factors in currency investing are political risks, credit risk, and the risks of devaluation, parallel markets, and inflation. **Table 1** provides a framework by comparing the rates and devaluations of currencies of five Latin American countries. Note particularly the relationship of the Mexican peso to the other currencies. Mexico's peso is an interesting and important currency in terms of past, actual, and potential developments. The peso should, like the Canadian dollar, be in the first tier of currencies; Mexico is far too advanced in actual and planned developments to be ignored by institutional investors. The second tier of currencies are those of Argentina and Chile; the third tier includes Brazil and Venezuela; and the fourth tier, which is not included in the table, comprises Bolivia, Colombia, Ecuador, and Uruguay.

Most Latin American currencies have both an official and a parallel exchange rate. In Brazil, for example, the official US$:cruzeiro exchange rate through December 1993 was 230,000:1; in the parallel market, the rate was 257,600:1. The situation is similar in Chile, where the official exchange rate is 416 pesos to the U.S. dollar and the parallel market rate is 438.50:1. Clearly, people trading in these markets—including exporters, importers, and investors—must be aware of what is happening in the parallel or floating markets.

Devaluation is not discussed often today, but it is a potential risk in these markets. Activities in the parallel markets often provide signals of future devaluations in the official rates. The foreign currency reserves of a country also provide valuable insights into whether a devaluation is likely.

Currency Markets

As is the case in most emerging markets, the Latin American countries provide limited derivative currency products with which an investor can hedge currency risk. Deregulations appear regularly, however, and changes are happening rapidly. For the five top currencies, the following contracts are available:

■ *Argentina.* Four- to six-month forward contracts are available. Liquidity is low to moderate.

■ *Brazil.* One- to two-month forward contracts are available. The commercial market for forwards is active. European options are available in Brazil for maturities of one to two months.

■ *Chile.* Forward contracts are available for maturities up to five years. Chile is developing well, and options on the Chilean peso are expected to be available before long.

■ *Mexico.* Forward contracts are available for maturities up to one year. The forward market is very active.

■ *Venezuela.* A small forward market exists for

Table 1. Currency Comparison: Selected Latin American Countries

Currency	Type	Rates as of December 1993	1992 Percentage Devaluation	1993 Percentage Devaluation
Argentine peso	Official	1.00	0	0
Brazilian cruzeiro	Official	230.00	1,058	1,756
	Parallel	257.60	1,180	1,664
Chilean peso	Official	416.00	2	9
	Parallel	438.50	2	14
Mexican peso	Official	3.40	3	7
	Libre[a]	3.37	1	8
Venezuelan bolivar	Official	105.00	27	32

Source: Swiss Bank Corp.

[a]Free market.

commercial transactions on a retail basis.

In addition, Colombia opened a three-month forward contract on October 1, 1993.

Because of the limited derivative products, investment in Latin American currencies involves taking total currency risk. Hedging is not possible for much of the risk, primarily because of the absence of liquid forward markets, which places many constraints on the development of options. The markets will develop and provide hedging instruments much faster with help than if left on their own; therefore, foreign institutions have a responsibility to help in the development of these markets. This responsibility includes helping the local authorities by training the people to understand and develop new products. Chile is a good example. The people there do not want to wait five years to launch derivative products; they are rapidly learning derivatives' potential applications. Foreign institutions can help, in part, by taking a proactive attitude toward training related to information systems and accounting procedures. Institutions can familiarize market participants with existing best practices in information technology and back-office procedures so that the participants in various countries do not need to reinvent the wheel every time.

The Investor's Perspective

Once an investor has decided to invest in emerging market currencies, he or she must select the right counterparty. Whether this counterparty is U.S., European, or locally based, investors should be concerned about the following basic issues regarding a counterparty:

- location and regional coverage,
- quality of the company,
- market knowledge and expertise,
- cultural adaptation facilities (that is, staff, years of presence in the country),
- technology, historical performance, and idea generation, and
- market position (whether the counterparty is a giver versus a taker).

The challenge is to find a counterparty that meets the investor's criteria in those key areas.

Conclusion

The major considerations for the international investor are, in order of importance:

1. Local economic, political, and monetary policies;
2. an appropriate counterparty—one with the right tools, staff, and market approach.

Emerging market currencies are being deregulated. The process may seem slow, but it should be, because it is important. In the years ahead before total liberalization of these currency markets, the worldwide financial institutions have the time to get to know market participants and to help the emerging countries develop their markets, procedures, and expertise. Giving this help will save time for all.

Question and Answer Session

Francisco Portillejo
Patrick O'Brien

Question: Do you think an inter-currency interest-rate swap market will soon develop?

O'Brien: Developing a swap market is complex. For a swap market to exist, banks must open credit lines to the countries and to the institutions in those countries, and opening those lines depends on the credit capacity of the entities involved. When the countries are not provisionable, an additional amount of long-term exposure to the country is possible.

Question: How good are the counterparties for the forward contracts available in Latin America?

Portillejo: Most of the counterparties are local, although some large, international firms, such as Citibank, are also involved in these transactions. Each country has three or four high-quality counterparties, but more players than at present are needed if the liquidity of these markets is to improve. The countries need more than one or two foreigners, and they need market givers as well as takers. More players will be good for the market, good for the people in these countries, and good for investors.

Question: Mr. O'Brien, please explain why you think the fixed-income market is dangerous now.

O'Brien: Companies with small capitalizations should not be accessing the Euromarkets, although these companies should be encouraged to issue private placements. The market is toxic because many issuers coming to the market in the second and third tier of institutions have come only because they have been swept along on a tide of euphoria, not because they can justify a placement in international capital markets on their own account.

For example, Brazilian banks do not generally make loans. They use those dollars for financial arbitrage. After those arbitrage opportunities disappear, the banks are highly unlikely to generate the currency required to pay their hard-currency debts. At that point, fixed-income investors will be disappointed.

Question: Is hedging prohibitively expensive over the long term in developing countries?

Portillejo: Hedging is not only expensive, but it is hard to do because so few products are available in the markets and liquidity is low. Investors have some options in the short term—up to about three months—but to hedge positions for one year is very difficult.

Look carefully at what instruments and types of institutions will provide this type of hedging. The cost can become extremely high, and the spreads between the bid and offer prices on some currencies can be extremely wide.

Question: How would you hedge an emerging country currency?

Portillejo: The development of such a complex and diversified question cannot be answered in a two or three paragraph explanation. Hedging emerging country currency exposures implies not only the consideration of the risks but also the local facilities (or products) available. Term structures, instruments, correlations, and investors' views and interest are some of the most important points to consider.

Question: Is hedging through local borrowing possible?

Portillejo: Interest rate markets in Latin America do play a significant role for local borrowers. We can even find a large number of derivative products available in the local bond market that, to a certain extent, are much more liquid than currency derivatives.

Question: How should U.S. and European investors adapt to think "Latin" when investing in Latin America?

Portillejo: First speak Spanish, then travel into the region and enjoy the local culture! Seriously, the "Latin" state of mind must be developed not merely by pure opportunistic approaches but by deep knowledge of the trends influencing these countries. The "Latin" mind should not be considered a fashion, but a real, true, and pure spirit. Their adaptation to difficult periods has shown an incredible power to manage change, and we can learn a lot from them. The success of international investors in Latin American countries will vary considerably on the basis of this understanding and perception.

Political Considerations in Emerging Markets Analysis

John F.H. Purcell
Director, Emerging Markets
Salomon Brothers, Inc.

> Political analysis should go hand in hand with economic analysis in the investigation of opportunities and risks in the emerging markets. The diverse factors that must be examined in a political analysis can be confusing, and the motivations unclear, but analysts avoid it at their peril. Because the creditworthiness of developing countries is dynamic, a cyclical model of political development is useful for framing a political analysis of the emerging market countries.

Political considerations can be extremely important in emerging markets research. Political developments often precede economic results, especially in developing countries, and if analysts are on top of political trends, they can often get ahead of the market. Political analysis is also crucial in analyzing the "willingness to pay" aspect of sovereign risk in an emerging market investment.

Explicitly avoiding politics can lead to serious investment mistakes. Some analysts erroneously conclude, for example, that a government must take certain economic measures because, from an economic viewpoint, the leaders cannot do anything else. The fact is, a politician can *always* do "something else," and ignoring political logic is a mistake. In Argentina, for example, when Juan Peron, an ex-military officer and "friend of the working man," headed the government, he told his cabinet ministers to ignore everything the economists told them: "Do not believe them. Just carry on with whatever you are doing." Eventually, that philosophy ran the country into the ground, but it went on for 40 years.

Analysts must understand that a political system is different from an economic system. For a company, the goal is profit, which is achieved through economy and efficiency. For a politician, the goal is office or power, which is achieved through popularity, compromise, and lack of clarity. People who think a country should be run like a company are missing what politics is all about.

Analysts would like to find a situation in which the motives of political leaders are the same as those of economic leaders, but that harmony does not happen often. Usually, the two kinds of actors have different sets of interests. For example, bankers assume a developing country has its debt payments at the top of its list of policy priorities, when in fact, debt payments may be far down the list. Russia is a case in point. The value of Russian debt depends on how high a priority debt payment has for the Russians. Even for President Boris Yeltsin, who is presumably more interested in paying the debt than many others in Russia, debt payment still comes far down on the priority list.

From another angle, many portfolio managers are surprised to learn they have been analyzing politics all their lives, even if they have only dealt with domestic markets. Political analysis is simply an element to be added to other kinds of analysis—in particular, economic analysis. This presentation will illustrate how political considerations can be incorporated into an emerging markets analysis—particularly, the analysis of creditworthiness.

Political Elements of Credit Analysis

Political credit analysis can be viewed in terms of three concentric rings, as illustrated in **Figure 1**. Short-term analysis considers the day-to-day motivations, strategies, and tactics of leaders and political actors. Medium-term analysis considers political systems and creditworthiness and encompasses a slightly longer period than short-term analysis. The ring called "Medium and Short Term" considers ev-

Figure 1. Political Credit Analysis in Emerging Markets

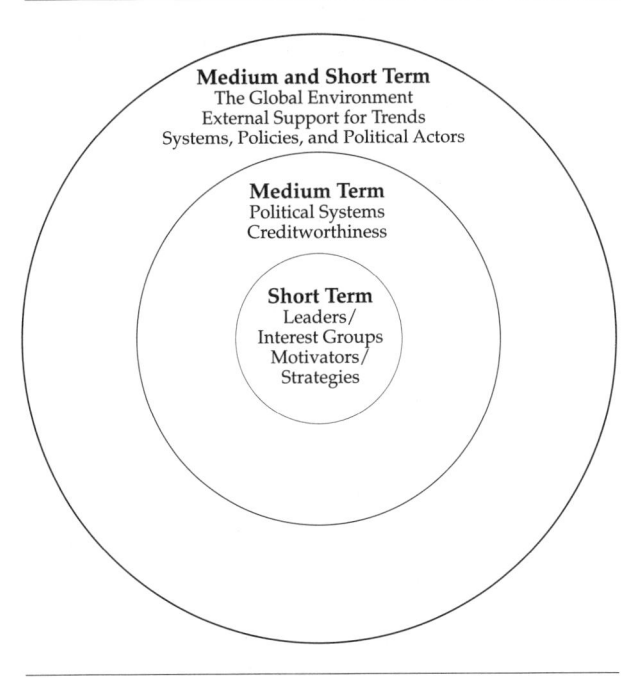

(Concentric circles diagram)
- Outer: **Medium and Short Term** — The Global Environment; External Support for Trends; Systems, Policies, and Political Actors
- Middle: **Medium Term** — Political Systems; Creditworthiness
- Inner: **Short Term** — Leaders/Interest Groups/Motivators/Strategies

Source: Salomon Brothers.

erything—the global environment (which, in many ways, is beyond the control of the country), the external support for or opposition to trends within a country, and the relevant internal systems, policies, and political actors. Keep in mind that political analysis must be informed by all three of these concentric rings of analysis.

With political analysis defined, now shift gears and consider the overall subject of comparative creditworthiness of emerging market countries (including political, economic, and financial analysis). Initially, the perspective is tiers of higher and lower credit quality. Emerging markets' debt can be categorized into five credit tiers, each of which requires a different type of credit analysis.

Tier 1: Brady Plan Countries or the Equivalent

This tier includes countries that are current on their payments. Their debt is often in the form of Brady bonds.[1] The debt of these countries is or "should be" rated in the Ba–BB range. Countries in this category include Argentina, Mexico, Venezuela, Morocco, the Philippines, and Costa Rica.

The type of analysis needed for these countries is basic, fundamental credit analysis. Questions the market asks are: What is likely to happen to this country's rating? Will it be investment grade? Is it climbing the ladder?

If Mexico does not receive investment grade rating, then those who have bought it and compare it with BBB bonds in the U.S. corporate market will be very disappointed, because the assumption in the market is that Standard & Poor's, at least, will upgrade Mexican external bond debt to the investment grade level.

Tier 2: Pre-Brady Plan

This tier encompasses countries that are possible Brady plan participants. They are currently making partial payments on their debt, and the debt is generally in the BB credit-rating range. Countries in this category include Poland (until its Brady plan is completed), Brazil, Ecuador, and possibly Peru. At some point, most of these countries will go through the Brady plan process and exchange their debt for bonds.

The type of analysis appropriate to these countries has a relatively narrow focus: analyzing a particular series of events that may lead to qualification for Brady plan status. Typically, under current market conditions, the prices of debt instruments in this tier move up rapidly during this process, so the purpose of the analysis is to anticipate a new Brady plan participant. This approach is a shorter term analysis than the approach for Tier 1 countries.

Tier 3: Pay/No-Pay Situations

This tier includes countries that are current on certain senior instruments but are priced almost as if they were about to default, so their rating levels are presumed to be below the BB range. Credit analysis involves looking for opportunity in disastrous credit situations, and this objective involves an even narrower set of issues than the Tier 2 credit analysis. Much of the analysis is short-term, strategic political analysis concerning the motivations of the particular leaders in power to continue payment on certain selected "senior" debt instruments.

Countries and debt issues in this category include Algeria (certain bonds and bank loans), Nigeria (par bonds and promissory notes), and Russia (Vneshekonombank bonds). These issues currently have yields in the high teens or even in excess of 20 percent, and investors profit if the debtors simply make the next few payments.

Tier 4: "Penny Stocks"

This tier contains nonperforming credits, with ratings below CCC—the penny-stock bonds. Before

---

[1] Brady bonds refer to rescheduled bank debt securitized under the Brady plan, which is discussed in the seminar overview beginning on page 1 and in Mr. Wenhammar's presentation, pages 58–64.

73

the major rally in this market beginning in June 1993, penny-stock debt was priced below 10 cents on the dollar. Now, many of these prices have shot up into the 30s and 40s.

The political analysis in these situations strives to determine whether a variety of factors that are not directly credit related support a price increase. Such a factor would be sponsorship from one of the developed countries, which might contribute money to a buy-back of the debt, or a privatization program sponsored by some multilateral agency.

Countries in this category have included the Ivory Coast, Bulgaria, and Nicaragua. The Sudan is one of the last remaining members of the category.

Tier 5: Legally Disadvantaged

Legally, none of the issues in this category can be traded in the United States, but they can be traded offshore. They are generally issued by countries whose policies have isolated them from global trade and financial flows.

The analysis in this tier involves trying to assess whether something drastic will happen that will be good for investors, such as a sudden change of government that would bring the country back into the international trade and financial system. In this tier, what makes the price move is the reverse of a good credit; for instance, the collapse of the government is good news in this tier.

South Africa has been in this tier (in the recent past but not today). Other examples of countries in this tier are Cuba and North Korea. Issues an analyst might evaluate are: Will Castro leave? Will North Korea join South Korea?

The Sovereign Policy Cycle

The creditworthiness of a country is dynamic, not static; it is illustrated in **Figure 2** as the sovereign policy cycle, or "the virtuous circle." Analysts looking at the sovereign policy cycle focus on how countries meet the challenge of shocks to the political and economic system. Every country suffers shocks and crises from time to time. The credit question is: How

Figure 2. The Sovereign Policy Cycle

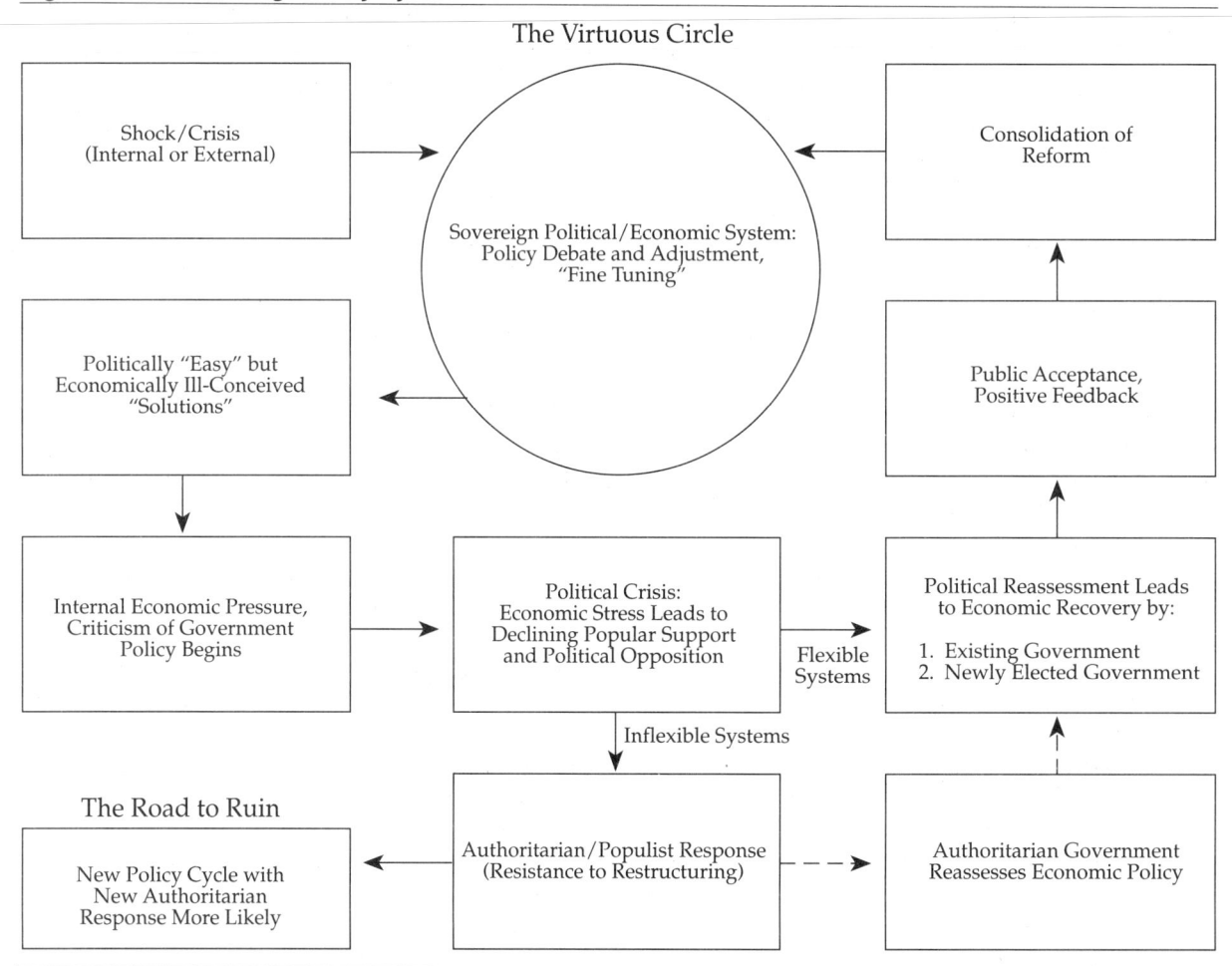

Source: Salomon Brothers.

does this country deal with them?

During the 1980s, many developing countries went through a period of overspending and overborrowing, followed by a series of shocks involving interest rates and a sudden drop in commodity prices, followed by the unwillingness of bankers to lend. These countries suddenly found themselves unable to pay external debt. Different political systems deal with such shocks and crises differently, and these differences define differences in creditworthiness.

The initial shock or crisis may be internal or external, such as a political upheaval or a sudden commodity price change. When the shock occurs, politicians usually take the easy way out. So, Stage 2 is typically to do something politically easy—subsidize something, pay somebody something, give some resources to key political groups making the most noise. The steps taken are usually economically ill conceived, however. In Latin America, for example, this approach led to huge budget deficits that, in turn, led to such negative economic results as inflation and a lowered standard of living for most people.

The third stage is characterized by internal economic pressure and criticism of government policy. Typically, the economic stress leads to the fourth stage, declining support for those in power and political opposition as people realize they are actually losing as a result of so-called popular economic policies.

At this point, the system can go one of two ways. It can take the path of a populist/authoritarian response, which is characterized by resistance to economic restructuring, or it can go directly into a period of political reassessment that leads to economic recovery. The populist response was typical in Latin America in the 1960s and 1970s. In many Latin American debt cycles, governments attempted solutions that ignored the difficult political decisions. Brazil tried such an approach in 1990 with the Collor Plan II (named for President Fernando Collor de Mello), through which it tried to eliminate inflation by freezing all short-term deposits in bank accounts for 18 months for a drastic reduction in the money supply. The intention was to reduce inflation, but the government did not take the other key measure necessary to reduce inflation, namely, the imposition of fiscal discipline. The result was a very quick reversion to extremely high inflation. Thus, the policy became one of simply confiscating private assets with no economic benefit.

Another response to political crisis is the imposition of authoritarian or military rule, also evident in Latin America and in the countries of Eastern Europe during the 1950s, 1960s, and 1970s. In this case, the crisis is "dealt with" by eliminating the democratic system, which is meant to eliminate the stage characterized by criticism of the failure of economic policy.

Unfortunately, the authoritarian/populist responses can send a country into a new cycle that might be called "the road to ruin" (refer to Figure 2). Many people argue that a dictatorship is a better credit risk than a democracy, but I believe that the important characteristics of a country that allow it to traverse the virtuous circle successfully are political openness and flexibility. These qualities are not usually characteristic of an authoritarian system.

In some circumstances, however, a country can move through the stage of an inflexible, authoritarian system back into the virtuous circle. Chile and China are good examples of countries that have moved into the virtuous circle through economic reassessment even during authoritarian phases in the 1970s and 1980s. Chile, at least, has also substituted full democracy for authoritarianism.

In the political reassessment phase, one alternative is that the *existing* government tries something new, as in the case of the Mexican government in the mid-1980s when the governments of Miguel de la Madrid (1982–88) and Carlos Salinas (1988–94) radically transformed Mexican economic policy along free market lines with disciplined fiscal and monetary policy. Another alternative is that a new government is chosen to try a different tack, as in the case of the countries in Eastern Europe after the fall of communism.

The next stage in the virtuous circle is public acceptance of the new policies and positive feedback that strengthens the system and the leadership. In an ideal scenario, the positive feedback leads to consolidation of reform, and the country moves back into macroeconomic balance. Argentina, Mexico, and Chile are examples of how the process can work.

Key Political Factors in Assessing Sovereign Credit

The process of analyzing sovereign credit risk is difficult to quantify precisely, but it can be made systematic. In my view, the seven key political factors in assessing sovereign risk are stability, policy coherence, political commitment to appropriate economic policies, the relative strength or weakness of the opposition, flexibility and adaptability, positive feedback, and external support. The following questions can help an analyst ascertain how well a country is doing in each of these areas. Examples from among the Latin American countries will be used to illustrate the factors.

■ *Stability.* Questions to be asked are: How stable is the political system? Have the country's policies been generally predictable? Do rules exist that limit what a political leader can do? Does an analyst need to know the psychology of the leader in order to know what the country will do, or can outcomes be predicted on the basis of written and unwritten rules and institutions that are broader than one individual. The more predictable the country, the more institutionalized and the more stable politically. By and large, countries that are doing well now, such as Mexico and Chile, are stable. Argentina is currently a dramatic departure from its history of instability.

■ *Policy coherence/political will.* Questions include: Is the government able to carry out announced policies, or are open policy disagreements apparent within the government? Are policy structures, such as ministries, in harmony or fragmented and at odds with each other? Brazil in the early 1990s illustrates multiple examples of the lack of policy coherence and political will.

■ *Political commitment to appropriate economic policies.* Appropriate economic policies promote integration of the country into the rest of the world. Questions to be asked are: Does the country encourage economic competitiveness? Does it encourage market solutions? Does it attract foreign capital flows? These characteristics can be seen in Mexico, Chile, and Argentina but are much less visible in Venezuela and Brazil.

■ *Opposition.* This factor is the other side of the coin of coherence and political will. The strength of the opposition is a measure of obstacles to how coherent a government's policies can be. Questions include: Is the opposition capable of radically altering policies or even the regime itself (as in a military coup), or is opposition simply making it difficult or impossible for the government to pursue coherent policies? Is the opposition trying to change the whole system?

An opposition seeking radical policy and regime change is not as common in the 1990s in Latin America as in the 1960s or 1970s, but one example is the Shining Path guerilla movement in Peru.

The possibility of policy fragmentation includes nonideological, personalistic opposition. In Brazil, for example, the voting of congress members cannot be predicted by what party they are in.

■ *Flexibility/adaptability.* Questions are: Can the system respond to external and internal challenges? Is it an open environment, where criticism and new ideas and ways of dealing with problems can be incorporated into the policy-making process?

An open system that allows criticism is more likely to be able to change, because the system can respond more quickly to complaints that signal the *need* for change. If criticism is repressed, the leadership may fail to receive important information until political pressures have built to a crisis stage.

■ *Positive feedback.* The question is: Does communication flow both up and down? Positive and negative feedback are encouraged by open systems, but positive feedback is important in its own right because politicians do not usually like to act unless they will eventually receive some positive feedback from the action.

■ *External support.* Questions are: Does the country have links to the major powers? What are the financial sources? Is the country a party to trade agreements and common markets? What are the security links with powerful neighbors?

What happens outside a political system can be almost as important as what is happening within it as far as a country's creditworthiness and future are concerned. For example, the North American Free Trade Agreement (NAFTA) is important for Mexico's creditworthiness (perhaps not as important as some observers believe but, nevertheless, important). Yet, the passage of NAFTA was virtually completely out of the control of the Mexican government.

The Virtuous Circle in Latin America

The preceding political questions can now be used to plot five major Latin American countries at differing stages around the virtuous circle (see **Figure 3**). All five countries experienced some form of crisis in the early 1980s, followed by easy solutions, increasing economic pressure, and criticism, and leading to political crisis. Since their crises, their paths have diverged. Chile has come the farthest around the virtuous circle, although it took the route of authoritarian response and reform rather than the more flexible direct route. Chile is probably the closest to being like one of the "Asian tigers" among the countries of Latin America and probably the closest to being in both political and economic equilibrium. The price of Chile's largest export, copper, has dropped dramatically, but the country has managed to get through this setback with a lot of equanimity and not much disturbance. Such a response is a good indicator of a creditworthy political and economic system.

Mexico took a semi-authoritarian path to reform and has come almost as far around the circle as Chile. Argentina has been a surprise because of its past history of extreme instabilities, but consolidation is occurring rapidly. Interestingly, the changes have been carried out in a fully democratic manner.

Venezuela went through significant reforms under Carlos Andrés Pérez, but the system has stalled because corruption remains high and the re-

Figure 3. The Sovereign Policy Cycle in Latin America, 1980–93

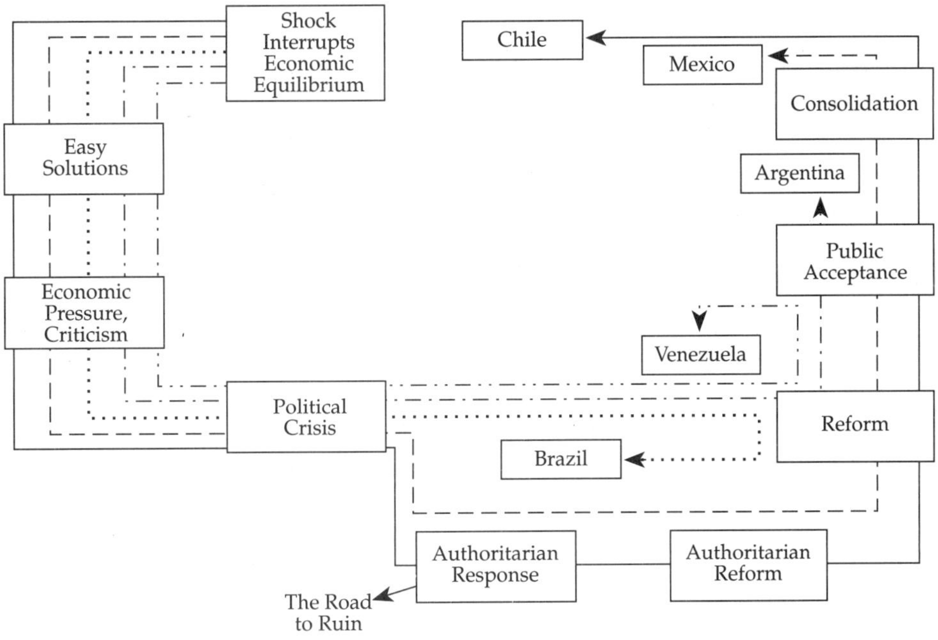

Source: Salomon Brothers.

formers have not been able to educate the public about the reforms. The reformers did not get the public acceptance that Argentine, Mexican, and Chilean leaders have received for similar reforms, and the Venezuelan system remains in serious need of both economic and political improvement. The new government under President Rafael Caldera faces an uphill task in moving Venezuela farther along the path toward economic and political reform.

Brazil did not even reach the reform stage before the system headed back toward political crisis. The system has been fragmented and weak, and political stability has been incomplete. For that reason, Brazilian leaders have been unable to drive reform through. Several leaders have tried, but they have had fatal weaknesses. Ex-President Collor, for example, was making some advances in the direction of reform but ran into trouble with the disclosure that he was simultaneously and secretly amassing a $1 billion campaign fund. When Collor faltered, the inherent fragmentation in Brazil's political system came to the fore and has stymied progress.

Value in Emerging Debt Markets

Emerging market debt prices have rallied strongly recently, so finding value is more of a challenge than it used to be. Should one choose instruments from countries that are already apparently quite expensive but where rapid, fundamental credit improvement is occurring? Or should one look for cheap instruments in low-credit-quality situations, under the assumption that things cannot get worse or at least the buyer will be able to spot the danger of oncoming default early? Political analysis can help in the assessment of value in emerging debt markets under both kinds of strategy.

The strategy of buying cheap instruments worked well in the past, but it may be less successful in the future. Salomon Brothers believes that a "flight to quality" could take place in emerging debt markets in the near future. In such a situation, the "cheap" opportunities are not necessarily cheap in relation to fundamental creditworthiness.

On the other hand, some rich countries, such as Mexico, show signs of continuing to improve. Based on political analysis, we are expecting Mexican debt to be upgraded to investment grade in 1994. The fundamental assumption is not that Mexico is not without problems. The Chiapas uprisings show that more reforms are necessary, but the Mexican political system is strong enough and the leadership sophisticated enough that, even with political upheavals in areas like Chiapas and in spite of economic imbalances like the country's current account deficit, Mexican political leadership will be able to handle the situation. Mexico has solid fundamentals and strong technical factors, such as commitment to its debt by institutional buyers, which is illustrated by the fact that investors are comparing Mexican yield spreads to those of BBB-rated, rather than BB-rated, bonds.

The situation in Argentina is interesting from a political perspective. The signs are that the *national interests* of Argentina are beginning to outweigh the narrow group interests that used to drive politics in Argentina. For example, a year ago, analysts were concerned that the desire of the current president, Carlos Saúl Menem, to change the constitution to give himself a second term would create a political breach between the president and his finance minister. Both of these leaders are considered necessary for economic policy to go forward. Analysts feared that the traditional Argentine political process would take over, producing policy conflict and breakdown; at that point, popular faith in the economic policy would die. That breakdown has not occurred; in fact, leaders have shown themselves to be very sensitive to maintaining policy continuity. The political system itself and the desires of the majority of the population appear to be making the politicians behave themselves, and the reforms continue. In late 1993, the political system of Argentina appears to be much more institutionalized, stable, and coherent than Argentine history would have led analysts to expect.

As pointed out in an earlier section, analyzing debt value in the lower-credit-quality countries is somewhat different from analyzing the Tier 1 and Tier 2 countries and is even more heavily dependent on political analysis. The assessment of Nigeria, for example, revolves around whether key individual leaders perceive a need to have a link with the rest of the world. This factor, in turn, depends on who is in power and how long that person will stay in power. Another concern, one that is absent in the major Latin American countries today, is the possibility of an extreme breakdown of political stability, as occurred in the Nigerian civil war of the 1960s. In that case, who is running the finance ministry will probably be irrelevant.

A similar type of analysis would be applicable to Algeria. The "bet" made by an investor in Algerian bank loans, for example, is that the military government will not be overthrown by the Islamic fundamentalist opposition. This conclusion requires a fairly sensitive assessment of the degree of support key European countries like France will give to the current government.

The fundamental analysis in Poland following the September 1993 elections revolved around the questionable commitment to reform of some new coalition partners versus the momentum of the reforms already underway. That Poland had just elected ex-communists to become the largest party in parliament and that this party might form a government with the so-called Polish Peasants Party, not known for its modernizing policies, has turned out not to be a matter for concern. Poland has probably already proceeded so far along the path of reform that a consensus has developed, and the country is unlikely to go back to earlier policies regardless of the party in power. Voters in Poland appear to have elected the current government for several reasons that were not directly related to the commitment to economic modernization, a goal that is widely accepted.

Conclusion

These few brief examples were chosen to illustrate the importance of an independent role, but not an isolated role, for political analysis in the overall analysis of investment opportunities in emerging markets. Economic and political analysis must go hand in hand. In the fall of 1993, however, much more consensus exists about economic policy for developing countries than about political arrangements. Vestiges of "old-fashioned" economic thinking remain, of course, as in the current Russian government, but many fewer governments than in past decades can afford an economic policy at odds with the rest of the world.

In the analysis of political forces, the situation is much more diverse and confusing for the analyst than in the analysis of economic forces. Is a democratic or authoritarian-type system more appropriate from a creditworthiness perspective? How will the newly liberated destructive forces of regional nationalism and religious fundamentalism affect the credit of certain vulnerable political systems? These very basic issues are grist for the emerging market political analyst's mill.

Question and Answer Session
John F.H. Purcell

Question: Why do you believe that the link to ultimate economic success is democracy? How does East Asia fit that model? Do you see the possibility of another kind of paradigm?

Purcell: The system does not have to be a Western-style, two-party system, but it must have flexibility and openness. Another paradigm is possible, but I would not call it dictatorship. Note that neither democracy nor dictatorship was one of the seven characteristics I listed.

A dictator who has successfully guided a country through the virtuous circle is rare. People often argue that former dictator Augusto Pinochet Ugarte was the only person who could have changed Chile, but Chile under Pinochet went through numerous permutations, combinations, troubles, and mistakes in economic policy before it finally found its way in the 1980s. Under Pinochet, Chile had a severe devaluation, extreme recession, and such a bad economic policy that the government had to take over the banks' debts. Chile's path was not a smooth process of open markets achieved under the tutelage of a wise, all-knowing dictator.

From a credit, rather than a moral, perspective, openness is more important than democracy, and the Western system of democracy is not the only way that a country can develop successfully. Indeed, democracy is not without its problems. Argentina is an example of a country under a fully democratic system that has gone through some severe adjustments while headed for success; some believe it is too early to say that it has succeeded.

The Mexican system is a good example of a rather open system that is not a democracy. Many of the Asian countries share this characteristic. The cultural paradigm is also different in Asia from that of the West, and this factor influences the appropriate political model. The greater degree of social/economic equality in Asia may make political authoritarianism more legitimate there than in Latin America. Note, however, that a process of political opening and, yes, even democratic opening, appears to be taking place among the most developed and creditworthy Asian countries—among others, Taiwan, Thailand, and Korea.

Question: Is there any correlation between emerging economies operating under the Brady plan and their equity markets? Do spreads or changes in spreads contain any information on perceived country risk?

Purcell: We haven't done such an analysis, but I do not think the correlation would be high. In most cases, the markets do not have good flows back and forth in terms of investments and investors.

The spreads indicate something about perceived country risk, but the validity of the measure depends on who is buying and who is selling. In Venezuela, for example, local investors come and go, sometimes influenced by factors that are less important to foreigners than to the local investors. Their actions obviously reflect perceptions, but so far, the local investors have been more pessimistic than hindsight would tell us was warranted.

Question: What are leading indicators of danger in Brazil?

Purcell: The politics surrounding the current presidential campaign and election are worth watching. Brazil will probably not be able to institute any substantive institutional reforms until after the October election. Finance Minister Fernando Henrique Cardoso is attempting to put in place a series of measures to eliminate Brazil's operational budget deficit, but major measures, including constitutional revisions, will probably be delayed until 1995.

The situation in Brazil contains two dangers; one is economic and the other is political. Economically, the question is whether the Brazilians can bridge this period to the election without hyperinflation: Will the measures the government can take prevent hyperinflation? Politically, the danger is that the Workers' Party (PT) candidate, Luis Ignacio daSilva (Lula), who almost won the last presidential election against Fernando Collor de Mello, will come to power this time. Signs that Lula will win would be the last straw for the Brazilian markets, both debt and equity. His election would set back the reform process for some time, perhaps years.

Regulatory Environments in Emerging Markets

Rudolf van der Bijl
Principal Investment Officer
International Finance Corporation

> The regulatory environment of an emerging market is important but not easy to analyze. Investors should be careful to include industry organizations in their analysis as well as government regulating bodies and should view regulations in the context of the market's total environment. The developmental role of regulators is as important as their disciplinary role, and the seriousness, professionalism, and credibility of regulators will have major effects on the market's short-term and long-term operations.

Assessing the regulatory environment of a country's securities market is a key factor in making emerging market investments. The ground rules embodied in laws and regulations, and the capacity and the intentions of governments and self-regulatory bodies to enforce those rules, affect the ability of portfolio managers to realize their key objectives: increasing returns, minimizing transaction costs, and managing risk.

The laws and regulations that have an impact on a country's markets are not limited to those administered by local securities commissions. Factors that contribute to the environment for investment include the ease of enforcing basic contractual and property rights, corporate governance practices and shareholder rights embodied in corporate statutes, and rules regulating the structure of industrial and financial ownership, including policies dealing with competition and controls over self-dealing and other conflicts of interest that protect markets from being dominated by a cozy set of insiders. Foreign portfolio investors also have special regulatory concerns not shared by domestic investors, such as taxation and currency rules that directly affect their abilities to remit capital and profits.

This presentation focuses on classic securities regulation by government and self-regulatory organizations. The other areas should be kept in mind, however, in the assessment of a given market. The presentation also gives an overview of the U.S. and international organizations that can provide information on the regulatory environments of the emerging markets and contains a list of published sources of information.

The Functions, Objectives, and Approaches of Securities Market Regulation

A serious regulatory effort is generally a precondition to the efficiency, transparency, and credibility of a securities market's operations. Moreover, how the investor puts specific techniques into practice in an emerging country's market will often depend on its regulatory environment. The research techniques the investor can use for a specific market, for example, must be tailored to the available types and quality of information about companies and trading—including financial and other disclosure requirements for issuers, information from such services as rating agencies, and data on trading volumes and prices. The amount of relevant information and its accuracy, timeliness, and completeness will be, in part, a function of the standards set by the government and self-regulatory organizations and the seriousness with which those standards are enforced. As a market grows and increases in sophistication, the demand by regulators for quality reporting often stimulates the emergence of information services that compete in delivering useful information to investors, including foreign investors.

In those emerging markets that have a strong regulatory capacity, the development and proper oversight of institutions to perform the functions of trading, clearing, and settlement and custody can dramatically enhance the efficiency and safety of the markets and improve their attractiveness for foreign portfolio investment.

In comparing the regulatory environments of different markets, the investor needs to remember that the classification "emerging markets" covers a remarkably diverse set of circumstances. Certain regulatory requirements, particularly financial disclosure by issuers and the accuracy and completeness of trade reporting, should be measured against high international standards. The adequacy of other regulatory requirements, such as qualifications and supervision of custodians, may depend on the particular stage of development of a given market. As in developed markets, the establishment of a regulatory framework in emerging markets is an ongoing process, not a one-shot event. Therefore, in examining a country's regulatory environment, consider not only the standards being enforced today but whether the regulators are supportive of, and responsive to, the continuing evolution of their market institutions and practices.

Since the early 1980s, the world has witnessed a growing trend toward economic deregulation and a rapid transformation from central planning to free markets. Countries are gradually abolishing restrictions on entry, ownership, and trade, are relaxing credit and interest rate controls, and are relying on financial markets rather than the state to allocate financial resources. In an apparent paradox, however, the same era of liberalization has introduced growing concerns over the safety and efficiency of financial systems and the need to regulate them.

In fact, no paradox exists. Economic deregulation means that restrictions on entry, operation, and exit are being relaxed to allow wider, more flexible market participation than in the past. It does not mean that regulations are simply being removed; rules that define the structure of markets and regulate their operation are still needed, sometimes needed more than in the past because of the wide participation made possible by deregulation. Regulation is, therefore, a necessary component of deregulation.

The Functions of Regulation

The regulation of securities markets, especially for new or emerging markets, serves both a disciplinary and a developmental role. The two roles are complementary, but the emphasis given to one or the other by a country's regulators will vary over time. Regulatory functions can be thought of as covering three types of activities, and each can have both a disciplinary and a developmental dimension.

■ *Definition of the financial system.* A regulatory framework must define the key features of the financial system and the role of securities market institutions within that system. At the broadest level, the regulatory process defines the basic structure of the system, such as deciding the debate between advocates of "universal" banking and partisans of separating banking from securities market activities. As markets develop, regulators must also define the basic standards for new types of market activities, such as for mutual funds, or clearing and settlement organizations, and the institutions that will be eligible to engage in those businesses.

■ *Provision of proper incentives.* Regulation provides incentives to market participants to engage in constructive behavior, such as following "best practice" or investing in the development of new market institutions. For example, the emphasis in U.S. regulatory philosophy on disclosure, whether by financial intermediaries or by issuers, gives much of the disciplinary role in the United States to the marketplace. That is, market participants often modify their behavior to avoid having to make damaging disclosures or because they want to publicize positive information.

In emerging markets, regulators will often require that a particular activity be performed in order to encourage the development of new types of institutions in the securities markets. For example, in Chile, public issues of securities must be rated by a licensed rating agency. This government requirement has force-fed the demand side of a domestic information industry and promoted the development of private rating agencies.

■ *Provision of disincentives.* The third type of regulatory activity is the one that most immediately comes to mind when people think of "regulation"—to provide disincentives for behavior that would be destructive to the market. This regulatory activity is particularly important in the financial sector because financial systems are characterized by systemic risk—that is, the risk of contagion for the entire system from the insolvency or collapse of a single institution or market.

Disincentives for such misbehavior as self-dealing and market manipulation are also required because of the special problems of information asymmetry (unequal access to information) in the financial sector. Although taking advantage of information asymmetry may be quite rational for a single economic actor in the short term, the long-term effects of such actions can have detrimental effects on the credibility of the market. These actions can dramatically reduce the number of investors and issuers willing to participate in the market, which will seriously impede the market's development and the at-

81

tractiveness of the securities industry as a business.

The Objectives of Regulation

The special characteristics of the financial sector just mentioned—systemic risk and information asymmetry—dictate the principal regulatory objectives that must be balanced by securities regulators. These objectives are market integrity, fairness, and efficiency.

Market integrity. This is the objective of regulatory activities that minimize systemic risk and encourage participation in the market, such as:

- prudential measures to safeguard the solvency of individual financial institutions and thereby maintain confidence in the financial system and protect individual savers;
- the encouragement of an effective, stable payments system, which can reduce the accumulation of significant counterparty risks, improve the ability of individual financial institutions to manage their risk exposures, and discourage contagion or financial panics; and
- prevention of fraud, manipulation, insider trading, and other such market abuses that threaten the market's integrity. Although few such cases are prosecuted and fewer result in convictions, rules preventing market abuse are a valuable deterrent; their absence would allow abusive behavior that would endanger the market.

Fairness. This is a regulatory concern not only for political and social reasons but also because it is a way to protect a market's competitiveness and integrity. For example, competition within the financial system is encouraged by allowing participants easy entry, operation, and exit. Measures to curb monopoly power prevent market domination by large participants.

Fairness also includes providing small, less sophisticated investors access to appropriate financial assets and protecting them from abuses by participants with greater market power.

Efficiency. This is the key to the ability of a financial sector to perform its principal function of pooling and allocating financial resources to economically viable businesses. As many countries open their economies and adopt market-based approaches to the development and operation of industrial enterprises, the allocation of capital and credit to industry must be responsive to new and shifting economic opportunities.

Both the developmental and disciplinary roles of securities regulation can contribute to rationally organized and efficient securities markets, but market efficiency can suffer from excessive regulation as well as inadequate regulation. Regulation should make its necessary contribution but not become an end in itself.

The three objectives of regulation are not easy to reconcile. In fact, the difficulty in structuring a regulatory system lies in the often contradictory goals of maintaining market integrity, fairness, and efficiency. A case in point is the degree of competition in the market. Although fairness might be enhanced by permitting any person to engage in a particular business, the goal of market integrity might depend on restricting participation to those with some minimum of capital, demonstrated expertise, and operating history. The constantly shifting emphasis among a country's regulatory objectives will always require of securities regulators a delicate balance.

Direct Regulation versus Self-Regulation

Virtually all securities markets comprise some degree of direct government regulation and self-regulation by the securities industry. As part of the dual trend around the world of increased reliance on market forces and expansion of domestic securities markets, the tendency is to formalize the respective regulatory responsibilities of government and industry.

Direct or state regulation. This means that the government assigns the regulatory role to one or more public agencies that set rules for the market and enforce their application. Whether securities regulation is in the hands of an independent entity or within one or more ministries, it is an integral part of the executive authority and under the control of the government.

Self-regulation. Questions about what rules to apply and how to monitor and enforce compliance are left largely to those who participate in the markets. For example, regulation of the securities markets may be primarily in the hands of the stock exchange, whose members draft their own rules and regulations governing trading on the exchange, the qualifications of members, and the business standards that members must meet.

Each approach has its virtues and drawbacks. Self-regulation allows the market's rules to respond to the real demands of participants, but the self-regulatory body may sacrifice market integrity for short-term gain when the interests of members and their clients conflict. Self-regulatory organizations are frequently the best sources of innovation in market practices and institutions, but they may also be anti-competitive. Self-regulatory organizations sometimes act like guilds, which promote the vested interests of their members; they may try to fix prices, restrict new entrants, and oppose changes in industry structure that could threaten the short-term interests of their members.

If government regulators have the necessary political and budgetary support, they are often better positioned than self-regulatory organizations to overcome the problems of vested interests and introduce necessary changes to the securities markets. Government may be handicapped by a lack of financial or human resources, however, in the development of detailed policies and standards and in the direct supervision and control of market activities.

A Global Perspective on Emerging Markets Regulation

The period of the 1980s into the present has been one of incomparable growth for emerging securities markets. By 1992, the emerging stock markets had increased their joint market capitalization about 11 times, to US$770 billion, and nearly tripled their share of world equity market capitalization, from 2.5 percent to 7 percent. Trading volumes have increased 25 times from 1982 levels, and the number of listed companies in these markets now represents about 40 percent of the approximately 30,000 listed companies worldwide.

The extensive growth in size of emerging markets has been accompanied by deregulation and liberalization, especially in such areas as foreign investment. The reasons are obvious: Foreign investment, portfolio and direct, has begun to play a significant role in developing countries because many of these countries are facing acute capital scarcities. The shortage of cash is manifested by deficits in their domestic budgets and in external balances of payments.

In the past, a primary source of capital for developing countries was foreign aid from the industrial nations. Because of recessions and deep economic disturbances in the latter, however, this source has shrunk considerably; thus, luring other capital has become extremely important for developing countries. Moreover, after the debt crisis in the 1980s, bank lending to the middle-income developing countries fell drastically, leaving a void in funding sources.

As emerging markets compete with each other for the scarce supply of investment capital, regulatory policies have evolved in light of the growing recognition that investment will head toward those countries that have the fewest barriers to entry and exit and that offer the most rewards in the form of after-tax returns. At the same time, these countries have realized the importance of developing their securities markets to channel their domestic savings and to reassure foreign investors of the economic and financial viability of their countries.

Furthermore, developing countries recognize the benefits to be reaped from globalization and the increased integration of financial markets. They are keen to share in these benefits by conforming with international standards, regulations, and norms. For example, a large number of emerging markets have adopted or are adopting recommendations made by the Group of Thirty, a Washington-based think tank, and by the International Organization of Securities Commissions intended to standardize and improve the overall quality of the countries' clearing and settlement procedures.

In addition to deregulation and liberalization, another change in the financial sectors of developing countries is the increasing importance of nonbank financial intermediaries. These institutions and their participation in the more active securities markets raise regulatory issues that go beyond traditional concerns with the performance and standing of commercial and development banks.

For foreign investors, an effective and efficient regulatory environment that meets international standards is a primary concern. For example, pricing information, trading fairness, efficiency, liquidity, and such matters as the clearing and settlement mechanisms of the host country—all contribute to reducing the risks of investing in a foreign market. In the emerging markets, restrictions on entry, operation, and exit are being relaxed, but fortunately, as mentioned previously, regulations are not simply being removed.

Wide disparities exist among developing countries regarding the extent to which liberal regulatory policies have replaced government controls. Some countries, such as Thailand and Chile, have had relatively open economies for a number of years; others, such as India, have only recently begun deregulation and are now in the process of easing rules and regulations.

Table 1 and **Table 2** provide comparisons of countries on the basis of treatment of foreign portfolio investment, dividend and capital repatriation, and withholding tax rates. Table 1 summarizes regulations governing foreign portfolio investment in 28 emerging markets. As can be seen, in countries such as Argentina, Brazil, Colombia, Malaysia, and Turkey, listed stocks are freely available to foreign investors. Others countries, such as Bangladesh, Kenya, South Korea, Mexico, and Thailand, require registration procedures to ensure repatriation rights. China, the Philippines, and Zimbabwe restrict foreigners to certain classes of stocks, while India and Taiwan

Table 1. Entering and Exiting Emerging Markets: A Summary of Investment Regulations as of March 31, 1993

Foreign Investor Access to Listed Stocks	Repatriation of Income	Repatriation of Capital
Free entry		
Argentina	Free	Free
Brazil	Free	Free
Colombia	Free	Free
Greece	Free	Some restrictions
Malaysia	Free	Free
Pakistan	Free	Free
Peru	Free	Free
Portugal	Free	Free
Turkey	Free	Free
Relatively free entry		
Bangladesh	Some restrictions	Some restrictions
Chile	Free	After one year
Costa Rica	Free	Free
Indonesia	Some restrictions	Some restrictions
Jamaica	Free	Free
Jordan	Free	Free
Kenya	Some restrictions	Some restrictions
Korea	Free	Free
Mexico	Free	Free
Sri Lanka	Some restrictions	Some restrictions
Thailand	Free	Free
Trinidad and Tobago	Free	Free
Venezuela	Free	Free
Special classes of shares		
China	Free	Free
Philippines	Free	Free
Zimbabwe[a]	Restricted	Restricted
Authorized investors only		
India	Free	Free
Taiwan	Free	Free
Closed		
Nigeria	Some restrictions	Some restrictions

Source: Emerging Stock Markets Factbook 1993 (Washington, D.C.: IFC Emerging Markets Database).

Note: Some industries in some countries are considered strategic and are not available to foreign/nonresident investors; in other cases, the level of foreign investment may be limited by national law or corporate policy to minority positions not to aggregate more than 49 percent of voting stock. This summary applies to "new money" invested by foreign institutions; other regulations may apply to capital invested through debt-conversion schemes or other sources.

Key to access:
Free entry — No significant restrictions on purchasing stocks.
Relatively free entry — Some registration procedures required to ensure repatriation rights.
Special classes — Foreigners restricted to certain designated classes of stocks. Foreigners restricted to certain designated classes of stocks.
Authorized investors only — Only approved foreign investors may buy stocks.
Closed — Closed or access severely restricted (e.g., to nonresident nationals only).

Key to repatriation:
Income — Dividends, interest, and realized capital gains.
Capital — Initial capital invested.
Some restrictions — Typically, some registration with or permission from a central bank, ministry of finance, or office of exchange controls required.
Free — Repatriation routine.

[a] At the end of April 1993, the government of Zimbabwe announced its intention to open the stock market on a limited basis to foreign investors.

Table 2. Withholding Tax Rates for U.S.-Based Institutional Investors
(percentage in effect at the end of 1992)

Country	Interest	Dividends	Long-Term Capital Gains on Listed Shares
Latin America and the Caribbean			
Argentina	0	0.0	0.00
Brazil	15	15.0	0.00
Chile[a]	32	32.0	32.00
Colombia	12	12.0	12.00
Costa Rica	0	5.0	0.00
Jamaica	25	33.3	0.00
Mexico	15	0.0	0.00
Peru	37	11.0	0.00
Trinidad and Tobago	25	25.0	0.00
Venezuela[b]	20	20.0	30.00
Asia			
China	10	10.0	0.00
India	10	10.0	10.00
Indonesia	20	20.0	20.00
Korea	12	15.0	0.00
Malaysia	20	0.0	0.00
Pakistan	10	10.0	0.00
Philippines[c]	20	25.0	0.25
Sri Lanka	0	15.0	0.00
Taiwan	20	20.0	0.00
Thailand	15	10.0	0.00
Europe, Mideast, and Africa			
Botswana	15	15.0	20.00
Cyprus	25	30.0	0.00
Ghana	30	10.0	0.00
Greece	15	0.0	0.00
Hungary	20	10.0	20.00
Jordan	0	0.0	0.00
Kenya	10	10.0	0.00
Mauritius	0	0.0	0.00
Morocco	20	15.0	40.00
Nigeria	15	5.0	20.00
Poland	0	10.0	0.00
Portugal	25	20.0	0.00
Russia	15	15.0	32.00
Turkey	0	0.0	0.00
Zimbabwe	0	20.0	30.00

Source: Emerging Stock Markets Factbook 1993.

[a] Rates if investment is made under Decree Law 600.
[b] Rate on capital gains in excess of 2 million bolivars.
[c] Transaction tax on gross transaction value, in lieu of capital gains tax.

allow only approved foreign investors to buy stocks.

Table 1 shows that most countries allow free repatriation of income and capital, but a number of countries, such as Indonesia and Kenya, require following some registration procedures or obtaining permission of the central bank or ministry of finance before repatriation is allowed, which may delay release.

Table 2 summarizes the withholding tax rates for

U.S.-based institutional investors in various emerging markets. Note that withholding tax rates are relatively high in Chile, Brazil, and Malaysia, countries to which foreign investors have nevertheless been favorably inclined. Investors do not always lean toward countries that give them the greatest tax concessions. In deciding whether to invest in a country, investors weigh the risks involved against the prospective returns. Lower risk in developing countries such as Chile or Malaysia, where economic conditions are more stable than in other countries, offset the higher taxes and offer the investor a more favorable risk–reward ratio. Furthermore, such countries generally are well regulated, have efficient market mechanisms, and possess relatively more sophisticated infrastructure, which facilitates operations in them.

Table 3 is a broad overview of market information and investor protection in selected markets. As can be seen, three countries in Latin America and three in Asia fare well with respect to investor protection. Those countries where investor protection is noticeably weak include Greece, China, and Taiwan.

Qualitative Comparisons of Regulatory Systems

An evaluation of a market's regulatory environment requires an appreciation of a number of factors that are harder to measure than the objective data in Tables 1–3, but not surprisingly, no comprehensive, up-to-date comparison of such qualitative aspects exists. The following discussion, although it cannot be comprehensive, is intended to flesh out some of the qualitative features of emerging market regulations that concern the foreign investor.

Financial-Sector Structure

The structure of the financial sector and its relationship to government and industry can have an important impact on the authority of the securities regulators, on their priorities, and on their scope for promoting market development. Structural features the investor should examine include the following:
- the relative roles of the banking system and the securities markets in pooling domestic savings and allocating financial resources to business;
- the extent to which the government is directly involved in credit allocation, such as through administered credit;
- the relationship between finance and industry, especially the degree of interlocking ownership.

As we all know, battles between banking and securities regulators are not confined to developing countries. Where the same institution or financial group can provide both banking and securities services, the allocation of oversight functions among different regulators and the methods of consolidated supervision are important to the effectiveness of prudential regulation. This factor is especially important in countries experiencing rapid introduction of new financial instruments. The risks of these new instruments are often not fully understood by either market participants or regulators.

In countries where industrial groups have an important stake in financial institutions (or vice versa), effective regulatory schemes for limiting self-dealing, market manipulation, and other common abuses are especially important to protect outside investors. Such controls reduce systematic risk and help assure the credibility, fairness, and competitiveness of the market.

Market Structure

The diversification of a country's financial sector will often be a function of the size, degree of development, and stability of the country's overall economy. The availability in the domestic market of diversified debt and equity instruments will depend largely on macroeconomic policies and a reliable term structure of interest rates. The manner in which a country's financial institutions are differentiated by function is often a result of historical accident, however, including whether an emerging market modeled itself on a developed market because of colonial history, common legal systems, or in recent years, the purchase of a specific market technology from a developed market.

Market structure presents a number of issues for foreign portfolio investors, for whom market transparency is especially important because they can never have the same degree of market knowledge as local "insiders." The following types of market characteristics can inform investors how regulators (including self-regulatory organizations) have been performing. These factors also affect regulators' future ability to promote the objectives of market integrity, fairness, and efficiency:
- the amount of trading that occurs in formal markets in relation to the amount that occurs outside markets, and the policy of regulators regarding limits on, or timely disclosure of, off-market trades;
- whether the country's securities are traded in well-defined markets, such as those segmented by class of security;
- the links, if any, with other markets, such as regional or foreign markets;

Table 3. Market Information and Investor Protection in Selected Emerging Markets

Country	Share Price Index[a]	Securities Exchange Publications[b]	International Electronic Coverage[c]	Regular Publication of P/E, Yield[d]	Market Commentaries in English[e]	Company Brokerage Reports[e]	Annual Statements[f]	Interim Statements[g]	Accounting Standards[h]	Investor Protection[h]
Argentina	X	AQMWD	X	C	LR,IR	LR,IR	X	Q	A	AS
Brazil	X	AMWD	X	C	LR,IR	LR,IR	X	Q	G	GS
Chile	X	AMWD	X	C	LR,IR	LR,IR	X	Q	G	GS
Colombia	X	AMWD	X	C	LR,IR	LR,IR	X	Q	A	AS
Mexico	X	AMWD	X	C	LR,IR	LR,IR	X	Q	G	GS
Peru	X	AMWD	X	C	LR,IR	LR,IR	X	Q	A	AS
Venezuela	X	AMWD	X	C	LR,IR	LR,IR	X	S (banks only)	A	AS
Greece	X	AMWD	X	C	LR,IR	LR,IR	X	S	A	P/NA
Jordan	X	AMWD	X	P	LR,IR	LR	X	NA	A	AS
Nigeria	X	AWD	X	P	LR,IR	LR	X	Q	A	AS
Portugal	X	AMWD	X	C	LR,IR	LR,IR	X	S	A	AS
Turkey	X	AMWD	X	C	LR,IR	LR,IR	X	Q	A	AS
Zimbabwe	X	AWD	NA	P	LR	LR	X	S	A	AS
China	X	AMWD	X	C	LR,IR	LR,IR	NA	S	P	PS
India	X	AMWD	X	C	LR,IR	LR,IR	X	S	G	GS
Indonesia	X	AMD	X	C	LR,IR	LR,IR	X	S	P	AS
Korea	X	AMWD	X	C	LR,IR	LR,IR	X	S	G	GS
Malaysia	X	A(M/2)WD	X	C	LR,IR	LR,IR	X	S	G	GS
Pakistan	X	AD	X	P	LR,IR	LR,IR	X	S	A	AS
Philippines	X	AMWD	X	C	LR,IR	LR,IR	X	S	G	AS
Sri Lanka	X	AMWD	X	C	LR,IR	LR,IR	X	S	G	AS
Taiwan	X	AMWD	X	C	LR,IR	IR	X	Q	A	PS
Thailand	X	AQMWD	X	C	LR,IR	LR,IR	X	Q	A	AS

Source: Emerging Stock Markets Factbook.

NA = not available.

[a]X indicates at least one share price index is calculated; most have several, and many also have sectoral indexes.
[b]A = annual; Q = quarterly; M = monthly; M/2 = biweekly; W = weekly; D = daily.
[c]X indicates daily coverage of the stock market on an international wire service.
[d]P = published; C = comprehensive and published internationally.
[e]LR means prepared by local brokers or analysts; IR means prepared by international brokers or analysts.
[f]X indicates consolidated, audited, annual accounts are required.
[g]Q means quarterly results must be published; S means semiannual results must be published.
[h]Ratings are: G for good (internationally acceptable quality); A for adequate; P for poor (requires reform); S indicates a functioning securities commission or similar government agency concentrating on regulating market activity.

- the standards, if any, for securities to be eligible for trading in each market, and how those standards are enforced;
- the standards, if any, for a securities intermediary to conduct business in each market, how those standards are enforced, and whether those standards affect the competitiveness or efficiency of the market;
- whether the functions of different types of market participants are well defined and, in instances in which combining functions could be risky (e.g., brokerage and dealing), whether the regulatory system segregates performance or provides reliable safeguards;
- whether the price-discovery mechanism in each market is reliable, and how it is regulated;
- the principal methods for supplying liquidity to each market, and whether they are formalized, mandatory, or otherwise regulated.

The rules governing a country's market structure may not be appropriate for the types of securities or investors with which the country's markets need to deal. For example, regulators in new markets commonly force all equities, regardless of size of float or volume of turnover, to trade on the same exchange in order to promote institutional development. In some cases, however, this policy may inhibit development by diluting standards for more heavily traded issues, by not providing cost-effective trading mechanisms for less liquid shares, or by poorly serving issuers and investors in regions outside a country's capital city. On the other hand, rules that permit the proliferation of uneconomic, competing trading structures may be equally destructive to the market unless a strategy exists for eventual consolidation of winning and losing trading systems. The most important factor for an investor to observe is whether the regulators are encouraging patterns of development that will increase the quality of services and promote efficiency, access, and transparency.

Market structure also dictates many of the ways in which securities regulators can perform their disciplinary role. First, the more transparent the market's operations, the more market competition, on the basis of price and quality of service, will discipline market participants without direct regulatory intervention. In addition, the better defined the market structure, the easier for government regulators to rely on self-regulation for detailed rule making and enforcement. Of course, a weakly structured market may be a sign that certain parts of the securities industry have had the political clout to block any serious attempts by government authorities to define appropriate market structures and behavior.

Broker/Dealer Activities

The ability of regulators to promote their key objectives—market integrity, fairness, and efficiency—is affected significantly by the relationship of the regulators to the broker/dealer industry. An investor will be concerned with such issues as:

- The minimum qualifications for broker/dealers—are there meaningful minimum capital requirements, net capital requirements, and professional standards?
- The principal customer protections against fraud and abusive practices—are the rules clear, and are they enforced?
- Does the government or industry provide collective protections against default or insolvency of its members, such as through protection guarantee funds?
- Do the regulators require good record keeping and risk-management practices, such as requiring trade documentation and appropriate marking to market?
- Are financial reporting standards adequate, and does the regulatory body with oversight authority have the technical capabilities to understand the financial condition of the firms it regulates?
- What is the frequency of disciplinary proceedings against broker/dealers?
- What investor redress mechanisms are available? Are efficient arrangements for dispute resolution available, or do regulators rely on lengthy or costly litigation?

The tension between direct regulation and self-regulation is particularly acute in the regulation of broker/dealers. As a rule, self-regulation is most effective in dealing with behavior that the industry members have a direct economic interest in seeing meets certain standards. For example, self-regulatory organizations often do well regulating broker-to-broker relationships, such as in enforcing rules to assure that both brokers are able to fulfill their sides of a trade. Self-regulation, at least in immature markets, is less suitable for protecting customers from members who engage in dubious practices. On the other hand, the extent to which self-regulation takes customer protection seriously speaks volumes about the overall integrity of a market.

Company Information

Many emerging markets have formal requirements that companies meet high disclosure standards, but the key issues are how seriously those standards are applied by regulators and, perhaps more importantly, whether issuers and securities professionals understand the benefit of timely and full disclosure. Some indications of the importance with which information disclosure is viewed by regulators and market participants can be gained from analyzing the following:

- the technical capability and resource commitment of regulators in their oversight of company disclosure, such as review practices for prospectuses and shareholder communications, or enforcement of listing standards by exchanges;
- how much the disclosure process is supported by well-qualified professionals, such as accountants and lawyers, for whom professional reputation is a valuable asset;
- whether regulators are encouraging the development of a financial advisory or information industry for the securities markets and whether they have meaningful safeguards against market manipulation or conflicts of interest by advisors or information providers. The involvement of regulators ensures that advisors meet professional qualifications.

Market Infrastructure

The development of infrastructure in emerging markets—trading systems, custodian and depository arrangements, and clearing and settlement organizations—often brings together the efforts of government and the securities industry. In this area, investors should look for a commitment by government not only to a realistic program of modernization but also to meeting international standards. The links between the securities markets and the banking sector, particularly the payments system and foreign exchange arrangements, are also important.

Foreign Participation

Access to emerging markets by foreign portfolio investors is meaningful only if no unacceptable restrictions on ownership, transfer of ownership, and foreign exchange movements exist. Some issues to investigate are the following:

- formal or informal limits on the degree of foreign participation permitted in the market;
- formal or informal limits on foreign ownership of corporations;
- the rules governing hard-currency repatriation of profits and capital by foreigners.

Although international investors prefer that countries not treat them differently from the way they treat domestic investors, a country's regulatory regime should also be judged by another factor: certainty. The reliability of government policymakers and regulators is frequently more important than the contents of the rules themselves. Investors can plan adequately only if they are certain that important rules that affect the economics of their investments will not be made more restrictive in the future. For example, an investor who knows that a rule relating to repatriation of capital will not be tightened can factor in the effects of the rule on the potential risks and returns of the investment.

This final major area of securities regulation illustrates one of the most important qualitative features of an emerging market's regulatory system: The credibility of the regulatory authorities, whether in the government or industry, is vital for foreign investors.

Agency Roles in Emerging Markets

Three agencies have been particularly involved in assisting the development of emerging markets—the International Finance Corporation (IFC), the International Organization of Securities Commissions (IOSCO), and the U.S. Securities and Exchange Commission. The IFC, IOSCO, and the SEC take different approaches to delivering technical assistance to emerging securities markets, but they have in common that their resources for assistance are quite limited relative to the explosion in demand. Even adding the resources of the Asian Development Bank and the World Bank, which have started to provide assistance in the past few years, cannot keep up with the global shift toward market economics.

The International Finance Corporation

The IFC is the largest source of foreign direct and portfolio investment from the private sector in developing countries. In addition, for more than two decades, the IFC has been fostering the development of capital markets in its client member countries. In 1971, the IFC established a Capital Markets Department to provide specialized advisory services and financing to initiate and expand financial institutions in developing countries. The Relations, Advisory, Technical Assistance and Specialists Unit of this department coordinates financial-sector technical assistance to IFC member countries and private entities. Technical assistance programs cover a wide range of activities:

- assisting with the drafting of securities laws and regulations;
- advising on regulations for new types of financial institutions and the adaptation of existing regulations for new forms of market activity;
- establishing supervisory and enforcement entities and mechanisms.

When a member country requests help in identifying necessary policy changes, the IFC examines the specific laws and regulations that inhibit financial market development. Together with the appropriate government agencies, it offers advice for adapting existing laws and policies. Discussions often lead to proposals for new laws and policies or for restructuring or reorienting regulatory entities.

Typical areas in which the IFC provides advice on regulatory issues are securities market laws and regulations (including the role and organization of securities commissions), financial market information in general (and securities market disclosure in particular), and regulations concerning foreign portfolio investment. The IFC has provided this type of advice to some 60 developing countries during the past 20 years.

The International Organization of Securities Commissions

IOSCO provides the major international forum for mutual consultation and collaboration on regulatory issues relevant to the securities business, including the growing cross-border business. The organization's broad aim is to help national regulators ensure that the business is conducted by adequately capitalized firms through safe and sound market systems that afford investors proper protection.

The member agencies of IOSCO have resolved through its permanent structure

- to cooperate together to improve the regulation of domestic and international markets;
- to exchange information on their experiences in order to promote the development of domestic markets; and
- to provide mutual assistance to ensure the integrity of the markets by a rigorous application of standards and by effective enforcement against offenses.

The IOSCO Development Committee endeavors to promote the emerging securities markets by, in particular, the exchange of pertinent information and the implementation of common standards. This committee has identified several priorities and set up working groups to deal with such matters as clearing and settlement, institutional investors, internationalization, derivatives, and disclosure. The Working Group on Disclosure, for example, aims to create a set of minimum disclosure standards and standardization of the norms for investor protection in member countries.

The Securities and Exchange Commission

The trend toward globalization of financial services and the rapid growth of new domestic markets have encouraged securities regulators from developed countries to focus on international regulatory matters. A number of these regulatory bodies are now offering technical assistance to regulators and market participants from emerging markets.

One of the more formalized assistance programs is the International Institute for Securities Market Development established by the SEC. The purpose of the institute is to promote market development, capital formation, and the building of sound regulatory structures. The institute's primary vehicle for assistance is an annual training seminar for officials from new or emerging markets. This program provides a series of lectures and workshops covering a full range of topics relevant to the development and oversight of securities markets. Participants have the opportunity to visit and consult with U.S. securities firms and other private-sector organizations that serve securities markets in the United States and internationally. Participants can also observe specific systems, such as trading and clearing, or settlement systems, in operation.

Sources of Information

Investors who wish to know more about the regulations and standards of the emerging markets than could be included in this presentation can consult the following publications:

- *Capital Asia*. Hong Kong: ISI Publications (monthly publication for Asia/Pacific region only).
- Chuppe, Terry, and Michael Atkin. 1992. *Regulation of Securities Markets: Some Recent Trends and Their Implications for Emerging Markets*. Washington, D.C.: The World Bank.
- de Caires, Brian, and Debbie Fletter. 1990. *Investing in Emerging Securities Markets*. London: Euromoney Publications.

- *Emerging Stock Markets Factbook 1993.* Washington, D.C.: IFC Emerging Markets Database.
- Fraser, K. Michael. 1993. *Emerging Markets IMF/World Bank Daily.* Washington, D.C. (September 27).
- *International Securities Regulation Report.* Washington, D.C.: Buraff Publications (biweekly news publication).
- van Agtmael, Antoine W., and Keith K.H. Park. 1993. *The World's Emerging Stock Markets.* Chicago, Ill.: Probus Publishing.
- Vittas, Dimitri. 1992. *Financial Regulation: Changing the Rules of the Game.* Washington, D.C.: The World Bank.

Conclusions

Securities regulation is not simple even in the small and relatively unsophisticated emerging markets. Every securities market must perform certain basic functions regardless of its trading volume, the extent of its diversification in instruments and institutions, or the degree to which it uses real-time information technology. These basic market functions must be well defined through laws and regulations and through commonly accepted industry practices. Fraud, abuse, and systemic risk are also common to all financial systems; therefore, prudential safeguards are essential. In summary, when analyzing the regulatory environment of any emerging market, the investor should keep in mind the following:

First, the regulatory environment is not limited to the activities of certain government agencies; it includes the manner in which the securities industry sets and enforces its own rules.

Second, regulation should not be viewed as an exclusively disciplinary activity; in emerging markets especially, government and industry regulators have vital developmental roles.

Third, the regulatory environment must be viewed as part of a country's broad environment of laws, regulations, and commercial practices that affect the value of financial assets and the rights of their owners. This issue is especially important in countries moving from a planned to a market economy.

Finally, for portfolio investors, one of the most important aspects of the regulatory environment of an emerging market is the seriousness and professionalism of the regulators. Their credibility will have a significant effect on the near-term operations of the market and the long-term prospects for development of the market. Both of these factors will, in turn, have an important impact on the risks and returns of portfolio investors investing in that market.

Question and Answer Session

Rudolf van der Bijl

Question: Which markets have the most to gain from improved regulatory protection, and which are also demonstrating improvements?

van der Bijl: The degree of seriousness with which the importance of foreign investment is taken has improved tremendously. An article titled "Money Managers Place Their Bets," which was published in the daily newsletter issued by the International Monetary Fund and the World Bank (see Fraser 1993, pp. 34, 39, in the Sources of Information), lists the 12 most important emerging market investors and some of the countries they see as having the best potential. It also gives a flavor for many of the techniques—bottom up, top down, and so forth. When they mention these countries, their choices are based not solely on returns but also on the regulatory environments with which they must deal.

Question: When you talk with emerging market regulators, do they ever object to some of the basic principles of regulation, and on what grounds?

van der Bijl: They do not object to these principles in favor of other principles, but their understanding of the principles and whether they can live with them in a given environment may be in question. This area has been improving because the influx of foreign portfolio investment—more so than rising domestic investment—has forced them to shape up.

The fundamental problem in a great majority of developing countries is that the securities commission is not a totally independent agency. It is either tied into the central bank or ministry of finance or is a department of the ministry of finance and, consequently, run by public servants working for civil service salaries. Therefore, the commission has difficulty attracting the right people. For example, among the 30 countries where foreign investors most frequently operate in the securities market, the technical capabilities of the securities commissions have great diversity.

For that matter, the capabilities on the self-regulatory side to deal with the issues discussed here also vary greatly. For example, Mexico, after having a fairly weak structure for many years, has in the past seven or eight years shaped up greatly. At this stage, Mexico's regulatory entity is very professional and competent. The same is generally true for the Mexican Stock Exchange.

In some other countries, the securities commission is a nonentity with a few underpaid people who have no clear idea of what is happening and are incapable of dealing with the complexities of controlling the market. In particular, they do not understand the perspective of actually helping to develop the markets, as opposed to sitting there like policemen and focusing totally on the regulatory function.

Question: Hot money is considered potentially dangerous for the country receiving the investment, but punitive short-term capital gains taxes intended to curb abuse are criticized. Do other regulatory options exist?

van der Bijl: Economists and, sometimes, the politically inclined people from the developing countries do not want hot money in portfolio investments because, according to a longstanding theory, it is bad for the market. It goes in rapidly and it will go out just as rapidly. Practice has not proved that conventional wisdom, however. Foreign portfolio investors obviously place their money based on a certain set of assumptions. If those assumptions do not work out or if the market takes a tremendous turn, they pull the money out.

On the whole, however, because of the increase in investors and because the amounts are becoming a substantial part of the investment in these markets, the money has become more and more permanent; it is there to stay. Therefore, the IFC has not focused any particular attention on how to control hot-money flows.

Trading and Execution in Emerging Markets

Alexander Peña
Head of Emerging Markets Trading
Morgan Stanley & Company, Inc.

> The lack of liquidity, inefficiencies, and distrust of foreign investors in many emerging markets place a premium on careful, timely, opportunistic, and realistic trading. Of particular importance to foreign investors is a satisfactory broker. In choosing a broker, investors must assess the advantages and disadvantages of using local and global brokers, issues of confidentiality, and transaction costs.

Although trading and execution in emerging markets should not be any different from what these tasks are in developed markets, problems with liquidity and inefficiencies may create difficulties for investors in emerging markets. This presentation will outline the key challenges in executing investment strategies in the emerging markets—in particular, the degree of liquidity in the markets and the factors that determine how investable a market may be. The presentation will conclude with a methodology for trading in the markets.

Determining Liquidity

Three key factors play a role in determining liquidity in emerging markets: the size of the market relative to the size of the country's economy, the volume and composition of the market, and regulatory limits on foreign investment in the country. The answers to the following questions can help assess the degree of liquidity in a market: Does the stock market offer a full exposure to the true economy, or are certain sectors missing? Is the market influenced by institutional investors, foreign or local investors, retail investors? Is the market fearful of or welcoming to foreigners?

Market Capitalizations

One of the key factors in determining liquidity is the size of the market relative to the size of the economy. **Table 1** compares the ratios of market capitalization to GDP in the United States and certain other developed countries with the ratios in emerging markets of Asia, Latin America, Europe, and Africa. Three of the Asian markets—Hong Kong, Singapore, and Malaysia—have highly developed markets relative to their economies; market capitalization-to-GDP ratios exceed 100 percent. Malaysia, with an economy a quarter the size of South Korea's, has a market capitalization equally as large as Korea's. China, Indonesia, and India will eventually become much more important markets as their local GDPs continue to grow and their markets develop.

Latin American capital markets, with the exception of Chile, lag the Asian markets in development. In most emerging markets, the major forces in improving liquidity are privatization and the efforts of those controlling the large family holdings to raise capital through the stock market, both of which allow market expansion. The privatization process of key sectors in Latin America—natural resources, energy generation, and telecommunications—is not complete, which has left key sectors of the economy out of the capital markets. In Argentina, for example, although the entire electricity generation and distribution sector has recently been privatized, these companies have not yet been listed on the stock market. They are expected to be listed within the next few months, however, which will expand the market capitalization of Argentina. Mexico's largest company, PEMEX, the national oil company, is not expected to be listed on an exchange unless the constitution is reformed to allow privatization of the company or sale of minor equity positions.

In the East European emerging markets, the capital markets are still relatively small and have limited exposure to the entire economy. As in Latin America, a good portion of the economy was or continues to be controlled by the government.

With the exception of South Africa and Nigeria,

Table 1. Comparison of Market Capitalizations as of September 1993

Country	Market Capitalization ($billions)	1992 GDP ($billions)	Market Capitalization/ GDP
United States	$4,000.0	$5,670	71%
Asia			
China	NA	402	NA
Hong Kong	243.0	96	253
India	65.0	238	27
Indonesia	25.0	130	19
Japan	3,811.0	4,000	95
Korea	115.0	277	42
Malaysia	116.0	57	203
Pakistan	8.0	49	16
Philippines	18.0	54	33
Singapore	63.0	45	140
Sri Lanka	1.0	7	20
Taiwan	128.0	207	62
Thailand	60.0	103	58
Latin America			
Argentina	30.0	229	13
Brazil	86.0	407	21
Chile	34.0	38	90
Colombia	9.0	51	18
Mexico	146.0	323	45
Peru	3.0	47	7
Venezuela	6.0	59	10
Europe			
Czech Republic	1.0	26	3
Greece	9.0	78	12
Hungary	1.0	36	1
Israel	34.0	65	52
Poland	2.0	76	2
Portugal	11.0	83	13
Russia	None	61	0
Turkey	23.0	155	15
Africa			
Botswana	0.3	4[a]	7
Egypt	1.4	42	3
Ghana	0.1	6[a]	2
Ivory Coast	0.3	10[a]	3
Kenya	0.6	8	7
Mauritius	0.5	3	17
Morocco	2.0	28	7
Namibia	0.4	1[a]	31
Nigeria	1.2	23	5
South Africa	143.0	163	87
Swaziland	0.1	1[b]	17
Tunisia	0.7	15	4
Uganda	NA	3[b]	
Zimbabwe	0.6	5[a]	11

Source: Morgan Stanley & Co.

NA = not available.
None = does not exist.
[a]1991.
[b]1990.

the southern African markets are in the early stages of market development. Northern Africa is further ahead in this respect. Several countries in the northern region have opened exchanges since 1988, and the region is beginning to take a market approach.

Volume and Composition

The general level of liquidity of a market is influenced by the volume traded and the concentration of that volume in certain stocks or sectors. **Table 2** shows various measures of the degree of volume concentration for Latin America for 1993. Often, when these markets are in early developmental stages, trading is concentrated in a few stocks, mainly the large-capitalization, blue-chip stocks. As the markets develop and more companies are listed on the exchanges, this concentration begins to subside. Latin America exhibits high market concentration in the top ten stocks with low market volume overall.

Table 2. Volume Concentration: Latin America

Country	Average Daily Volume ($millions)	Percent of Trading by Top Ten Stocks	Percent of Trading by Benchmark Stock
Argentina	$29	73%	25%
Brazil	97	74	43
Chile	8	77	25
Colombia	1	79	34
Mexico	112	65	40
Peru	5	67	12
Venezuela	4	95	62

Source: Morgan Stanley & Co., Inc.

Note: Based on data collected for the 12 months to September 1993.

Latin American countries tend to focus on a "benchmark" stock, which is generally the largest capitalization stock on the exchange—in most cases, the telecommunication stock. Investors, believing that this stock provides the best exposure to the market, tend to trade the stock heavily. As Table 2 shows, with the exception of Peru, trading in a benchmark stock accounts for more than 25 percent of the activity in these markets. The markets are thus usually strongly affected by this one stock: If the stock moves up, the market moves up; if the stock declines, the market declines.

Investment Accessibility

If the market is not friendly to foreigners, that attitude probably stems from one of two reasons—fear that foreign companies are buying out local companies, or the perception that foreigners are investing in the local market only for short-term gains rather than long-term investment.

The free float presented in **Table 3** provides a good measure of investment accessibility in the emerging markets. Free float is defined as the amount of a company's outstanding equity not held by the company and/or the government that is available for purchase in the open market. Although the numbers vary, the Asian countries tend to have a greater level of free float than the Latin American

Table 3. Investment Accessibility of Emerging Markets: Asia, Latin America, and Europe

Country	Free Float	Theoretical Availability to Foreigners
Asia		
Hong Kong	46%	100%
India	NA	24% including conversion of convertible debentures; 5% limit per investor
Indonesia	18	35%; banks 25–45%
Korea	30	Authorized investors 10%; companies may apply to increase limit to 25%
Malaysia	44	100%; banks and financial institutions 30%
Pakistan	NA	100%
Philippines	14	Up to 49%; generally, foreign investment restricted from mass media, retail trade, and rural banking
Singapore	56	49%; banks, media, and airlines 27–46%
Sri Lanka	NA	NA
Taiwan	72	10%; $2.5 billion ceiling on total foreign cash inflows
Thailand	65	49%; 25% most banks
Latin America		
Argentina	36	100%
Brazil	53	Up to 49% voting common stock; 100% nonvoting preferred stock; no foreign individuals
Chile	36	25% of listed company's shares
Colombia	15	100%
Mexico	47	100%; financial institutions 30%
Peru	52	100%
Venezuela	20	Nonfinancial 100%
Europe		
Czech Republic	NA	
Greece	25	100%
Hungary	NA	
Israel	30	100%
Poland	40–50	100%; management 10–15%, government 20%, strategic investors 10–15%, 18 stocks
Portugal	25	100%; family oriented, 100 companies, 60 traded regularly
Turkey	15	100%; family oriented, 160 companies, 60 traded regularly

Source: Morgan Stanley & Co.

NA = not available.

[a] The percentage for Brazil without Telebras would be 22.
[b] The percentage for Mexico without Telmex would be 38.

countries, which is consistent with the ratios of market capitalization to GDP.

Table 3 also summarizes the theoretical limitations on foreign investment for selected countries. The practical limitations may be quite different, however. In Hong Kong, for example, a foreign investor cannot buy 100 percent of a company, even though regulations permit it, because either the stock is not available or management holds a good stake in the stock. In practice, either the local investors and owners will not let the sale to foreigners happen or the government will intervene.

Taiwan and Korea limit foreign investors to 10 percent of a company's equity, which is the lowest in the world of countries open to foreign investment. One explanation may be a fear of foreigners in these markets. Another is that the markets do not need foreign financing. The cost of funding in Korea is 9 percent; equity financing is not attractive. The free float in Korea is very small because of some fairly large corporate cross-holdings. (Korea has no such thing as a holding company; therefore, "sister" companies own large equity stakes in each other.)

Limitations on foreign investment are different in Latin America. The countries love foreign financing and foreign technology, and welcome foreign ownership. Foreign corporations have been large participants in many of the privatizations throughout Latin America, especially in Argentina. The free float is relatively low in Latin America because local families, corporations, and the government have significant stakes in numerous industries.

Formal limitations on foreign investment are virtually nonexistent in the emerging markets of Europe, but the free float is low, and buying sizable positions through the market is virtually impossible. In Poland, for example, foreigners can theoretically buy up to 100 percent of a company, but realistically only about 50 percent is available for sale. Management is generally required to hold 10–15 percent, the government will hold 20 percent, and strategic investors will hold 10–15 percent. Family and bank holdings are large in most companies in Europe, and many companies are not listed on the exchange at all. (Families fear foreigners buying up their companies, so they do not list them.) In addition, borrowing is easy for local owners in the East European markets.

In Africa, volumes are very low and investors face various hurdles in trying to invest. Calculating free float is not relevant, so **Table 4** shows the investment accessibility for Africa using average daily volume as a measure of accessibility. The most prevalent "limitation" is that foreign investors must go through an arduous application process (paper and legal work) to gain access to the market. Although foreign investors want to invest in the African countries, these markets, with the exceptions of South Africa and Nigeria, are not yet ready for foreign investors. The markets are still in the process of setting up stock exchanges and regulations.

A commission has been established in Sub-Saharan Africa to centralize and standardize trading, accounting, and stock exchange procedures for the region. This commission will allow South Africa and Nigeria to develop some of the other markets in Africa, which should lead to cross-listing for some stocks in South Africa. This commission should also generate improvements in brokerage services in Africa overall.

Market Expansion

The rate of market expansion is another indication of liquidity. **Table 5** uses Mexico and Argentina to illustrate this concept. These markets are relatively small and have low liquidity, but they continue to grow, and liquidity should improve. In both countries, primary and secondary offerings have been numerous and sizable since December 1991. Many of the issues in Mexico have been primary offerings of existing listed companies, however (as was the case in 1992 for Telmex, the Mexican telecommunications company, and some of the leading financial institutions), which has not increased the market capitalization.

During this period, Argentina experienced strong market expansion, with initial public offerings by YPF, the national oil company, Baesa, a beverage company, and an automaker. Also affecting the market was the privatization of Telefonica and Telecom, the two telecommunication stocks.

Trading Issues

Trading strategies in emerging markets must account for the characteristics of the markets, such as low liquidity and inefficiency relative to developed markets. Investors in emerging markets must be much more sensitive to issues of paying for premiums, looking for blocks, taking the opportunities to buy certain stocks when they appear, and timing. In many of these markets, if you take your time investing, you will have a hard time building a sizable position in the stock.

Purchasing top-tier stocks in the open market is much easier than purchasing second- or third-tier stocks. Often, with second- and third-tier stocks, you must seek blocks of stock; you will not be able to go into the open market.

Liquidity in some of the stocks can range from $10,000 to $250,000 a day, so investors must seek out an opportunity. You must be prepared to act swiftly if a block is offered, even if the timing or the price is

Table 4. Investment Accessibility: Africa

Country	Average Daily Volume	Theorectial Availability to Foreigners
Botswana	35,300	49%; no single foreign investor may own more than 5% of company
Egypt	NA	Closed
Ghana	19,000	74%; no single foreign investor may own more than 10% of company
Ivory Coast	NA	Closed
Kenya	46,600	Foreigners must apply
Mauritius	NA	Foreigners must apply
Morocco	$100,000	100%
Namibia	25,000	100%; foreign exchange control
Nigeria	80,000	Foreigners must apply
South Africa	NA	No restrictions
Swaziland	822	Foreigners must apply
Tunisia	100,000	Foreigners must apply
Uganda		No stock market
Zimbabwe	50,000	25%; no single foreign investor may own more than 5% of company

Source: Morgan Stanley & Co.

NA = not available.

Table 5. Market Expansion: Argentina and Mexico

	Market Capitalization ($millions)	Equity Issues ($millions)	Market Capitalization Increase ($millions)
Argentina			
August 1993	$29,600	$2,194.0	$6,732
June 1993	26,733	0.0	0
March 1993	18,769	6.0	22
December 1992	18,706	0.0	0
September 1992	18,462	0.0	0
June 1992	25,607	293.0	1,953
March 1992	25,542	1,210.0	4,056
December 1991	18,785	848.0	2,829
Mexico			
August 1993	146,000	42.8[a]	—
June 1993	130,000	108.0	—
March 1993	133,000	583.0	—
December 1992	139,000	174.0	—
September 1992	108,000	0.0	—
June 1992	129,000	2,672.0	—
March 1992	136,000	1,029.0	—
December 1991	102,000	5,134.0[b]	—

Source: Morgan Stanley & Co., Inc.
[a]$826 million pending.
[b]Full year.

---

not ideal; you may never have another opportunity.

Companies often issue different series of stocks for foreign and local investors, and the relative price performance reflects that difference. **Figure 1** and **Figure 2** illustrate relative price performance of the stocks of two financial institutions in Mexico—Banacci (Figure 1) and GF Bancomer (Figure 2). Each company has three series of stocks—two for local investors (A and B) and one for foreign investors (C). In November 1992, the B series of Banacci was opened to foreigners, so the spread between the Bs and Cs began to narrow. In the middle of 1993, the company started to hint that it might come out with an American Depositary Receipt linked to the C series, so the premiums started to increase, which is characteristic of a stock with an ADR link in these markets.

For Bancomer, the premiums for the C series grew to as much as 30–40 percent over the B series in 1993. In August 1993, the B series was opened to foreign investors, which resulted in a reduction of the premium; the C series declined and the B series in-

Figure 1. Relative Price Performance: Banacci A, B, and C

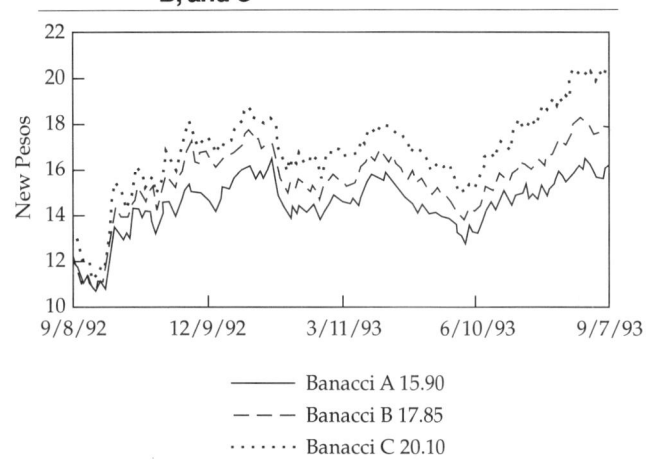

— Banacci A 15.90
- - - Banacci B 17.85
······ Banacci C 20.10

Source: Bolsa de Valores data.

Figure 2. Relative Price Performance: GF Bancomer (GFB) A, B, and C

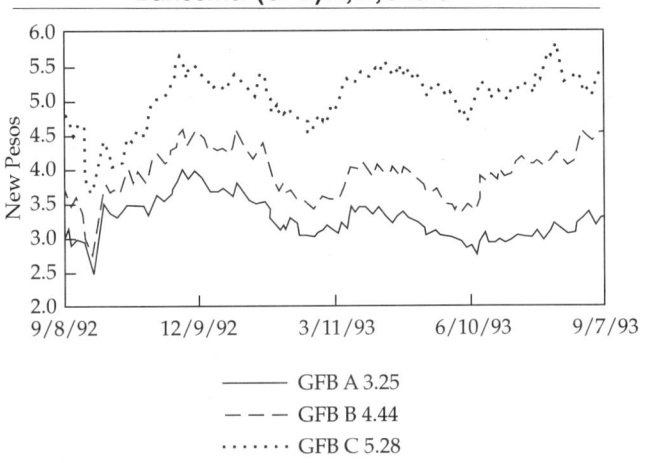

— GFB A 3.25
- - - GFB B 4.44
······ GFB C 5.28

Source: Bolsa de Valores data.

creased. The spread in September 1993 was about 15 percent, which is consistent with the fact that there is an ADR linked to the C series.

Local or Global Brokers

Trading in emerging markets requires a combination of local and global brokers. Experienced global brokers offer research, credibility, trading experience, and the ability to see blocks of stocks. Local brokers offer experience with the local markets; they know the key players and the corporations. Local brokers can often supply blocks of stocks being sold by the company, local investors, or local pension funds, particularly for second-tier companies. Another advantage to using local brokers is lower costs than using global brokers.

One important advantage of using a global broker is that the global broker will take responsibility for seeking the best prices and looking out for your best interests. Local brokers may believe they should not have this responsibility because many of them trade from their own books. Placement is another advantage when dealing with global brokers. The global brokers will lead primary and secondary offerings, such as the Telmex or YPF deals, that can be as large as US$1 billion, so as the markets develop, they will add liquidity in the markets. Local brokers in emerging markets do not have the distribution capability or expertise to manage billion-dollar deals.

The primary disadvantage of using a local broker is lack of experience with foreign institutions. Local brokers may not understand how foreign investors prefer to transact orders. Also, the research effort is fairly limited in local brokerages. It generally focuses on macro, micro, and sectorial issues; local brokers usually cannot provide earnings estimates, for example, for a company for the next two-to-three years.

The primary disadvantage in using a global broker is cost. Another disadvantage is timeliness of information, because the global brokers are as new to these emerging markets as the investors; information from a global broker is generally information that was received from a local broker. The lack of settlement experience is sometimes an issue when using global brokers. In many of these markets, the brokerage sector is closed to foreign participation; therefore, everyone, both foreign investors and foreign brokers, must transact with local institutions.

Confidentiality

Confidentiality is one of the most important issues when trading in emerging markets. Information about orders leaks out quickly in some markets, particularly in Asia and Latin America. I have placed orders seeking to sell a very liquid stock, and within 30 minutes, a broker will call offering that same block of stock. Developing strong relationships with the local brokers and being able to trust that they will not advertise your order is important.

The entry of foreign buyers strongly affects sentiment in all the emerging markets. Small markets in particular, such as Peru, may be very sensitive to a foreign investor coming in with a large order. When local or other foreign investors see another foreigner coming in to buy, everyone starts buying or holds off selling.

Confidentiality is particularly important when selling stock. A stock price can collapse 5–6 percent before the order is actually sold because someone found out a sale was being considered. Confidentiality is one of the big advantages with using global brokers; they have experience dealing with institutional investors and know how to handle the orders.

Transaction Costs

Commissions are fairly high throughout the emerging markets. **Table 6** shows local commissions for selected countries in Asia and Latin America. Argentina has local commissions of 50 to 75 basis points; other countries can have costs as high as 100 basis points. In some countries, the commissions are fixed by the local security exchange, while in others,

Table 6. Transaction Costs in Selected Emerging Markets

Country	Local Commissions (basis points)	Stamps/Fees (basis points)
Latin America		
Argentina	50–75	17
Brazil	20–50	5
Chile	30–50	NA
Colombia	30–100	NA
Mexico	40–50	NA
Peru	65–100	NA
Poland	50–100	NA
Portugal	15–50	20–50
Turkey	20–50	1–2.5
Venezuela	90+	NA
Asia		
Hong Kong	25–50	17
India	45–100	NA
Indonesia	55–100	18.8
Korea	50+	NA
Malaysia	75–100	10–15
Philippines	50–100	Board lot fee, 2.5 basis points on sales
Singapore	75–100	5
Thailand	75–100	NA

Source: Morgan Stanley & Co.

NA = not applicable.

costs are somewhat negotiable. In Chile, commissions usually decline as an investor's activities in the local market increase. Foreign institutions (global brokers) will probably charge commissions between 25 and 50 basis points for their research and experience in addition to local brokerage fees. Few of the emerging market countries have stamps or other fees, but some markets do.

Conclusion

When investing in emerging markets, realistic investment goals and approaches are extremely important. Placing large orders in these markets will scare the local owners and make purchasing stocks difficult. Trading in emerging markets plays a much larger role in the investment process than it does in developed markets, because many of the stocks are illiquid and, therefore, hard to trade. Investors must depend on brokers for information and execution. Individual investors do not have much control unless they want to spend an entire day monitoring their order and the activity of their brokers. Investors must understand the underlying local market, how stocks trade, and the key players. These markets are sensitive to rumors, government activity, foreign institutions, and local investors, and they are also subject to manipulation.

Question and Answer Session

Alexander Peña

Question: What is the best way to determine whether a large trade has occurred in a particular emerging market stock?

Peña: The best way is to compare the total volume traded with the number of trades on a specific day. This ratio tells you whether the stock is trading in big chunks through one specific broker, in which case the broker may be manipulating the stock.

Question: Please provide some examples of market tricks or manipulations by local investment managers about which investors should be aware.

Peña: A classic example occurs in Colombia; because very large holding companies there own cement stocks, beverage stocks, brokerage houses, and banks, the banks and brokerage houses can manipulate the activity in some of their other listed stocks. Similar manipulations occur in Mexico, where certain important individuals have holdings in banks, industrial companies, and brokerage houses. In these cases, there is a tendency for a specific brokerage house or bank to be the primary trader of that industrial company.

Question: Do you find it difficult to get daily prices on emerging market securities to use in valuing shares of open-end mutual funds?

Peña: Yes, daily prices are difficult to get. For example, only in Brazil, Mexico, and Venezuela, can you pull up stocks individually to obtain pricing. For Peru, Colombia, Chile, and Argentina, you must depend on brokers to send you faxes of information for pricing.

Question: In markets such as Thailand, Korea, or Indonesia that have a foreign board (a separate exchange for designated eligible foreign securities) but the foreign shares do not trade often, which prices do you use for valuing your emerging markets fund? Do you use the local share prices, or do you use foreign board prices?

Peña: In most cases, we use the last trade price, regardless of which shares were traded, unless a significant spread normally exists, in which case, we would use the average between the bid and ask prices.

Question: Do you agree that custodial operations are loss leaders and that the banks really make all their profits on foreign exchange?

Peña: The answer depends partly on the market. Different markets have different regulations for holding cash. In Mexico, for example, the local authorities do not allow investors actually to hold cash or have a checking account. The Mexican currency must be immediately converted or invested in something else, such as an overnight T-bill.

Question: How strictly enforced are restrictions and limitations on shares, particularly those relating to foreign versus local ownership?

Peña: The degree of enforcement depends on the market, but this type of regulation is easy to implement, so the area is heavily regulated. For example, most exchanges require an account number for each trade. This number signals whether the party is local or foreign.

Question: Please discuss the advantages and disadvantages of using ADRs rather than local shares.

Peña: An ADR is usually much more liquid than the underlying stock. The primary example is Mexico, where three or four of the biggest companies have ADRs and the liquidity has actually been removed from the local market into the ADRs. Generally, the spreads will be about 0.5 percent, but the investor must shop around for them. The best spreads—typically one-fourth to three-eighths—are generally with the U.S. institutions that originated the deal.

Question: Would foreign investors be penalized for holding ADRs instead of domestic issues?

Peña: No intrinsic penalizing would be involved. The investor owning ADRs should have the same rights as in owning the local shares as far as dividends and voting are concerned. The ADR may be issued on an underlying series of stocks that has different rights from the stocks that trade locally. Prices may be a bit higher to cover additional administrative charges.

Question: Would the spreads of SEC Rule 144a ADRs and the traditional ADRs differ?

Peña: The spreads are wider on the 144a shares, but the liquidity continues to be fairly strong.

Question: How might emerging market equity derivatives (basket and index warrants, options, and swaps) affect liquidity, volume concentration, and so forth?

Peña: Liquidity can be improved. Basket trades are possible only in the less concentrated markets, such as Asia, and will add equity flow. In Brazil, options and futures create volume surges near expiration.

Question: What is the best way to monitor foreign ownership ceilings and available shares for purchase?

Peña: Ask the custodian or broker. Some markets publish these data.

Settlement, Custody, and Regulatory Challenges in Emerging Markets

Andrew Summers
Principal
Morgan Stanley & Company, Inc.

> Much progress has been made in developing the stock markets of the emerging economies and in custodial services. A market may still present difficulties, however, in carrying out settlement, foreign exchange transactions, and obtaining information about corporate events. Investors must be fully educated about the processes and regulations in the emerging markets, try to anticipate problems, and work with top-flight professional custodians.

Settlement, custody, and regulatory issues are important considerations for investors in emerging markets. Global custody and settlement procedures have changed somewhat since the early 1980s, but foreign investors still face challenges in these areas in most emerging markets. Most local brokers are not used to dealing with a global custodian, so education is vital.

Settlement Issues

Settlement is not as big an issue now as it was ten years ago, when foreign investors began going into countries such as Italy and Spain. Some of the emerging markets, however, have imposed more regulations since then. In many countries, licenses and approvals are required to enter the markets, and some stock exchanges impose penalties on late settlement. The five key settlement issues are settlement periods, penalties for failure to settle, delivery versus payment, foreign exchange, and communication barriers.

■ *Settlement periods.* The Italian market in the 1980s provides a good example of the problems that can beset settlement procedures. Settlement was a nightmare in Italy at the time. Between 1985 and 1987, settlement took between 6 and 12 months. The delays caused considerable problems for fund managers trying to liquidate positions. Then, if a broker went bankrupt during that period, the fund manager had no idea what might happen to his or her position. In the meantime, managers could neither reinvest the proceeds of a sale nor get out of the lira position. Other difficulties with Italy included suspension of dividend payments for two to three years, no opportunity to recover withholding taxes, and central registers that did not know who owned what. Now, however, the Italians have sorted out the difficulties. Today's emerging markets have learned from others' past mistakes and, indeed, present less of a problem with settlement periods than most EAFE markets. (Settlement in France, Spain, or the United Kingdom, for example, can take six weeks. The delay causes cash flow problems for managers who want to invest the proceeds in, say, Japan or Germany, which have three-day or five-day settlement periods.) In emerging markets, most settlement is within two-to-five days. Two-day settlement periods are found in countries such as Turkey and Brazil, for example, where inflation is significant and people want to keep their money at work.

■ *Penalties for failure to settle.* Most emerging countries now emphasize quick settlement, with penalties if it does not happen. Singapore, Malaysia, and South Korea, for example, have instituted buyback solutions whereby the stock exchanges force brokers to buy back the shares sold, which cancels the transaction at a loss to the investor. In Korea, in addition, brokers and managers risk losing their licenses to invest if they are continual late settlers. In India, the stock exchange watches brokers and fund managers closely, and sends warning letters to those who are too slow. Brazil has some onerous fines; they can be 1–2 percent of capital a day for missettlement.

■ *Delivery versus payment.* Delivery versus payment is relevant to ERISA funds or any fund that complies with the Investment Advisers Act of 1940, under which the seller is required to deliver shares on receipt of payment in a simultaneously timed transaction. Consequently, the ERISA or Act 40 investor should not be dealing with U.S. brokers and settling in U.S. dollars, because the dollars are paid into a U.S.-based bank account but delivery of shares is a free delivery in the local market. Without DVP (delivery versus payment), the fund is not operating within the spirit of ERISA and Act 40 regulations. Therefore, investors must deal increasingly with local brokers, which involves the complications of time zones, language, and foreign exchange execution.

■ *Foreign exchange.* Settlement of emerging market trades involves foreign exchange transactions. The challenge is to be able to execute a foreign exchange trade in conjunction with the underlying asset trade. Most people use their global custodians to execute the foreign exchange trades, although the worry is that the custodian may be executing the trades at a time and rate that is most convenient for them. Ideally, the fund manager would monitor the custodian's foreign exchange transaction.

■ *Communication barriers.* Communication is another challenge. Dealing with local brokers means possible language and time zone differences. Morgan Stanley recruits Spanish-speaking employees in our New York office to help with the language challenge and has three hub offices—in Singapore, London, and New York—to deal with the time zone problem. Other companies have chosen to set up 24-hour trading facilities.

Local execution can be difficult, and the fund managers must participate in the settlement process. The fund managers serve as middlemen between brokers and custodians.

Example: Brazil

The problems we faced in Brazil recently are a good example of what can go wrong with settlement. On a Friday afternoon in early August, a fund manager decided to invest in Brazilian treasury bills for settlement on Monday. He was trading for two accounts with two different custodians. We got all the allocations on Friday night. On Monday, the $10 million trade with one custodian settled smoothly, but the $5 million trade with the second custodian did not settle, and we incurred a $50,000 fine.

The problem began when the custodian's subagent in Brazil refused to take new instructions beyond 10 a.m., even though the local exchange in Brazil settles up until 4 p.m. Sometimes investment managers are successful in getting subagents to bend their rules; other times, they are not.

A few days later, the Brazilian government changed the rules and prohibited foreign investors from holding treasury bills. We were given three-to-four weeks to liquidate our treasury bill position. Then, when we repatriated our money, we took off 25 basis points for a recently passed tax, but a few weeks later, the Brazilian supreme court decreed that the tax was illegal. We had to make claims against the Brazilian government to recover the tax it illegally took from us.

Summary

The investment firm is the administrator and must pass instructions to a global custodian. The global custodian then passes instructions to its subagent, and the subagent must get a local administrator involved. The foreign exchange trade must be tied into the details of the amount being repatriated. If two different custodians are involved, then there are 12 people in the chain, and they must all be focused on the one trade the investor is trying to settle—no lunch, no coffee breaks, no meetings. It is an exercise in coordination and strong management.

Settlement in emerging markets involves a wide variety of processes and issues that must be negotiated. The secret is to keep on top, try to anticipate problems, and work with professional people wherever possible.

Custody Issues

Custody issues are important in all international markets, not only emerging markets. Investors depend heavily on custodians to look after their interests. The key issues with regard to custody in emerging markets are the characteristics of the custodian bank, the extent and quality of the subagent network, the custodian's foreign exchange capabilities, the custodian's corporate actions department, and the custodian's fee structure.

■ *Custodian bank.* A custodian bank should have experienced staff and should be professional, oriented toward problem solving, and flexible—because you never know when a problem will occur requiring immediate resolution. Forged and fraudulent shares are probably the biggest, although not the most frequent, problem. Some of the controls in these markets are not as mature as they might be in the U.S. market.

In India, for example, seven stock lines have been frozen because the shares are considered tainted. Someone made very good forgeries of those shares and used them as security on a loan. When the loan defaulted, the bank tried to liquidate the shares to recover its loan. Now delivery on those shares is pending the completion of investigations by the appropriate authorities.

Another example of fraud is the China Light & Power shares marketed in Hong Kong. Someone forged the transfer document and sold the shares to a broker. The broker sold them to us, delivered the forged shares, and transferred the document to our custodian. All parties involved disclaim responsibility.

Some custodian banks do not handle certain instruments, such as the settlement of investments in loans to less developed countries (LDCs). The documentation in buying an LDC loan is complicated, and skill is involved in those settlements. The custodian's settlement staff must make sure the lenders are getting the appropriate issues.

Investors must make sure that custodians handle the types of instruments the investor wants to use or are ambitious to add those instruments.

■ *Subagent network.* A good subagent network expands an investor's opportunities for investment. The subagent network of the better custodians cover 50 or 60 countries, whereas others cover only 40. Persuading a custodian to add a new agent to the network can be difficult. Setting up a subagent takes between 3 and 12 months and costs about $50,000. Consequently, the custodians want a sizable commitment—say, $5 million to $20 million in business in the country—before they undertake to add a new subagent. The delay can be frustrating for a manager who wants to be the first investor in a country.

Another problem with expanding the agent network is meeting 17-F5 qualifications requiring an agent to have at least $200 million of capital. This amount of capital is virtually unheard of in many emerging markets, so the custodian has to find a British or U.S. bank to set up a branch in the country and obtain an SEC exemption from the requirement in order for the bank to act as the custodian's subagent. Getting the SEC exemption can take months.

■ *Foreign exchange capabilities.* Another important qualification of a custodian is having the capability to carry out foreign exchange transactions. This requirement includes wide coverage. In addition, of course, the investor wants to be able to trust that the custodian will execute the transactions in the investor's best interest.

Custodians are responsible for most of Morgan Stanley's foreign exchange transactions. Having custodians handle the foreign exchange is advisable because of issues involving, in a country with exchange controls, the repatriation of funds in dollars.

■ *Corporate action department.* A key requirement is that the custodian have a strong corporate action department. The custodian should be helpful in supplying good, accurate information and should be responsive if any problems develop.

■ *Fees.* Fees vary widely according to the activities the custodian is providing and the client's mix of countries and trading volume. For the whole portfolio, the minimum the investor might expect to pay is about 20 basis points and the maximum might be 1 percent.

Some custodians are considering adding insurance to their services and, accordingly, to their fees. The insurance would protect the investor from loss in the event that, for example, assets are frozen and cannot be traded. Those investors that are aware of the political risks involved in investing in these countries might choose not to take out this insurance; other investors might like the coverage.

Regulatory Issues

Regulatory issues are another consideration for investors in emerging markets. The five key regulatory concerns are licenses, local representation, SEC regulations, ERISA regulations, and commingled funds.

■ *Licenses.* Licenses are required to invest in some countries—Korea, Taiwan, and India, for example—and obtaining the license is a laborious process; approval for a new investor's license can take three-to-six months. The delays often come from the clients themselves, however, because their corporate legal departments do not understand what is going on. (If a client invests through a commingled fund, a license is not needed, because the fund already has one.)

■ *Local representation.* The use of local brokers means local representation, which creates various problems. First, the fund manager must be precise with names. In Peru, one of our local agents held stock for a client in three different names, all varying slightly. The problem came when we tried to sell the position. The authorities would not allow us to match one name against the other. The securities had to be reregistered, which cost about $10,000, just because of the lack of precision in the names used by the local administrator. In Brazil, the investor must confirm that the custodian has set up an annex arrangement. In countries such as Chile, Colombia, and Peru, a local administrator must be appointed.

■ *The SEC and ERISA.* The investor must comply with SEC and ERISA regulations, but problems arise in doing so in emerging countries. The main problem in opening up new markets is with 17-F5. In addition, although using the broker's settlement capabilities would be a convenient way of getting started, that route is discouraged under the 1940 Investment Advisers Act and ERISA, as previously explained, because of DVP issues.

The commingled approach. The commingled approach is helpful in emerging markets because it eliminates many of the hurdles in entering the markets. With commingled funds, adding new accounts incurs no delay, custody and settlement are simplified, and the client avoids potential problems associated with managing the custodial relationship.

Conclusion

Much progress has been made in the past ten years in the stock markets of the emerging economies and in custodian services. The markets may still be difficult for settlement, foreign exchange, and obtaining information about corporate events, but the settlement process is somewhat easier than previously. Nevertheless, investment managers should always be aware of potential problems, such as the Brazilian treasury bill situation, and anticipating problems depends on everyone being fully educated. Managers should also work with a top-class custodian, and they should be mindful of regulatory issues. No investment is so complex that it cannot be done; the doing, however, may be arduous.

Question and Answer Session

Andrew Summers

Question: Whose money is on the line if one is delivered counterfeit securities?

Summers: If we had counterfeit securities delivered to us, we would look back to the broker who made the bad delivery. We expect the custodians to apply due diligence in the receipt of securities, because the custodians are using our client's money to acquire the securities. The custodians have clauses in their contracts, however, that require only that they apply best efforts. If the forgery is of high quality, the custodians could say they were not responsible or did not have an opportunity to pick up the forgery. Thus, we look to the brokers.

Question: What is the best source of information on corporate actions in emerging markets? Is the custodian's information satisfactory, or do other vendors do a better job?

Summers: By and large, global custodians do a satisfactory job in their delivery of this information. Other vendors do supply data on corporate actions, but their efforts so far have not been great. At best, they might cover 60–70 percent of the issues.

We work with five custodians, two who are good and three who are not so good on emerging markets. By using five, we achieve an acceptable breadth of coverage; if one misses an event, the others will probably provide information on it.

Question: With regard to open-end funds, how would investors be made whole if a corporate action ever worked to their disadvantage?

Summers: If one of our clients was affected, through an administrative error on our part, we would feel responsible to step in and make the client whole. The investor would not be disadvantaged or suffer any loss.

Question: The convertibility of foreign currency to dollars can be a problem, especially for stock sale trades. Do you have any solutions or tips for solving this problem?

Summers: For foreign exchange, we always depend on our custodian to have a strong treasury department and to be able to execute the foreign exchange trade either through the custodian's own markets or directly with a local subagent. Local subagents are always banks, which also have foreign exchange capabilities; so the foreign exchange will often be carried out with the local bank.

Question: Do you agree that custodial operations are loss leaders and that the banks really make all their profits on foreign exchange?

Summers: The answer probably depends on the custodian and its relationship with its client. Custodians' profits come from custody and servicing fees, foreign exchange services, and cash services; so, an element of the fees is invisible. Some custodians have "cleaner" custody and servicing fees and thus expect little contribution from their foreign exchange or cash services. But it is a murky area. For that reason, a number of fund managers prefer to execute foreign exchange trades with some other institution. In many emerging markets, however, as noted previously, the custodial bank is the only place to do foreign exchange because of the repatriation administration.

Question: How many of the emerging markets are headed toward electronic settlement?

Summers: In the next 10 years, probably all of them will have electronic settlement. The countries that have made good progress include Hong Kong, Singapore, and Malaysia. Keep in mind, however, that London has been trying to effect electronic settlement for 20 years and has not yet succeeded.

Understanding Emerging Market Life Cycles

Marc Faber
Managing Director
Marc Faber, Ltd.

> Investors who rightly look to the future must always be aware of the cycles in emerging markets; opportunities are falling in countries that rely on exports of industrial products and rising in markets with large resource bases. The most exciting opportunities may lie in entrepreneurship. Moreover, all future investment opportunities will depend on certain critical factors in the world economy; the most important: developments in China.

International investing has come a long way since 1970, when most U.S. institutions were not interested in investing overseas. In the early 1970s, the Boeing 747 made transcontinental travel practical and affordable, so people started traveling overseas on business and vacations. They became familiar with foreign countries and foreign corporate names. In addition, new technologies made international communication and broadcasting easy. Furthermore, the dollar weakness in 1970 and again in 1985 and the incredible economic success of Japan and other newly industrialized countries in Asia following World War II were all factors convincing people that a well-balanced portfolio had to contain international investments.

People began to focus on emerging markets in about 1989 because of the almost unprecedented bull moves in Mexico, South Korea, and Taiwan. The question now is whether the current popularity of investing in emerging markets is a bad omen for the future. To answer that question, this presentation will examine the life cycle of markets and note under what conditions stocks are undervalued and how to identify when they have become fully priced or overvalued.

The second topic will be Asia. The Asian stock markets have the heaviest weighting within the emerging economies universe. The reason for looking at their markets now is to determine if Asia had some particularly favorable conditions between 1985 and 1991 that propelled it to above-trendline growth.

Third will be a review of the global economy to see how the 1990s may be different from the 1980s—particularly in terms of stock performance. Which regions of the world will be the most attractive? If stocks are not the investment vehicles that will perform well, are alternative investment opportunities available?

Market Life Cycles

The life cycle of emerging markets is illustrated in **Figure 1**. Essentially, markets—whether they are stock markets, commodity markets, or real estate markets—move from obscurity (Phase Zero) to a high degree of recognition and popularity (Phase Three). Fundamentals often exceed expectations during Phases One through Three, and stock prices can rise significantly, but then following Phase Three, the fundamentals disappoint expectations, liquidity tends to shrink, and stock prices decline.

Phase Zero to Phase One

In Phase Zero, little or no foreign direct investment is entering the new market, and no portfolio investment. During this phase, countries are in a period in which everything has gone wrong. A typical example would be Latin America in the early 1980s, when it had a depression, real wages fell, economic growth was negative, and corporate profits were disappointing. Phase Zero usually also contains many political and social problems. Things are so bad that people who do invest in a Phase Zero economy run the risk of being sued by their shareholders.

During this phase, stock market volume is extremely low, and no new issues, no conferences about investment vehicles, and no country funds exist. Also, the headlines in the press, particularly in the United States, are extremely negative. During this

Figure 1. The Life Cycle of Emerging Markets

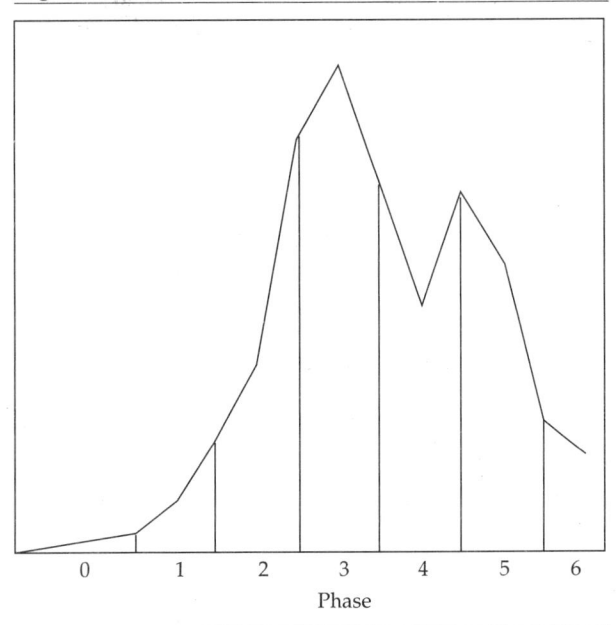

Source: Marc Faber, Ltd.

phase, even the local investors do not trust their country's economic conditions, and they move capital overseas. Stocks are unbelievably undervalued.

The transition from Phase Zero to Phase One is the most important time. In this period, the economy usually grows rapidly. For the transition to occur, a catalyst for a secular improvement in economic conditions is necessary. Three primary types of catalyst are possible—a major displacement, major changes in economic policies, and major social and political changes.

■ *A major displacement.* Such a displacement acts as a catalyst and could be a sharp rise in the price of an important commodity, which produces an inflow of liquidity and direct investment in a region. In the 1970s, for example, the rapid rise of oil prices created a business opportunity for oil-producing countries, principally in the Middle East but also in Nigeria, Venezuela, and Mexico. The price rise was the catalyst for the boom in the Middle East. During the 1975–81 period, the best-performing stock market in the world was the Kuwait stock market.

The application of an important new invention or a sudden increase in product demand, particularly exports, are other examples of a major displacement. For instance, in the 19th century, the growth of railroads opened the American West and allowed businesses to transfer their factories to inland America. The railroads acted as a catalyst for development of the Midwest and, later, the West Coast. The rise in the demand for manufactured goods from Asia is an example of a displacement that led to trade surpluses, which in turn, stimulated local Japanese businesses.

■ *Major changes in economic policies.* These can also act as catalysts. For example, a favorable change in tax laws can improve an investment climate and attract foreign direct investment. Other examples are changes in laws governing foreign direct investment and replacement of a planned with a market economy. Changes in an economic system have stimulated many new regions in the world to above-trendline growth.

■ *Major social and political changes.* These include changes in geopolitical conditions that lead to peace treaties; a lifting of embargoes or other constraints; settlement of a civil war or domestic strife; elimination or reduction in terrorism; establishment of "the rule of law" through a fair legal system; and the rise of an efficient commercial infrastructure. For example, the peace treaty being negotiated in the Middle East may stimulate business there by increasing political stability. Stability in northern Asia may increase because diplomatic relations have been established between South Korea and China and between South Korea and Russia.

Following the catalyst comes the transition from economic chaos to the strong economic growth of Phase One. In this phase, corporate profits usually improve. Local entrepreneurs recognize the local business opportunities, and instead of capital flight, repatriation of capital begins to take place. Citizens with large Swiss bank accounts return their money to the country to take advantage of the new opportunities. Capital spending and consumption increase, which is the catalyst for the next phases.

Phases Two and Three

During Phase Two and Phase Three, the country's stock markets become popular, liquidity improves, and stock prices rise rapidly. Often, excess capacity develops because businesses and investors commit the so-called error of optimism. In contrast to Phase Zero, when they were overly pessimistic, businesses now project continued above-trendline performance indefinitely into the future. As a result, they overexpand in real estate, hotels, and other industries. Major new projects are undertaken, such as the construction of subways, airports, canals, or port facilities.

The same optimism is evident in the stock markets during Phase Three. Investors project continued rises in stock prices, and the stock exchange volume is extremely high. New issues abound. Local investors are participating in the market; indeed, many people who never bought shares previously are in the market. The activity is euphoric. The headlines are extremely positive, and waves of foreign brokers open offices in the country. The research reports are thick, and competition for people with experience in the market is strong.

Exhibit 1 summarizes the contrasting conditions associated with cheap, undervalued Phase Zero and expensive, overvalued Phase Three stocks. Examples of cheap stock markets include European markets in the late 1970s, the Philippines and Mexico in 1985, Thailand and Chile in 1986, Argentina in 1989, Sri Lanka in 1990, and Peru in 1991. Examples of expensive stock markets are today's Singapore, Malaysia, and Hong Kong markets.

Phases Four and Five

The conditions in Phase Three cannot continue indefinitely. Toward the end of Phase Three, inflationary pressures start to build and liquidity begins to tighten. Inevitably, conditions deteriorate, and stocks begin to decline. Typically, Phase Four includes, as drawn on Figure 1, a steep decline but also one more powerful bear market rally. In that rally, the index may reach a new high, but when it is adjusted for inflation, it may not be a true new high.

The rally is fueled by the activities of the brokers and fund managers who just opened offices in the country (to generate revenue, these people must continue to recommend securities) and by investors who believe they missed out on the first big rally.

The rally cannot be sustained, and in Phase Five, corporate profits are disappointing, social conditions deteriorate, liquidity tightens, and stock prices decline sharply.

Phase Six

Phase Six is the "give-up" phase, a period of desperation and disappointment. Investors and businesses now commit the error of pessimism.

The Asian Markets

The recently developed Asian markets are a useful illustration of the concept of the emerging market's life cycle. Most of the Asian emerging markets are in Phase Three or Phase Four. (Although several countries—namely, Vietnam and those in northern Asia—are in transition from Phase Zero to Phase One, these countries do not have stock markets, so

---

Exhibit 1. Characteristics of Cheap and Expensive Stock Markets

Characteristics of cheap stock markets
- Long-last economic stagnation or slow contraction in real terms.
- Real per capita incomes flat or falling for several years.
- Little capital spending, and international competitive position deteriorating.
- Unstable political and social conditions (strikes, high inflation, continuous devaluations, terrorism, border conflicts, etc.).
- Corporate profits depressed.
- No foreign direct or portfolio investments.
- Massive capital flight.
- Little tourism, run-down hotels, low hotel occupancy rates, and no new hotels built for several years.
- Curfews at night
- Little volume on the stock exchange; no new issues.
- Stock market moving sideways or moderately down for several years.
- In real terms, stocks ridiculously undervalued; stocks selling at a fraction of their net asset or replacement values.
- No visits by foreign fund managers.
- No foreign brokers establishing offices, no country funds launched, and no brokerage reports published for a long time.
- Headlines in the press very negative.

Characteristics of expensive stock markets
- Overinvestments leading to excess capacity in several sectors of the economy ("error of optimism").
- Strong inflationary pressures brought about, via rising wages and real estate prices, by infrastructure problems and excessive credit expansion.
- Slowing rate of corporate profit growth; in some industries, beginning of falling corporate profits.
- Many condominium, housing projects, new hotels, office buildings, and shopping centers completed.
- City that is the business capital resembles a "boom town"— lively nightlife and heavy traffic congestion.
- Frequently, a new airport inaugurated and a second one in planning stage; megaprojects such as "new cities," subways, high-speed railways, or highways being planned and developed.
- Real estate and stock market speculators flourish, make the headlines with their rags-to-riches tales, and fill the nightclubs.
- The stock and real estate markets become a topic of discussion; active retail and speculative activity, much of it on borrowed money; local investors beginning to invest overseas in things they may not understand (art, real estate, stocks, golf courses, etc.)
- Stock exchange volume high (thus, back-office problems) and stocks selling at a premium to their net asset values.
- New issues of stock and bonds at peak levels.
- An avalanche of thick, colorful, and bullish country research reports published by foreign brokers; foreign brokerage offices opened up; record salaries paid, and staff turnover high; poaching of entire trading, sales, or research teams common practice.
- Many country funds launched.
- Headlines in the international press extremely positive.

investing in their growth opportunities would be difficult.)

The catalyst to move Asia from Phase Zero to Phase One was a sharp rise in exports, which provided liquidity, which in turn, led to capital spending and above-trendline consumption during the 1985–91 period. The tremendous growth in the Asian markets was fueled by the dramatic increase in capital flowing to these countries from the Western world in the mid-1980s. During the 1982–85 period, when the U.S. economy was growing rapidly, both U.S. imports and consumption increased dramatically. As a result, a rapid expansion in the U.S. trade deficit began in 1984; it reached a peak in 1986. Because the United States maintained a balanced trade account with Europe, the trade deficit of the United States was offset by trade surpluses in Japan, South Korea, and Taiwan. This surplus stimulated economic activity in Asia through the acceleration principle and multiplier effect.

The inflow of liquidity that accompanies such tremendous growth is sometimes so substantial, however, that not all the liquidity can be used immediately in the real economy. This surplus liquidity creates inflation pressures, usually in the real estate and financial markets, so the financial markets of emerging economies that have this capital inflow experience enormous increases.

Figure 2 illustrates these huge moves in Korea, Thailand, Indonesia, and Taiwan. When the bull moves came, they were very powerful; many of these markets went up 10–20 times earnings, and many stocks went up 40 times.

Interestingly, these countries did not all move at the same time. The U.S. stock market began to pick up in August 1982, but most of these countries did not show bull moves until 1986 or later. The initial inflow of liquidity came to Japan, Taiwan, and South Korea, causing increases in price levels and production costs. As a result, those three countries began to shift production to countries with lower costs, such as Thailand, Malaysia, and Indonesia.

Foreign direct investments in Thailand began to increase dramatically in 1988. The absolute level of foreign direct investment is not as important, however, as the rate of change. As foreign direct investments pick up, GDP accelerates. When the rate of growth of foreign direct investment slows or declines, a tremendous deceleration occurs in the economy. Today, foreign direct investment in Thailand is still higher than in 1987, but the rate of economic growth is slower than it was in 1987.

In the developed economies, recessions occasionally result in negative GDP growth rates. In emerging economies, negative growth rates are infrequent, but recessions are often caused by a slowdown in the growth rate—from, say, 9 to 5 percent. For example, the total vehicle market of Malaysia peaked out at 123,419 units annually in 1984. Thereafter, it deteriorated rapidly. Total vehicle sales contracted by 20.8 percent in 1985, 22.8 percent in 1986, and 27.7 percent in 1987. Most assemblers were incurring losses. Passenger car sales shrunk from 101,511 units in 1983 to only 39,628 units in 1987, a decline of 61 percent. The contraction in commercial vehicle sales during the same period was less severe—from 20,237 units to 14,894 units, a drop of 26.4 percent. The motor industry recovered rapidly after 1988, however, because of an economic recovery. Total sales of 123,232 units in 1990 surpassed the earlier peak of 1984. Note that although Malaysia is a rapidly growing economy, six years were required for total car sales to exceed the 1984 high. Even rapidly growing economies have serious recessions.

Since 1990, the financial markets in the Asian Phase Three and Four countries have grown disproportionately to real value in underlying assets, which is dangerous. Eventually, these markets will top out and decline sharply (in some cases, by more than 50 percent from their peaks), and the impact of that decline on economic growth may be severe.

Changes in the 1990s

This section forecasts changes for the world economy and contains a discussion of investment opportunities in the old and new markets of Asia.

The World Economy

People frequently say that globalization is wonderful and point specifically to the international capital market. In the context of globalization, however, the capital market is usually overemphasized. Technically, globalization means an arbitrage effect between countries with enormous populations combined with extremely low wages and Western societies with their relatively small populations and extremely high wages. **Figure 3** illustrates real wages in the Western world as exemplified by the United States. The U.S. trend toward lower real wages is expected to continue for several years and to spread over to Europe. It will thus have a dampening effect on consumption throughout the Western world.

Interest rates in the West have declined significantly during the early 1990s. The impact of these lower rates on consumption and economic growth is not clear, however. Despite economic predictions that lower interest rates will stimulate Western economies, capital spending will not be affected positively in many industries. If, for example, overcapac-

Figure 2. Selected Asian Stock Markets: Nine-Month Moving Averages, 1975–93

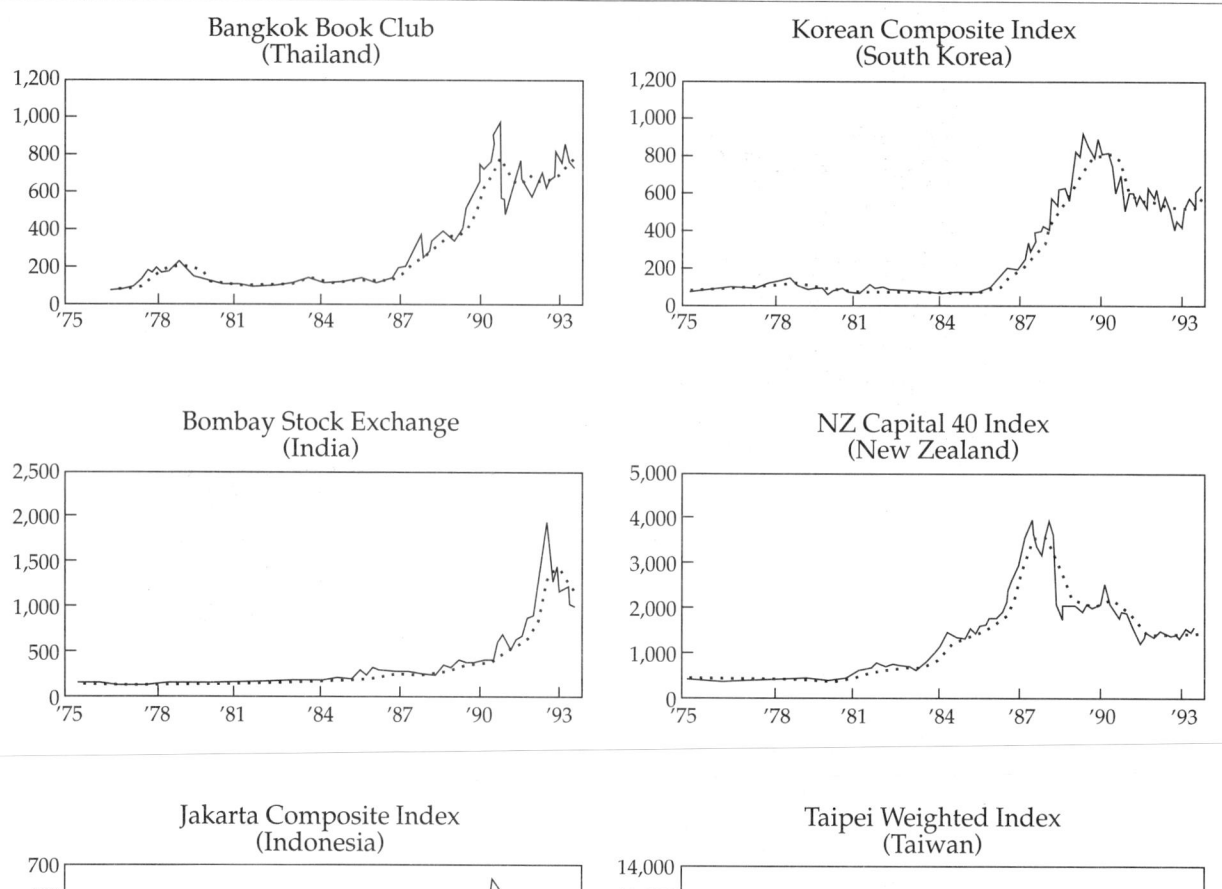

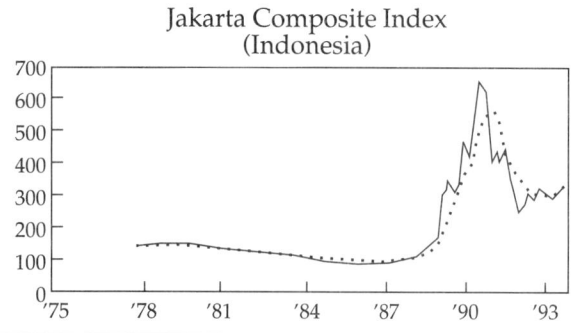

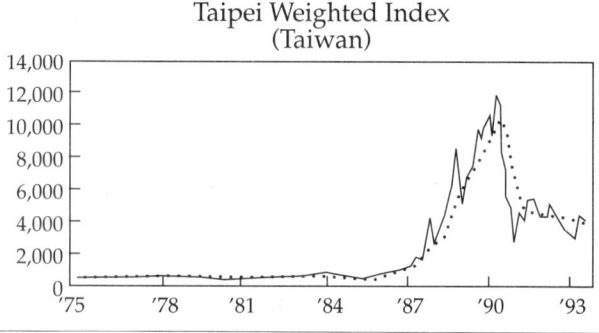

Source: Baring Securities.

ity is plaguing the steel industry, lower interest rates will not cause increases in steel industry capacity.

Falling interest rates can also have a negative effect on employment and consumption if companies start to substitute capital for labor. Clearly, this incentive toward substitution is at work in the United States, where in the first six months of 1993, labor costs rose at a rate of 3.6 percent a year and capital costs fell at 7.7 percent a year. These rate movements made it advantageous for many companies to lay off people and replace them with machinery.

U.S. consumption can also be adversely affected by lower interest rates, because most U.S. households are larger interest recipients than interest payers. When interest rates fall dramatically, their incomes fall, which causes a slowdown in consumption.

Another trend already visible in the 1990s is declining real estate markets in the Western world. During the rest of the decade, real estate will not perform as well as it did between 1984 and 1986. New-home prices may stabilize, but the big boom years that had such a positive effect on the balance sheets of individuals will not occur.

Finally, a secular trend is apparent in the world toward slower growing labor forces in Europe, the United States, and particularly, Japan. As shown in **Figure 4**, between 1990 and the year 2000, all labor forces will grow at a slower rate than they did in the two prior decades. The growth will be particularly slow in Western Europe. Starting in the year 2000, as **Table 1** indicates, both Japan and Europe will actu-

Figure 3. Annual Growth Rate of Real U.S. Average Hourly Wages, 1964 to Mid-1992

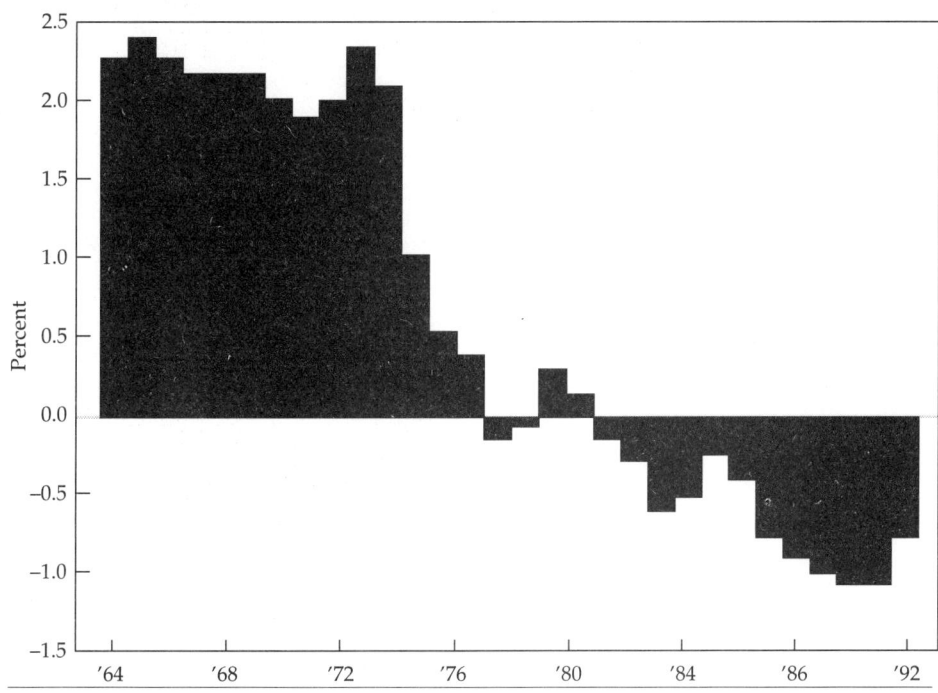

Source: Comstock Partners.

Note: Data points are five-year moving averages of the year-to-year percentage change in average hourly earnings minus the year-to-year percentage change in the personal consumption expenditures deflator. Data for 1992 are only through May 1992.

ally experience a decline in the labor force. This slowed growth is likely to have a negative effect on consumption.

Current Asian Markets

Negative consumption growth in Western countries will have a negative impact on exports from

Figure 4. Rate of Growth of Labor Forces for Selected Areas

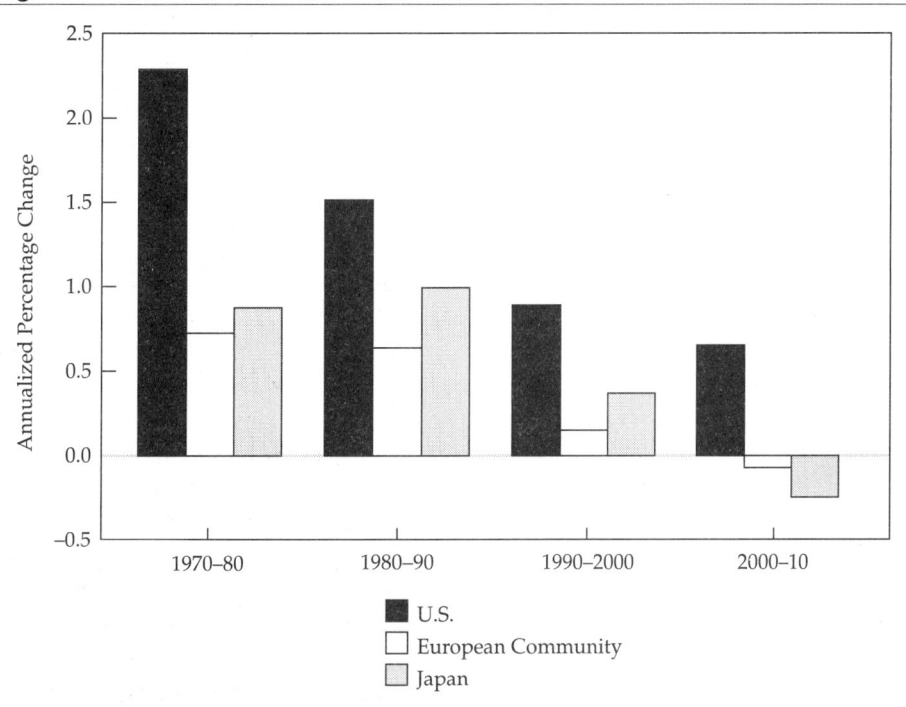

Source: Richard F. Hokenson, Donaldson, Lufkin & Jenrette.

Table 1. Projected Increases in the Labor Force by Decade Relative to 1980–90

	1980–1990	1990–2000	2000–2010
Developed countries			
United States	100	66	52
Japan	100	43	–43
Europe Community	100	17	–18
Selected newly *industrialized countries*			
Singapore	100	44	22
South Korea	100	82	58
Taiwan	100	65	32
Southeast Asia			
Indonesia	100	109	96
Malaysia	100	121	138
Philippines	100	128	154
Thailand	100	87	58
South Asia			
Bangladesh	100	140	173
India	100	117	138
Nepal	100	142	165
Pakistan	100	130	208
Mexico	100	121	128

Source: Richard F. Hokenson.

Figure 6. Average Export Growth versus Average Import Growth: Non-Japan Asia

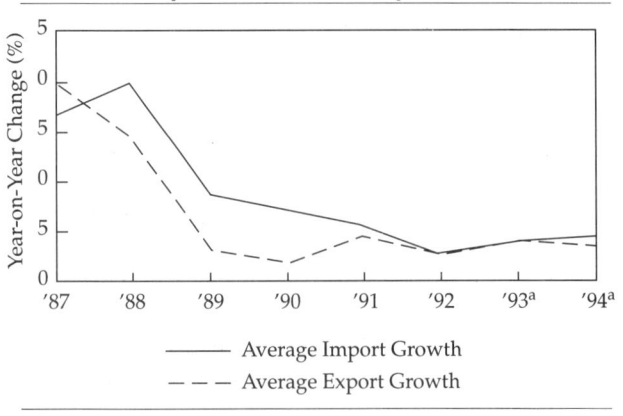

Source: CS First Boston.
[a]Forecast.

Asia, which will, in turn, have a negative impact on Asian liquidity flows. **Figure 5** compares the levels of exports from seven Asian countries in 1986 with the levels in 1991. In most countries, exports doubled. In the next few years, exports from Asia will probably grow by only 5–8 percent. **Figure 6** shows the average export growth and average import growth for non-Japan Asia from 1987 through 1992, with estimates for 1993 and 1994. Since 1988, export growth has been slowing and imports have begun to outperform exports because rising prosperity in these countries has led to increasing demands for high-quality foreign goods. The result of this lower export growth is that trade balances and current account balances turned negative between 1989 and 1992.

The Asian countries are also experiencing tightening liquidity. Between 1987 and 1992, the savings–investment gap was a positive US$94 billion; between 1993 and 1998, the gap is expected to be a negative US$158 billion. Clearly, liquidity is tightening at a time when Asia is embarking on enormous infrastructure projects, which are forecasted to cost between $600 billion and $800 billion in the next five years. The shortfall between gross domestic savings and gross domestic investment as a percentage of GDP is illustrated in **Figure 7**.

The infrastructure projects may be good for growth in Asia, but they will be bad for liquidity. Therefore, the Asian markets will have lower P/Es than they had in the boom years of 1985 through 1987. **Figure 8** shows the history of P/Es for Hong Kong, Malaysia, Singapore, and Thailand. In all of these markets, P/E multiples have not reached 1986–87 levels.

The situation in Asia now may be similar to the one in Europe between 1962 and 1986. Following World War II, German, Swiss, Italian, French, and English stocks performed extremely well. All these markets peaked around 1962, however, and did not reach another new high until 1986. The Asian market—including Japan, Taiwan, and South Korea—has not performed well in the past few years. (When Japan was doing extremely well, it "belonged" to

Figure 5. Exports from Asia to the United States

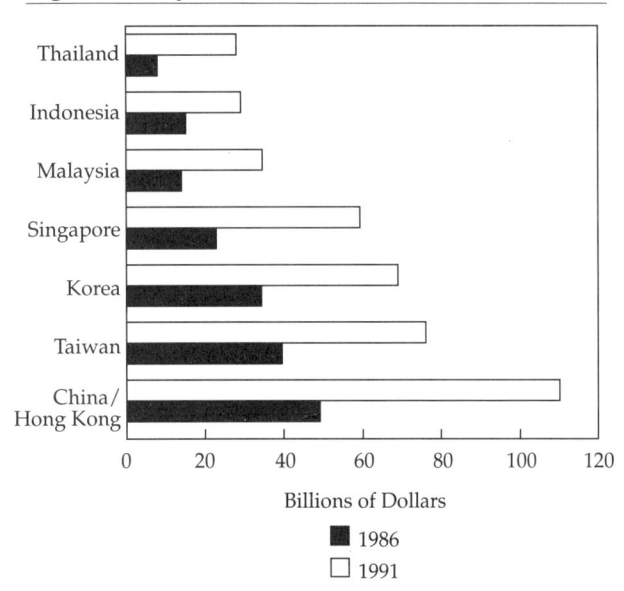

Source: W-I-Carr.

Figure 7. Gross Domestic Savings and Gross Domestic Investment: Regional Totals

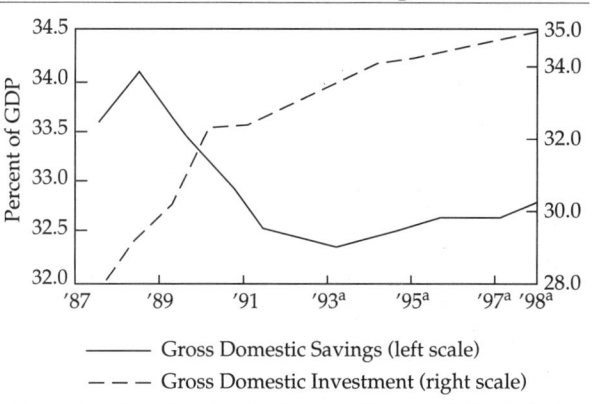

Source: CS First Boston.

^aForecast.

Asia. Now that it is not doing well, people are suddenly illogically looking at Asia *ex* Japan.)

Another consideration for investors in Asia—and, indeed, other regions of the world—is that one may correctly anticipate growth but invest in a vehicle that does not participate in that growth. Consider the computer industry of the early 1970s. At that time, an analyst who correctly anticipated rapid growth in the computer industry probably would have bought IBM, the largest computer manufacturer, under the assumption that IBM would participate in that growth. Unfortunately, although the computer industry has grown beyond anyone's expectations, IBM has not. The people who invested in IBM in the 1970s lost money.

The same happens in regions and countries. For example, before 1800, America's most populous cities were Baltimore, Boston, Charleston, New Haven, New London, Newport, New York, Norwich, Philadelphia, Providence, and Salem. By 1986, only three—Boston, Philadelphia, and New York—remained in the top ten; the newcomers were Chicago, Dallas, Detroit, Houston, Los Angeles, and San Francisco. Detroit was also one of the most prosperous industrial cities between 1910 and 1930, but since then, it has declined.

Similarly, although a region may grow in general, the shifts of economic activity within that region can be tremendous. Asia can be considered an enormous region—almost 3 billion people—in which the centers of prosperity today may not be the centers of the future. Six areas in Asia could be identified in 1989 with above-trendline growth: moving from south to north, (1) Singapore, southern Malaysia, and Indonesia, (2) Vietnam in combination with Taiwanese and South Korean capital, (3) Hong Kong and

Figure 8. Falling Liquidity and Contracting P/Es in Asia

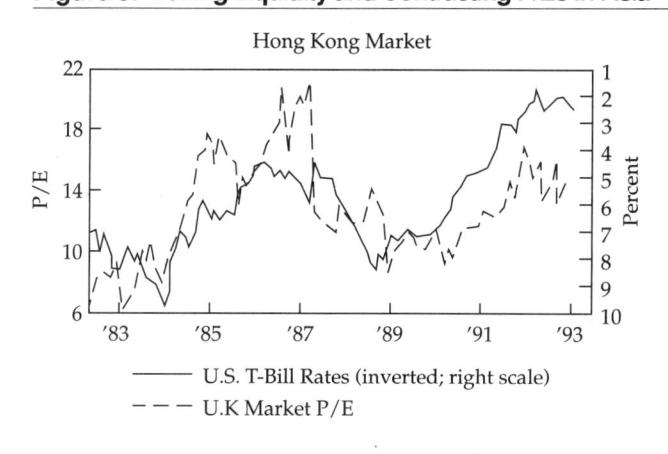

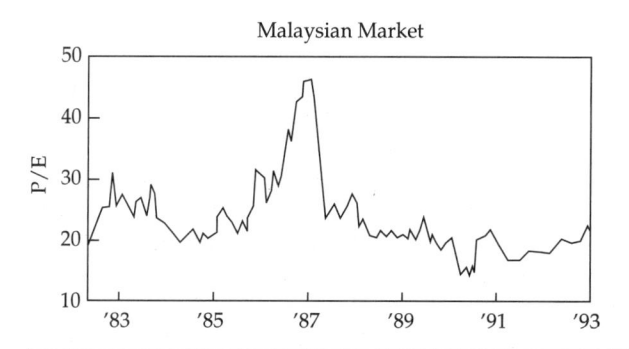

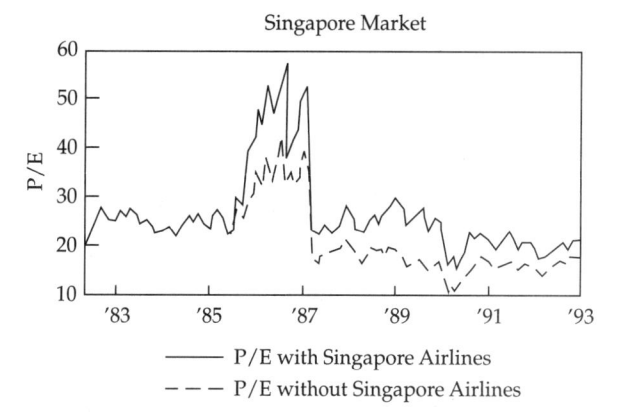

Source: CS First Boston.

Guandong Province (China), (4) Xiamen (China) and the Kaohsiung region of Taiwan, (5) Shanghai (China) combined with Japanese, Korean, and Taiwanese capital, and (6) northern Asia, including parts of South Korea, North Korea, northeastern China, and far eastern Russia. These regions have several features in common: They usually combine a rich country or prosperous city with a poor hinterland. The rich city or country has few resources other than capital, know-how, technology, and a well-established commercial and legal infrastructure. The poor region is disorganized, but it has a lot of such resources as cheap labor, land, and sometimes, natural resources—copper, gold, and so forth. The two benefit from doing business together.

A price-level difference between the well-developed area and the poor hinterland leads to an arbitrage effect. Land prices usually rise more rapidly in the poor region than in the well-established economy. Some developing regions have already reached a relative price level that makes them no longer attractive.

Some of the listed regions have already developed well, and some will develop rapidly in the future. Some regions are just emerging. The two areas that should do particularly well in the near future are Vietnam and northern Asia, the regions around the Korean peninsula.

As noted previously, foreign direct investment has a pronounced effect on an economy. As an example, **Figure 9** shows where Taiwan has invested since 1986. Taiwanese investments rose rapidly in Thailand between 1986 and 1990 and then began to decline. The Philippines, Malaysia, and Indonesia also experienced rapid rises and declines in Taiwanese investment. In 1990, Taiwan's direct investments shifted into China and Vietnam. Following such movements is very important for an investor, because where direct investments increase, growth will accelerate, and where they decrease, growth will decelerate.

Prior to World War II, northern Asia, not the

Figure 9. Direct Overseas Investments by Taiwan

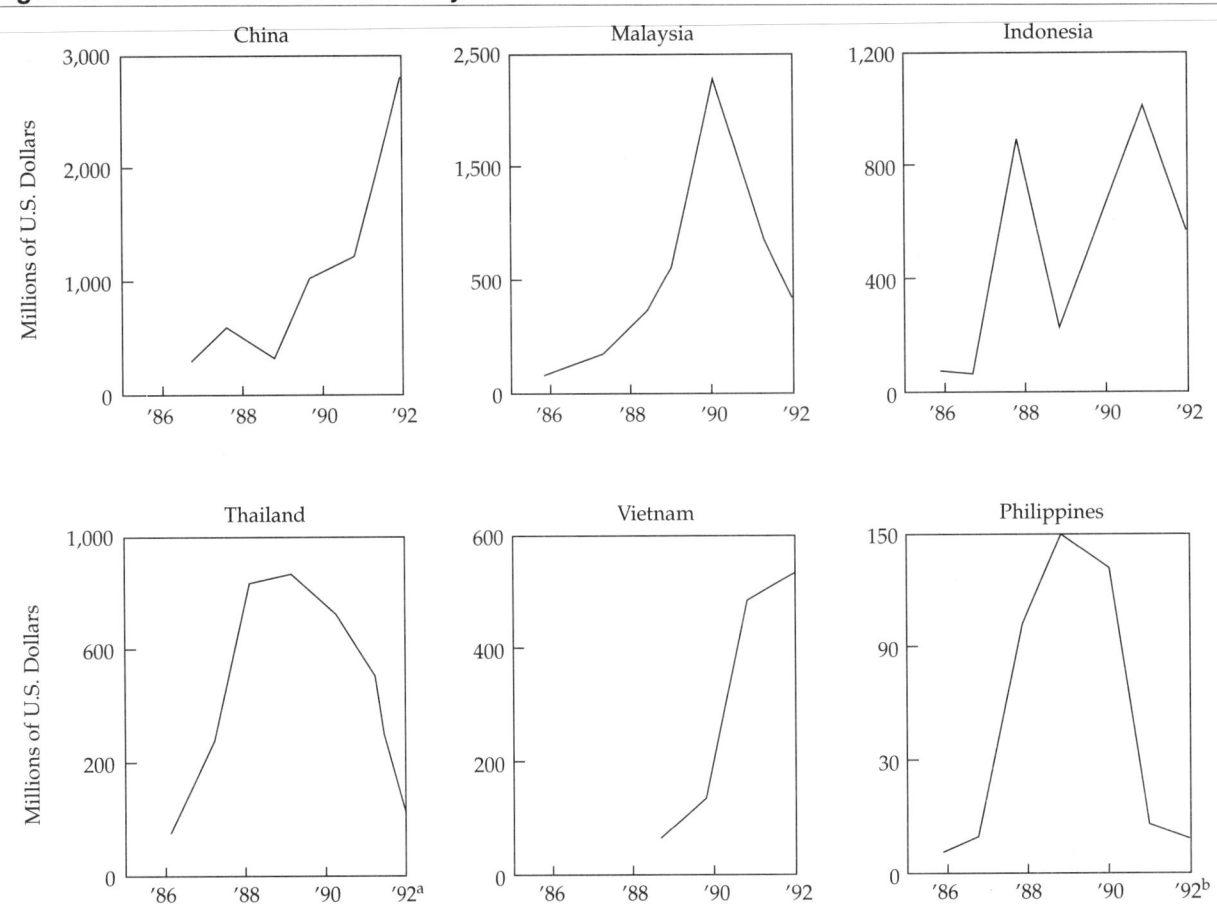

Source: Ministry of Economic Affairs and Chung-hua Institute for Economic Research, Taipei, Taiwan.

[a] January–September.
[b] January–October.

Figure 10. Foreign Investments in China, 1902–31

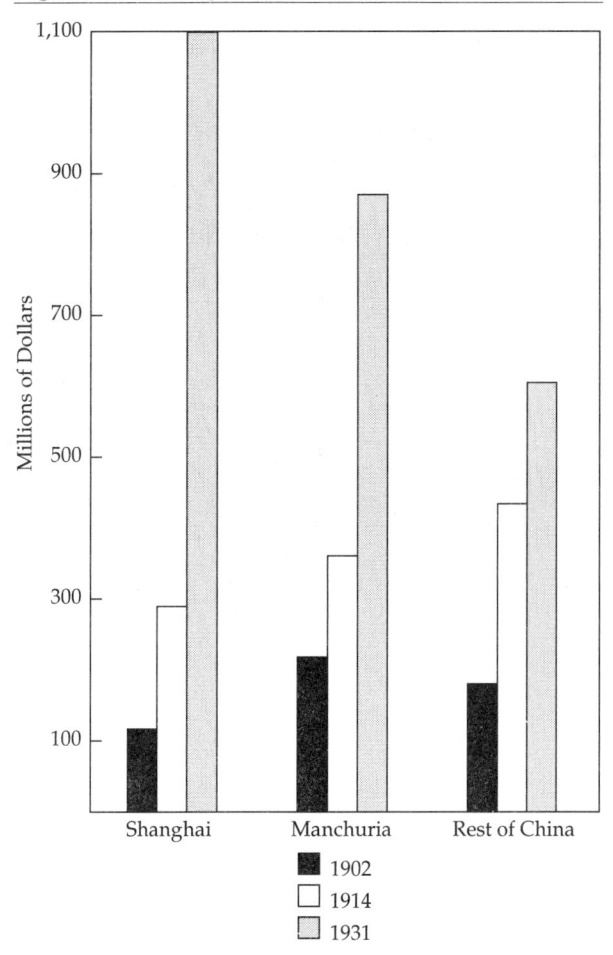

[Bar chart showing foreign investments in millions of dollars for Shanghai, Manchuria, and Rest of China in years 1902, 1914, and 1931]

Source: C.F. Remer, *Foreign Investments in China* (New York, 1932).

south, was the industrial part of China. As **Figure 10** shows, the bulk of foreign investments in China in 1902, 1914, and 1931 went to the northeastern provinces of Shanghai and Manchuria. Little went to Guangdong Province, because the south was at that time essentially an area of poorly educated peasants. Obviously, these patterns change: In recent years, the foreign direct investment in China has gone predominantly to the southern Pearl River Delta region.

The Opening of China

The opening of new markets in various parts of the world is an important economic event. The opening of China may prove to be the most important economic event since World War II. Indeed, it may define a Kondratieff long cycle, illustrated in **Figure 11**. According to Kondratieff cycle theory, an upward wave occurs when a displacement takes place that leads to new business opportunities. In this wave, corporate profits rise rapidly and the economy has tremendous energy. Recessions are usually short, and debt accumulates. When a plateau is reached, an economic decline follows, with sticky recessions, debt liquidation, bankruptcies, and so forth. These long waves have occurred with a regularity of roughly 45–65 years.

According to this theory, the world economy is now in a downward wave, and what is happening now in the Western economies suggests that the theory is accurate. In that case, the opening of such large emerging markets as China and Russia will stimulate rapid economic growth in the world and introduce the next upward wave, which is due to begin between 1995 and 1999.

The conditions are not yet in place, however, for this latest stimulus to act positively on the global economy. Several conditions must be met before China can become as important and as big an economy as the covers on most magazines suggest.

First, for an economically strong China to emerge, growth must move from the south coast provinces to the rest of China. The growth in Asia during the past few years was export driven. The growth was thus especially strong in coastal regions of China—Guangdong Province, for example—because of the regions' proximity to Hong Kong, which had the infrastructure to channel investments and handle the exports.

Second, the export-led growth will have to be replaced by domestic-led growth. China has been growing principally through rapid exports. The Chinese now have a trade surplus of approximately $20 billion with the United States, and if that surplus were to grow in the next five years at the same rate as the past four, it would reach $50 billion—an unlikely development. More likely is that exports from China to the United States and other Western countries will decrease. For China to become an important economy, therefore, domestic growth within China must take over, and for that purpose, purchasing power will need to increase. Export-led growth is usually encouraged by low wages and depreciating currencies; domestic-led growth requires high wages and high purchasing power. Now, it takes most Chinese more than 50 years of wages to buy a car because wages are so low. Unless wages rise significantly, China will not have a prosperous system.

In addition, China will have to overcome its lack of education, technology, and innovation. The United States did not become rich in the last century and early part of this century because of cheap labor. It became rich because of inventions and industrialization. People like Cyrus McCormick, John Deere, Henry Bessemer, and Thomas Edison made major contributions to the industrialization of the United States. Society must attract the leading thinkers and

Figure 11. Kondratieff Long Waves, 1787–2058

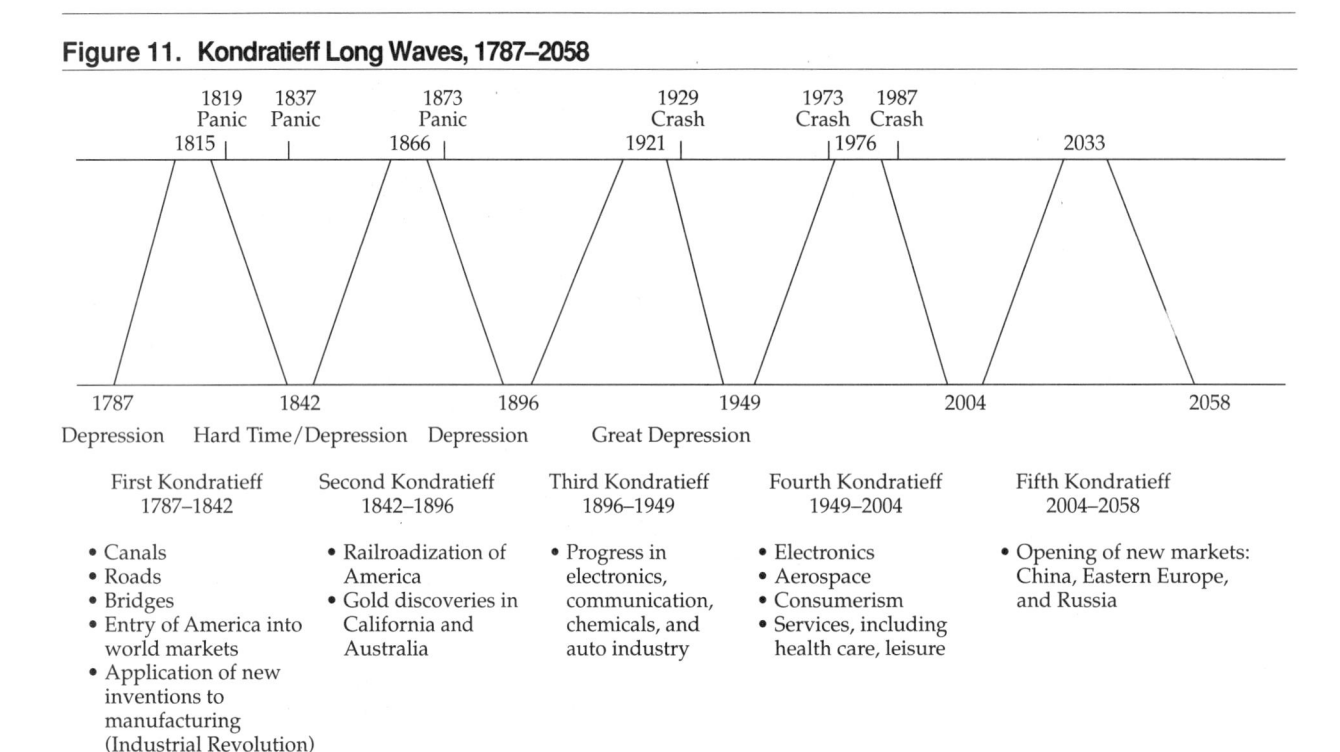

	1819 Panic	1837 Panic		1873 Panic		1929 Crash		1973 Crash	1987 Crash		
	1815			1866		1921		1976		2033	

1787	1842	1896	1949	2004	2058
Depression	Hard Time/Depression	Depression	Great Depression		

First Kondratieff 1787–1842	Second Kondratieff 1842–1896	Third Kondratieff 1896–1949	Fourth Kondratieff 1949–2004	Fifth Kondratieff 2004–2058
• Canals • Roads • Bridges • Entry of America into world markets • Application of new inventions to manufacturing (Industrial Revolution)	• Railroadization of America • Gold discoveries in California and Australia	• Progress in electronics, communication, chemicals, and auto industry	• Electronics • Aerospace • Consumerism • Services, including health care, leisure	• Opening of new markets: China, Eastern Europe, and Russia

Source: Marc Faber, Ltd.

---

scientists. China has many intelligent people, but they tend to move to the United States where the monetary rewards for their efforts are much higher. In China today, a worker at McDonald's earns more than a university professor. This disparity in pay leads to a continuous brain drain.

Another problem in China is population growth. When a population grows rapidly, wages remain low, and the impact on GDP per capita can be negative. For China and other emerging economies, the population explosion has led to tremendous wealth disparity: The wealth generated by the boom in China has been distributed principally in the cities on the coast; the countryside, where approximately 800 million peasants live, has remained extremely poor. In urban centers, for example, about 50 percent of the households own refrigerators; in rural households, only 1.5 percent do.

China will also have to overcome a lack of commercial and legal infrastructure. Changing a market economy to a capitalistic economy often results in chaos when the commercial and legal infrastructure is not in place. Under a socialist system, China did not have lawyers, tax laws, or courts, because disputes between state enterprises that needed to be resolved through courts never arose. Neither did China have any property rights.

Another problem is that China may fragment itself into different states during the next few years. The succession after Li Peng has not been settled, and when he passes away, some internal strife may follow.

China will also have to make sure its market is competitive once it is no longer closed. Emerging economies such as China are not all that competitive vis-a-vis Western countries if the markets are really open. Many emerging economies enjoy easy access to Western markets but are competitive in some products at home only because they keep their own markets closed. For instance, until 1989, Taiwan did not allow the import of foreign beer. Today, beer manufactured in Milwaukee and shipped to Asia can be marketed in Taiwan and, provided no high import duties existed, could be cheaper than Taiwanese beer. Another example is the automobile industry. With open markets and no import duties, countries like Malaysia, Indonesia, and Thailand would not have competitive automobile industries. In the next few years, the Western countries will no doubt put pressure on emerging economies to open up. Such a move will have negative implications for companies that have enjoyed some kind of monopolistic positions in their domestic markets.

Finally, if China is to become the catalyst for a growth wave, it will have to become one of the world's largest consumer markets. The impact of such a development would be enormous, especially on the commodity markets. China is extremely poor in terms of resources. It has practically no trees, coffee, or cocoa. If the Chinese drank as much coffee as the South Koreans do today, they would absorb 25 percent of the world's coffee. If they equaled U.S. coffee consumption (South Korean coffee consumption is one-fourth U.S. coffee consumption), they would absorb twice the global production of coffee. China's purchases and sales will thus have a dramatic influence on prices. When they overstock, they may become heavy sellers and depress prices.

A rich China will have significant implications for the entire Pacific region. First, a prosperous China will radically change the political and economic landscape of Asia. China will dwarf everything else in Asia. **Table 2** illustrates the effect the Chinese market can have on its trading partners. The

Table 2. Taiwan's Exports to China
(dollars in millions)

Year	Via Hong Kong	Direct	Total	Percent
1986	812	0	812	NA
1987	1,233	0	1,233	51.8%
1988	2,248	0	2,248	82.3
1989	2,889	428	3,317	47.6
1990	3,282	1,099	4,381	32.1
1991	4,667	2,832	7,499	71.2
1992	6,288	4,146	10,453	39.4
1993[a]	8,300	5,498	13,798	32.0

Source: Marc Faber, Ltd.
NA = not applicable.
[a]Forecast.

table shows that Taiwan's exports to China have been growing rapidly during the past few years. If China becomes the dominant economy in Asia, many Asian countries will become dependent on Chinese buying, and the Chinese will have a very strong position within Asia.

Another implication is that current centers of prosperity—such as Hong Kong, Singapore, Taiwan, and possibly even South Korea and Japan—may become insignificant. Prior to the communist takeover in 1949, China, Taiwan, Korea, and Hong Kong were all insignificant places. The communists shut down the whole of China—including Shanghai, which until the end of World War II had been the most important city in Asia. The result was that other cities grew and prospered. Moreover, the growth of Taiwan, South Korea, and to some extent, Japan during this period was assisted by the United States and other Western countries' hopes to turn these centers into a fortress against the threat of communism. Without the communists, Taiwan would be nothing more than a little island. Why produce in Taiwan when you could produce in Manchuria or Shanghai?

A geopolitical realignment of such dimensions is likely to create economic and political tensions not only in Asia but throughout the world. From the Age of Exploration all the way up to World War II, the European community was continually fighting for economic and political hegemony. The fights tended to accelerate when a change in leadership occurred—from Portugal to Spain, from Spain to Holland, and from Holland to England. China cannot become economically powerful without creating similar tremendous tensions, especially between China and Japan and the other countries of southeastern Asia. The Asian borders are not likely to be the same in 20 years as they are today.

Conclusion

Emerging markets go through pronounced economic cycles. Asia benefited during the 1985–92 period from unusually favorable conditions—rapidly rising exports to the Western world and the liquidity inflow that led to increases of almost unprecedented dimensions in capital spending, consumption, and financial markets. The slowdown in exports from Asia to the Western world that is expected in the next few years is the result of sluggish growth in Europe, the United States, and Japan, and will tighten liquidity in Asia. Asian and other emerging markets where liquidity is tightening may not perform as well in the years to come, therefore, as they did during the 1984–90 period. Frequently, moreover, when the growth rate slows down, individual industries perform particularly badly, as was the case for the Malaysian motor industry between 1984 and 1987.

Are emerging markets overrated or overvalued? This question cannot be easily answered. Generally, the financial markets are fully priced in today's emerging economies, but other opportunities exist. Since the early 1980s, the emerging financial markets have performed well, but the commodity markets have been in an incredible secular bear market. Commodity prices have recently hit a secular low, however, and will begin to rise—a trend that may last for several years.

The outlook for the emerging economies is positive overall, but investors should focus less on countries exporting industrial products and more on countries that have a big resource base with a lot of agriculture, such as some of the African countries.

Finally, the real opportunities in emerging markets will involve direct investment, which means going to eastern Europe or eastern Asia. Do not necessarily go as a stockbroker/trader in derivative products or a fund manager. Those who will make the most money in emerging economies are those who migrate there and start a business. In 19th century America, the people who became rich were those who came to the land, not necessarily those who were sitting in their comfortable clubs in England and buying the canals, railroads, and cattle farms at the wrong time. Watch the emerging world and consider moving to a newly upcoming region that will provide opportunities for people on the spot.

Question and Answer Session
Marc Faber

Question: To what extent will interregional trade driven by consumerism offset the weaker Western demand for Asian imports and boost GDP growth in the Asian economies?

Faber: Interregional trade will become very important, but it will not boost liquidity like trade to the United States or other Western countries does. Two major trade links are the North Korean–South Korean–Chinese link and the link between the Far East and Russia. Both will boost economic activity in these regions, but they may not boost liquidity. Therefore, the result may be economic growth but lower P/Es for some of the companies in those regions.

The amount of interregional trade should not be overestimated; the end market is frequently the Western world. Part of a computer is manufactured in Taiwan, another part in Malaysia, another part in China, and they are brought together somewhere in Asia, assembled, and shipped to the West.

Question: Won't the relatively low interest rates in the international capital market help those emerging markets that can tap that market expand their economies?

Faber: Since about 1988, emerging economies have had unprecedented access to the international capital markets. In 1985, who would have bought a bond issued by an Argentine or Brazilian company? Today, because of the Brady plans the countries had to impose, investor optimism, and greedy investors chasing high yields, many emerging economies can issue lots of bonds in the international capital market, and this situation should continue, at least for a while.

Enormous amounts of foreign capital are needed, however, to open up an economy. For instance, to move a million peasants into the city to produce industrial products, a country must build the factory, buy the machinery, build the roads, install the telephone system, and so on. The cost is roughly $10,000 per worker shifted from the farm into the city. That capital will have to be raised and provided by foreign investors, banks, the mutual fund industry, and so forth.

As long as the climate is favorable for emerging markets, these countries will have access to capital and their growth will be stimulated by that access. Whether this situation will continue remains to be seen. When the tide changes and becomes less favorable, the emerging countries will not have that access and their growth could suffer badly.

Question: What is your opinion of the North American Free Trade Agreement (NAFTA)?

Faber: NAFTA is the high spot of the move toward free trade. From it, the pendulum will swing back to more restrictive trade policies—not just in the United States but throughout the world. The world has moved about as far as it will move toward free trade and the free movement of labor from one part of the world to another. In Europe, a cleaning person earns $20 an hour; in Asia, most people earn $50 a month. If markets were totally free, half of Asia would move to the Western economies, depressing the wages in those economies dramatically.

In the next ten years, especially if the Western economies remain sluggish, protectionism will increase. It will not be called protectionism, but it will have the same effect—limiting the access of both labor and products to the domestic market.

Question: During the 1962–82 period, did new, small companies grow in Europe? Could we see new highs in Asian markets in the same kind of stocks?

Faber: Yes, growth on the part of new and smaller companies is most likely to happen in Asia as it did in Europe. The market will be more and more a market of individual stocks.

Question: Relative to the International Finance Corporation's Investable Global Emerging Markets, which countries would you overweight and which would you underweight during the next three years?

Faber: I would overweight only commodities, which are not in any index. I would underweight Hong Kong, Singapore, Malaysia, and Thailand.

Question: Because Asian governments have tended to invest in their population (that is, education) and infrastructure, will substantial growth in Asia in the 1990s come from domestic demand and a rising middle class?

Faber: Investment in education was limited to Japan, South Korea, Taiwan, Malaysia, and Singapore. In other countries, education is still very poor.

Question: Do you try to participate in Phase Four rebounds, or is doing so too risky?

Faber: I do not usually participate in Phase Four rebounds; it may be a mistake.

Question: Does a transition from an export-dominated economy to an import-dominated economy necessarily lead to P/E contraction?

Faber: If liquidity shrinks, yes, but not in all cases, because markets may be pushed up by foreign investors, as was the case recently.

Question: Does the life cycle you discussed apply to mature markets, companies, industries, and societies? If so, are cycles of companies and markets usually parallel?

Faber: The cycle does appear to be relevant to more mature economies and to emerging industries (for example, gaming in the United States, software). The cycles of companies and markets are not necessarily parallel, but they often are.

Question: How does your life-cycle model explain successful emerging markets such as Japan, which made the transition to developed status and achieved considerable, sustained growth in stock market returns over time?

Faber: Japan is an exception, but it did move through several of the cycles. It may now be in Phase Five or Phase Six.

Adventures of the Russell 20–20

Teresa E. Goodale
Vice President, International
AT&T Investment Management Corporation

> Travelers to Poland, the Czech and Slovak republics, and China are struck by the spirit of free enterprise that is apparent as these countries move from a planned to a market economy, but significant differences in competitive advantages exist. In particular, China faces major challenges if it is to become a successful world competitor: in population density; infrastructure; political leadership; accounting, legal, and financial systems; and in investor protection.

The Russell 20–20 is an organization of 20 large corporate plan sponsors and 20 investment managers. The group was established in 1990 to study investing in the economies that were transforming from a command to a market system. During the first two years, the group invited people from various investment management firms to discuss the economic policies that were being established, the development that was occurring, and prospects for the future in these countries and economies. In 1992, the group decided to visit the countries to see firsthand what was happening. In May 1992, the group went to the former Czechoslovakia and Poland, where we met with foreign ministers and U.S. and foreign businessmen, and visited plant sites. In 1993, the group visited the People's Republic of China. This presentation will summarize what the Russell 20–20 learned in each of these countries.

Eastern Europe

The trip to Eastern Europe in 1992 provided numerous insights. Poland and Czechoslovakia exhibited both positive and negative investment characteristics.

Poland

The group decided to visit Poland for several reasons, including the country's reform efforts, the attractiveness of its geographical location, and its growth opportunities. Poland is situated advantageously; to the east is Ukraine, with a population of over 50 million, and to the west is Germany, with access to the European Community. Poland's population in 1992 was about 40 million.

In 1990, Poland started a reform program in which some drastic measures were taken. Prices were freed, currency convertibility was provided, restrictions were removed on establishing businesses, and trade was liberalized.

The Russell 20–20 group experienced a sense of growth in the grass roots of the private sector in Poland. In 1989, the private sector represented about 10 percent of the total economy. By 1992, it had grown to at least 30 percent, and it is now probably about 50 percent. A free enterprise spirit can be seen clearly in the parks, where the people have set up kiosks to sell a whole range of items—primarily clothing, but also such goods as food, toys, and household goods.

In Poland, the group visited several new businesses. The group went to a clothing manufacturer, for example, that operated a clean, modern factory. Although the fashion was not Fifth Avenue style, the clothing was fashionable. The designs were created in Germany and shipped to Poland. The clothing was manufactured in Poland and then sent back to Germany, without hems or cuffs in order to avoid some of the import duty.

This company had a unique way of compensating its employees. They received a basic wage plus a wage based on the quality and quantity of items produced. This approach was unexpected in Poland, but given freedom and the resources, the company had tapped into the capitalistic spirit.

Czechoslovakia

Czechoslovakia is a much smaller country than

Poland, with a population of about 11 million. What is unique about Czechoslovakia is that it has much less foreign debt than the other countries in the region. In addition, before World War II, Czechoslovakia was the 15th most developed nation in the world, but its current economy reflects more than 40 years of Soviet influence. The group was interested in whether the prewar status could be captured again in the 1990s.

The factories in Czechoslovakia contrasted sharply with those in Poland. We visited a factory that had previously manufactured cars and motorcycles (the entrance still showcased a beautiful silver trophy awarded for winning the 1934 Le Mans race) and now manufactured jet engines. The factory was very dirty, few people were about, and the operations showed no sense of an assembly line; something was done in one place and then carried to another place.

We wondered if the people understood what they were facing in the way of free market competition. Did they know General Electric was making engines and had made a commitment to that market?

The group also visited a new trolley car factory in Czechoslovakia. Although the plant manager said the factory had 1,000 employees, the employees were not visible. He also said there was a significant interest in the plant's product but countries could not pay for it. He said the plant was bidding for a project in the Philippines. Six months later, it won that bid.

Outlook for Poland and Czechoslovakia

The outlook for these countries is cautiously optimistic. Opportunities exist, but so do some serious negative factors. One of the largest concerns is politics. In 1992, Poland had more than 29 different political parties. When someone expressed concern about how things will move forward, given the political challenges, the response was, "We can work around that. Things will get done." This faith made us very cautious, but during the past two years some changes have occurred. For example, in the last election, some of the rules were changed so as to reduce the number of parties.

The breakup of Czechoslovakia into two republics was being discussed at the time of our visit and was official on January 1, 1993. These countries have in the past depended heavily on trade with each other and with the former Comecon countries (Communist Eastern European trading bloc including the Soviet Union); for example, 61 percent of Slovakia's exports in 1992 went to the Czech Republic and the former Soviet Union. Moreover, the Czech Republic has much more opportunity than Slovakia for future development. A predominant concern in 1992, therefore, was that the breakdown of the Comecon trade agreement between the republics had significantly decreased exports.

Another concern, in Poland and the Czech and Slovak republics, relates to banking and the overall business environment. In Poland, the people said, "If you are going to do business here, bring some banking expertise with you." In addition, the commercial code, laws, and accounting standards—all needed to be updated. The people we met understood that our group represented a staggering amount of capital, but we were not sure they understood the role of investing and that we were looking for a certain risk–reward trade-off. Hopefully, in time, we can educate each other about investments.

A third concern, although this problem is more apparent in China than in Poland or Czechoslovakia, relates to insufficient infrastructure. Telecommunications and power generation are both needed, as are transportation systems for moving products from the farm to the factories.

China

The trip to China covered Hong Kong and three mainland cities—Beijing, Shanghai, and Shenzhen—in 12 days. The contrasts between the cities were interesting and highlighted the growth that has occurred. Beijing was rather colorless and is still tied to the central government. Shanghai has a European flavor stemming from its history prior to World War II. Shenzhen, the center of the booming coastal province of Guangdong, is an ultramodern city with skyscrapers and freely traded Hong Kong dollars. Hong Kong is a shopper's paradise.

What is unique about China is the sheer numbers. Shanghai has over 3,000 foreign investment operations, handling $7 billion in investments. In the first six months of 1993, another $3 billion of investment was received. In Shanghai, the group stopped at the welcome center of the Paudong special economic zone and toured the zone's commercial/industrial real estate development area. Phase I of the development called for the construction of 50 buildings; 22 were currently under construction! The scope of the project is staggering. The Chinese approach to real estate development is that, if they build the buildings, the business/people will come.

In Shenzhen, the population growth is amazing; it rose from 27,000 to 2.6 million people in ten years. During the same period, the average growth rate was 46 percent for gross domestic product and 60 percent for industrial output. Currently, the number of foreign investments is more than 10,000, and the value is more than $10 billion. According to the mayor of

Shenzhen, the goal of Guangdong Province is to "overtake" the other emerging nations of East Asia within the next 20 years. The leaders of Shenzhen were not specific about how this extremely ambitious goal could be achieved. They probably have the opportunity, but as investors, we are concerned about whether the growth can be managed successfully and without chaos.

From an investor's point of view, China has several challenges to overcome. One obvious challenge is dealing with the population density, which is 323 persons a square mile, compared with 79 persons a square mile in the United States. Throughout the trip, the group had police escorts just to get through traffic.

Related to population density are some basic infrastructure problems, such as power generation and telecommunications. All the businesses we visited mentioned the need for improvement in these areas.

Politics is another concern. Who will be the next leader? Will the new leadership continue the economic reform program? The people are much more prosperous now than when the program started in 1978; therefore, economic reform is likely to continue. However, the country certainly has a huge task to manage.

Investors are also concerned about the accounting, financial, and legal systems. A representative of Arthur Andersen in the Russell 20–20 group said record keeping is very good but knowledge of accounting principles is weak. Only 130 accountants exist for a population of 1.2 billion people. As for the legal system, the challenge is how the new laws will be interpreted.

Another concern is how well investors are protected. Our group wanted the two stock exchanges (the Shanghai and Shenzhen) to establish more rules and regulations than they presently have.

China lacks the level of innovation and technology necessary for a country to become a predominant player in today's world markets. This deficiency could be seen when we visited some of the factories. Where technology existed, it was usually brought in by a joint-venture partner. Money is spent on research and development, but it is not of the same magnitude as what corporate America spends on research and development.

Finally, the businesses must learn how to manage large groups of people in a market rather than a command system. The country does not clearly have those skills in place.

Conclusion

The Russell 20–20 trips enlightened us about the different cultures and systems of the countries. Each has a unique approach to managing the evolution to a market economy. By visiting the countries, we learned firsthand what has developed, what the future prosperity could be, and the potential investment for a plan sponsor.

Question and Answer Session

Teresa E. Goodale

Question: Please contrast the sense of the capitalist spirit and the understanding of the profit motive in China and in the Eastern European countries you visited?

Goodale: The capitalist spirit is alive in both places. In China, for example, many people work two jobs. During the day, they work for someone else, and at night, they are constructing their stores.

Question: When did AT&T Investment Management first invest in emerging markets, and how much money does AT&T have invested in those markets?

Goodale: In 1987, the AT&T pension fund entered emerging markets with a small investment commitment to Brazil. Currently, emerging market investments represent about 1 percent of the total AT&T pension fund. These investments are spread among 20 countries.

Question: Has AT&T invested in China?

Goodale: In October 1992, we invested a small amount in China through a fund. It is primarily invested in listed securities on the Shanghai or Shenzhen exchanges, in Hong Kong, and in Malaysia. We wanted to learn from small first investments. Some investors are investing privately in China rather than through the stock exchanges because putting a significant amount of assets into China through the stock exchanges is difficult.

Question: Will the current program in China of instituting a market system but with controls on the people's freedom persist into the future? Will it be successful?

Goodale: My sense from talking to the people is that prosperity is their first priority, not freedom. The real challenge for China is creating prosperity within central China. Because we spent all of our time in the cities, I do not have a feel for the atmosphere in the countryside.

Question: Do companies in Eastern Europe understand the competition they will face? What is their competitive advantage compared with Western Europe and the world?

Goodale: Typically, the small, start-up companies recognize the competition. Obviously, the jet engine manufacturer we visited did not. The competitive advantages of these countries are low wages, a well-educated work force, and people willing to work.

Trends in Emerging Markets

Jayant S. Tata
Head, International Securities Group
International Finance Corporation

> Investing in emerging markets is expanding beyond equity assets to encompass debt, real estate, and venture-capital investing. In addition, investors that have not been participants in emerging markets are entering the field, and the emerging markets themselves are offering more specialized opportunities than in the past—opportunities in infrastructure, telecommunications, and mining.

The International Finance Corporation (IFC) sees three major trends in emerging markets: expansion of the asset class, expansion of the investor universe, and deepening of the markets.

Expansion of the Asset Class

As an asset class, emerging markets have come into the mainstream and are widely accepted by sophisticated institutional investors and the retail market. So far, most of the activity has been confined to the equity arena, and most people consider emerging markets a subclass within the equity category. That view is beginning to change, however. In the not-too-distant future, emerging market investment opportunities will be available in each of the major asset classes. Debt, real estate, and venture capital investments are beginning to grow.

Debt

Interest in debt issues—corporate debt in particular—is increasing. Through the end of 1992, the commercial banks handled most of the emerging market debt securities, and most of the buyers were "flight-capital investors" (high-net-worth individuals from developing countries who hold a significant part of their wealth outside their countries). Institutions started to become interested in emerging market debt in 1993; interest rates were relatively low in the United States and Europe, and inflation expectations were stable and low. In this environment, the higher returns on emerging market debt looked relatively attractive. Among the public funds, Morgan Stanley & Company has successfully completed an emerging market debt fund, Templeton recently raised $600 million for emerging market debt investment, and Bear, Stearns & Company has two emerging market debt funds.

The reluctance of some investors to venture into emerging markets is caused by their memory of the 1982 debt crisis. They must overcome this hurdle. The equity portfolios have done well with the inclusion of emerging market equities, and the IFC thinks the same will hold true for the debt side.

Real Estate

Real estate funds are beginning to broaden their horizons. Some real estate portfolios that previously invested primarily in, for example, the United States have already expanded into European and other developed markets. Now people are beginning to ask, "Why not an emerging markets real estate fund?"

Venture Capital

Venture capital is another potential area for investing in emerging markets. Investments in these markets are not going to be high-technology, state-of-the-art ventures but low-tech, entrepreneurial ventures. Currently, lively entrepreneurial groups are active in Latin America and Asia. At this stage, the opportunities are significant, but the risks are extremely high in these types of investments.

Expansion of the Investor Universe

The base of investors in emerging markets is expanding. A major segment of the institutional market in the United States—the passive investors—has not yet been exposed to emerging markets. Most large state pension funds, for example, index about 80 percent of their funds. The IFC wants to attract these investors to emerging markets by launching an emerging markets investable index based on the IFC Investable Index. An index fund already exists for the India market. Institutional investors may also use derivatives to gain exposure to these emerging market indexes.

Deepening of the Emerging Markets

The third trend, deepening of the emerging markets, has two aspects. The first is sectoral deepening, meaning the targeting of funds that invest in one sector of an emerging economy. The second is increased access by emerging market corporations to developed capital markets.

Sector Funds

Sector funds can provide financing to specific areas that need investment support. Infrastructure, for example, is key to further economic development in emerging markets, and the financing need for infrastructure projects is in the billions of dollars. The investor universe for emerging markets is now large enough that some of the largest institutional investors might be interested in tilting their exposures to various sectors. For example, the IFC is establishing funds for Latin American and Asian power companies. Power generation is very important to infrastructure and is a bottleneck to development in Latin America, Asia, the Philippines, and Thailand.

Telecommunications is another area that might be attractive to investors. Thus, the IFC is launching a fund of telecommunications operations in East European countries.

Another interesting sector of emerging markets is mining investments, particularly gold. Gold-mining companies of the developed countries are shifting their emphasis and exposure to emerging markets, where low-cost resources are available. Some fundamental changes have occurred in the worldwide demand for gold. Many industrial uses for gold have been declining, but demand by individuals is growing. As emerging markets become more affluent, their rapidly growing middle classes buy more gold and gold jewelry. This pattern has been apparent in India and the People's Republic of China. Other commodities may also be experiencing fundamental shifts in demand.

The IFC is not sure whether the demand exists for these types of funds, but without funds from the capital markets in the developed countries, the World Bank Group will not be able to service all of the requests for financing of projects in these emerging markets sectors.

Access to Capital Markets

The second trend in the area of deepening of emerging markets is increased access to developed capital markets. The first wave of investing in emerging markets could be characterized as money from the developed countries looking for investment opportunities in the emerging markets—in effect, an exploration process by the investors. The second wave will be emerging market companies going to the sources of capital. This trend is already underway, with emerging market companies beginning to list their securities on exchanges throughout the developed world, such as Telmex (in Mexico) and the CTC (in Chile). The same trend should follow on the debt side.

Conclusion

Emerging market investments are an integral part of global portfolios of sophisticated institutional investors. This trend is likely to grow stronger in the future.

One reason access to capital markets is increasing for emerging markets is that diversification and the need for diversified portfolios are driving the globalization of capital. As the different pools of capital bump against their diversification needs, they begin to seek out different asset classes and investment opportunities in emerging markets.

Another cause of increasing access to world capital markets is that the local capital markets in the emerging economies are developing rapidly. These markets may not develop as evenly and properly as one would like, but they are developing, and these local capital markets must continue to grow, be nourished, and be encouraged.

Emerging Markets Allocation: The Plan Sponsor's View

René T. Goupillaud
Director of Outside Investments
ARCO Investment Management Company

> In the experience of one in-house investment fund, investing in emerging markets requires commitment and the devotion of resources to research. The indispensable element of the research is travel to the emerging market countries.

Each plan sponsor has a different perspective on investing in emerging markets, and that perspective is influenced by many factors—whether the plan's pension plan is over- or underfunded, the plan's cash flow requirements, whether the fund is a mature fund or a new fund, and the sponsor's organizational culture. This presentation uses the experience of ARCO Investment Management Company (AIMCO) to illustrate how a plan sponsor might approach emerging markets investing.

Investment Philosophy

AIMCO is a unit of Atlantic Richfield Company, a large, integrated, domestic petroleum company. AIMCO is separate from the parent and is responsible for managing the assets of several trusts that benefit retirees and employees of Atlantic Richfield and its subsidiaries. These plans, all of which are well funded, include defined-benefit-plan trusts, defined-contribution trusts, and a welfare benefit trust.

AIMCO's primary efforts are directed toward the $2.5 million in defined-benefit plans, which are managed as a pool of assets for the benefit of about 16 retirement plans. The defined-benefit plans are mature; that is, benefits are paid out each month and the plans receive no contributions from the parent company. About 10 percent of the aggregate fund is paid in benefits each year, and the asset allocation must be made with that situation in mind.

The foundation of AIMCO's investment approach was established in 1977 when the company began managing some of the domestic equity assets in-house. Then in 1979, AIMCO made its first venture into international investing by hiring some EAFE managers. Those two approaches came together in 1983 when AIMCO initiated in-house management of international equities with the funding of a Pacific Basin portfolio. Since 1986, more than 60 percent of the assets have been managed internally and about 20 percent of the assets have been in foreign markets. The international equities have been as high as 28 percent during the past five years.

By 1986, asset allocation had become a primary focus at AIMCO and the principal responsibility of the chief investment officer. The process is active and involved: In addition to weekly meetings, we meet monthly to review the markets of all our in-house portfolio managers; I represent the external managers. We have management information systems that provide timely information on recent performance and attribution of that performance, as well as a snapshot of what our exposures are at the end of each month. The review is performed in a timely manner and concentrates on management information as opposed to accounting information.

AIMCO's managers are not market timers. Our allocation decisions must be made carefully because we must make benefit payments from the fund every month. By philosophy, we spend a great deal of energy and resources on asset allocation. Changes are usually on the margin. We forecast cash flows, review what we think the market performance will be during the next few months, and make a judgment about where the cash should be raised to pay future monthly benefits. That decision may change as a particular month approaches, because not all months' benefit requirements are the same and forecasts frequently change. Many people take lump-sum retirement payments, so some volatility exists for the cash that must be raised, which encourages careful attention to asset allocation.

Emerging Markets

AIMCO took steps to invest in emerging markets in 1985 through the Emerging Markets Growth Fund at Capital International and has been investing in emerging markets since 1986. AIMCO invests in about 22 emerging market countries out of a total of about 34 foreign countries.

One reason to invest in emerging markets is the reduction in risk through diversification. However, although emerging markets have provided risk-reduction benefits to a world equity portfolio in the past, those benefits are based on historical relationships, which change over time. To make an asset allocation decision based on that history is to presume the relationships will remain consistent.

The major reason AIMCO invests in emerging markets is the pursuit of superior returns. The expectation is not for triple-digit returns or even for consistently superior returns; indeed, the volatility of the emerging markets is well known. But these markets offer significant opportunities for superior returns to those who are willing to devote resources to evaluate the markets and commit to them. The developed world does not look promising for robust growth. Our view is that the best opportunities for growth have been and will be in the emerging markets. The fastest growing economies produce the fastest growing equity markets.

Most of the emerging markets have low costs and resource advantages or other advantages that make them competitive in the evolving world economy. Their governments are moving toward prudent fiscal and monetary policies (such as efforts to reduce inflation), reducing restrictions on trade and ownership, privatizing state-owned companies, implementing tax reforms, offering investment incentives, and instituting political reforms. All of these changes create a positive environment for superior investment returns.

Each country moves at its own pace, and not every country is moving in the same direction with the same set of reforms. Therefore, questions about structural aspects are important in the evaluation of specific emerging markets. In addition, the country allocations must reflect what is happening in the markets. AIMCO's investment managers make the decisions about the appropriate countries, while AIMCO employs a regional approach in its top-down allocation process.

Implementing the Decision

AIMCO's investment activity in emerging markets developed gradually. After the small investment in the Emerging Markets Growth Fund, our commitment to emerging markets grew with subsequent subscriptions to that fund and to other private closed-end funds, such as the Emerging Markets Investors Fund run by Antoine W. van Agtmael. We have also used publicly traded closed-end funds to increase our exposure to these markets.

Our implementation of an emerging markets investment strategy consisted of entry, expansion, liquidity, and allocation. In other words, as these investments became an increasingly larger portion of the fund assets, we needed to be able to increase or decrease our allocation easily.

We do not view emerging markets as a separate asset class but as a segment of international equity, which, in turn, is a subset of world equities. At present, although the figures could change in the future, approximately 40 percent of our international assets are in emerging markets.

AIMCO makes allocation changes on the margin and regionally. The capability to make changes on the margin has been enhanced through in-house management and the use of publicly traded closed-end funds.

In-house management offers several potential benefits. AIMCO's first in-house emerging market portfolio, launched in 1987, had somewhat greater flexibility than the outside funds. It was regionally focused and could make investments in the more developed markets, with the exception of Japan and Australia. The purpose of that flexibility was to give portfolio managers substantial discretion in choosing and weighting markets in order to optimize their performance. Another justification for allowing investments in the more developed markets is exemplified by the case of Hong Kong, which today can be considered a China play. Excluding a manager from Hong Kong might result in missing the best way to invest in China.

In-house management also provides more liquidity than the private funds. For example, at one time, we had an investment in a Latin American closed-end fund. When we wished to withdraw from the fund, the process was difficult and took several months. In 1990, AIMCO added an in-house Latin American portfolio. Now, we can quickly alter our exposure to this region.

AIMCO's strategy for investing in emerging markets involved getting to know these countries by traveling to and within them. At a minimum, the investment officer and the managing director for international equities go to each region once a year. I go to one or two regions a year, and the in-house managers go as many as four times a year and stay longer than the other managers. AIMCO employees also participate on boards of directors and find other ways to obtain data and views about structural, political, social, and economic issues in the emerging economies.

The most important step, however, is to go to the countries. On these trips, employees meet with local policymakers, visit the companies, and observe the society and the marketplace. The stock exchange is not the only place to go. In fact, seeing what is happening in the streets of the cities, even outside the cities, is more important. In Chile in 1992, for example, going outside Santiago was more informative than staying in town. It is also important to hear directly from, say, Argentina's minister of finance what his intentions, views, and policy are.

Some examples may help illustrate the kinds of impressions one can gather in country visits. Early this year, the media reports and the consensus view seemed to be that Argentina would soon decouple its currency from the U.S. dollar because that was the only way it could manage its trade problem with Brazil. I did not share this view, and a meeting with the minister of finance reinforced my belief. Now, eight months later, Argentina's currency remains linked to the dollar.

In Brazil, I was surprised that the size of the governor's mansion in São Paulo was much larger than the White House. I was also surprised that at 10:00 p.m. every light in the place was on. These signs reinforced my perception that the federal government did not have control, that power was too decentralized, and that issues such as the lack of central bank control of monetary policy and the rights of the states to follow independent fiscal policies were all very real.

I visited Hong Kong in 1992, just prior to Chris Patton's appointment as governor. From meetings with local activists, U.S. State Department representatives, business leaders, and People's Republic of China officials, I came away with the impression that the risk to the markets came from the outside. The level of economic activity in southeastern China and the relationship between Hong Kong and southeastern China makes Hong Kong critical to China. The discount reflected in the market was too great, and since that time, the market's P/E has indeed increased.

A final example of the importance of travel comes from China. The only way truly to appreciate the magnitude of the Chinese population and the implications of that magnitude is to go to China. You can be standing a few feet from the gate to an airplane and take 10 minutes to board because of the mass of people funneling through doors. In highly populated Shanghai, where the streets are narrow and the level of activity is great, you can sense the power of numbers. At night, every other doorway in Shanghai has an awning with a light hanging from it and a table set up with goods for sale—generally, fruits and vegetables. These people probably work in state-owned stores during the day and run their own businesses at night; they are gradually building up their own businesses so that one day they can leave their state jobs. This activity is a strong indicator of what is happening in China. China may have a bumpy road ahead, but its huge population gives it power (if every person in China had only $100 to invest, the total would be $120 billion available for investment), and it will solve its problems.

Question and Answer Session
René T. Goupillaud

Question: How does AIMCO measure in-house performance to be sure that the considerable resources devoted to asset management are included in the analysis?

Goupillaud: Since 1986, we have compared our costs with those of outside management, and based on this analysis, in-house management is considerably cheaper. The comparison is part of our budget process and helps justify our organization to the parent company. Cost is not the only reason for selecting a manager, however. We are looking for an overall blend of strategies and capabilities to maximize the total fund's performance.

Question: What type of benchmark does AIMCO use to evaluate international equity returns?

Goupillaud: Arjun Divecha illustrates some problems with using one index for comparing all your managers—those managing EAFE and those managing emerging market investments.[1] AIMCO has done some custom benchmarking—more for qualitative than quantitative assessment—and also looked at peer-group performance. Peer performance is difficult to obtain in the case of emerging markets, but we believe peer performance is more important than performance relative to an index.

Question: What percentage of AIMCO's international equity exposure is hedged?

Goupillaud: We approach hedging in two ways. First, a manager's decision to hedge a portfolio is independent of AIMCO's decision on hedging. If the manager wants to hedge, he or she is permitted to do so. In any event, AIMCO can override the currency allocation, and we have done so.

Second, in those cases in which managers opt not to do their own hedging, we include their portfolios in a currency overlay program. This program is in the pilot stage; we have been doing it for about three years. At this point, our approach is to revise the benchmark as a way of influencing the behavior of managers to accommodate our view of trends in currencies. Currently, our exposure is 50 percent hedged for continental Europe and 25 percent hedged for Japan.

Question: Does the lack of liquidity in emerging markets predetermine AIMCO's asset allocation to that sector and result, at some point, in AIMCO being overweighted in that sector?

Goupillaud: Yes, it does. One problem is low liquidity in the market itself, and the other is restrictions on liquidity in the vehicles through which we invest in that market (i.e., private funds). We have no control over liquidity in the market itself, and the portfolio managers must take this into account in their decisions. We do choose the investment vehicles, and liquidity is a consideration.

Question: As a mature fund, are any of your fund's pension payments made in currencies other than U.S. dollars? If so, does that influence your global allocation?

Goupillaud: No, the pension trusts are for U.S. plans and the benefit payments are in U.S. dollars.

---

[1] Please see Mr. Divecha's discussion of benchmarks on pages 131–35.

Choosing an Emerging Markets Benchmark

Arjun Divecha[1]
Managing Director
BARRA

> Global investors in emerging markets must choose a benchmark for measuring portfolio performance from among a variety of offerings, none of which is at present overwhelmingly accepted as the best. The study of major international indexes reported here investigated the indexes' differences in light of this task. A primary decision in the choice is investable versus global scope.

Both the investment manager allocating funds to emerging markets and the plan sponsor need to know what benchmark should be used to judge performance. This presentation discusses global and local benchmarks—what they are, the countries the different benchmarks include, their selection criteria, how they allocate weights to each country or each stock within the index, and the implications of some of those characteristics for choosing a benchmark. The presentation then analyzes correlations between the indexes, because if they are all highly correlated with each other, it does not make much difference which one is chosen.

The Appropriate Benchmark

The appropriate benchmark depends on the investment strategy and what performance is being measured. For example, is the investment being viewed from a local investor's perspective or a global investor's perspective? The benchmark to be used from a local investor's perspective may be very different from a global investor's benchmark because of investment restrictions on foreign investors, such as liquidity. For clients in Thailand, for example, the issue will be whether to use the Securities Exchange of Thailand Index versus another index within Thailand, not whether to use an MSCI Index or an International Finance Corporation (IFC) index.

The three major purveyors of global benchmarks are the IFC, MSCI, and Barings. As shown in **Table 1**, the IFC and MSCI indexes have categories termed "global" and "free"; free, meaning an open market, is basically the same as investable, so the terms will be used interchangeably here.

The IFC and MSCI indexes have broad bases and capture many stocks among many countries. The Barings Index is narrower; it covers only 12 countries and about 200 stocks. Barings is more like the DJIA than, say, the S&P 500 Index. It can be computed daily with some accuracy, so it is a good bellwether, but it does not represent the broad index that a true global investor would care about.

The IFC indexes cover more countries than those of the MSCI, although Morgan Stanley has announced plans to increase its coverage to India and other countries. In time, the IFC and MSCI indexes will probably be very similar. The IFC indexes also cover more stocks than the MSCI.

Selection Criteria

The IFC Global Index has been around for many years and is the standard most people use who have considered emerging markets. This index focuses on actively traded issues but makes no adjustment for investability by local or foreign investors. Although it is a good, broad index that includes many countries, a global investor in the United States or Europe cannot really buy stocks in the proportion they are in the index. In fact, the global investor cannot buy some of the countries at all because of restrictions.

To avoid this problem, the IFC developed the investable index, which adjusts the index's country and stock weights for float, liquidity, market capitalization, and investability by foreigners. It does not adjust for industry weights.

Morgan Stanley's global index is similar to the IFC's global index, although the selection criteria are

---

[1] Mr. Divecha is currently with Grantham, Mayo, Van Otterloo & Company.

Table 1. Characteristics of Global Benchmarks

Benchmark	Number of Countries	Number of Stocks
IFC		
Global	20	877
Investable	18	647
Morgan Stanley		
Global	14	567
Free	13	511
Barings	12	200

Sources: IFC; MSCI; and Barings Securities.

Table 2. Country Weights in Key Benchmarks

Country	IFC Investable[a]	IFC Global[a]	MSCI Global[b]	MSCI Free[b]	Barings[a]
Argentina	5.18	2.55	2.98	4.27	5.43
Brazil	11.05	7.62	10.51	15.08	15.60
Chile	1.69	3.51	5.16	7.39	NA
Colombia	1.50	0.83	NA	NA	NA
Greece	2.70	1.31	1.41	2.02	3.06
India	2.45	5.47	NA	NA	NA
Indonesia	2.19	1.99	2.27	3.26	2.68
Jordan	0.32	0.43	0.34	0.49	NA
Korea	3.34	15.08	18.05	5.18	NA
Malaysia	23.94	14.64	15.37	22.04	19.46
Mexico	28.27	13.99	18.87	23.26	32.98
Nigeria	NA	0.16	NA	NA	NA
Pakistan	0.53	0.81	NA	NA	NA
Philippines	2.69	2.43	1.84	2.64	4.14
Portugal	2.14	1.53	1.45	2.07	2.69
Taiwan	1.07	15.12	13.15	NA	2.93
Thailand	7.84	11.86	6.93	9.14	7.68
Turkey	5.47	2.44	2.23	3.20	2.26
Venezuela	1.08	0.87	NA	NA	NA
Zimbabwe	NA	0.06	NA	NA	NA

Sources: IFC; MSCI; and Barings Securities.

NA = not applicable.

[a]May 30, 1993.
[b]June 30, 1993.

different. MSCI does not include closely held companies or certain classes of companies, such as multi-industry companies. MSCI does adjust for industry coverage. Each index within each country has the same industry representation as the local market index or the local market itself. If 30 percent of the local market in Indonesia is in banks, for instance, MSCI will make sure 30 percent of the Indonesian index is in banks.

Clearly, a trade-off is involved between being correct on industries versus being correct on stocks. To be right on industries, MSCI must make certain assumptions and must add or delete stocks to get the right industry weights. The IFC does not care about getting the weight of industries right; it cares only about getting right the weight of stocks the investor can actually buy. Which index is best depends on which weighting is considered most important.

The Barings Index covers basically large, liquid issues in major countries. Barings has stringent criteria for including a country in the index and stringent criteria for liquidity and market capitalization for a stock to be included. Investability by foreign investors is essential.

Country Weights

An implicit assumption is often made that each stock or country should be weighted in an index on the basis of market capitalization, but that decision may not be correct. **Table 2** shows how each of 20 countries is weighted in the five indexes. These weights illustrate the differences between an investable index and a global index. For example, the weights of Mexico and Malaysia, which are essentially open to foreign investment, increase dramatically in an investable index, and the weights of Taiwan and South Korea, which restrict the amount of money that can come in, decrease dramatically. The Korean and Taiwanese markets are large emerging markets, but the amount of money that can be invested in them is small because of the restrictions on investment by foreigners. Thus, two of the largest country weights in the IFC Global Index, Taiwan at 15.12 percent and Korea at 15.08 percent, are very small parts of the IFC Investable Index.

An often-debated issue is whether an index should be capitalization weighted or equal weighted. The theory behind capitalization weighting is market efficiency. Capitalization weighting may not make sense in the context of benchmarks, however. What does market efficiency mean when the weights can be as disparate as they are in Table 2?

Choosing an Index

Malaysia and Mexico together make up over 50 percent of the IFC Investable Index (see Table 2). As Korea and Taiwan open their markets more, however, and become a bigger percentage of the market, Mexico and Malaysia will become a smaller part. Dynamically, the weights change as local markets go up and down. This change brings up the problem posed by Japan's weight during 1987 through 1990. Japan was at the time 50–60 percent of the EAFE Index, but many managers did not want to have 60 percent of their money in Japan. Doing that did not make sense to them. The dilemma was that a manager who did not put 60 percent in Japan was making a huge bet against Japan relative to the EAFE Index.

Whether investing 60 percent of the money in, say, two of the most developed and accessible markets is appropriate depends on the type of manager and the purpose of the investment. If the manager's purpose is to manage an index fund or a passive portfolio, then an investable index is the appropriate benchmark because it reflects the investable set. An active manager, however, may go beyond the investability criteria and put money in places that are hard to invest in. Something other than an investable index, therefore, may be appropriate as the benchmark for an active fund.

Correlations among Indexes

A final aspect of choosing the appropriate index as a benchmark is whether they are truly different. A quantitative model was used to examine two dimensions of this issue—fundamental betas and predicted tracking errors. The result is shown in **Table 3**, which presents the fundamental beta and tracking error for 18 countries and the composite of the IFC Investable Index relative to the IFC Global Index.

The fundamental betas of the investable index and the global index are similar. Most of the betas are close to 1, and whether the market is defined as investable or global causes little difference when the market moves. The exceptions are Portugal, Venezuela, and Greece, for which the beta of the investable is higher than the beta of the global index.

Another phenomenon found in this analysis of the world indexes was that the betas of the bigger companies are usually higher than the betas of the smaller companies. This finding is, of course, exactly the opposite of what is found in the United States, where the betas of small companies are usually much higher than the betas of large companies.

The other dimension of the study, a comparison of predicted tracking errors, sought to find out how different the returns of these two indexes could be from one another in any given year. The finding is a statistical measure of how different the indexes are. The bigger the number, the more different they are. If the number is zero, the implication is that the two will move in lockstep. Table 3 shows a range of 17 percent in Venezuela to almost zero in Taiwan and Korea. For Taiwan and Korea, the investable index is the same as the global index except that all the stocks are reduced a certain percentage; that is, each stock has a smaller weight. Therefore, the two indexes are effectively the same; one simply has bigger positions than the other.

The lists of stocks for Venezuela, Greece, and Brazil would be significantly different, however, because the investable index excludes the stocks that cannot be bought by foreigners, which may be a large part of the market. In addition, in certain countries, the banking sector is off-limits to foreigners. The investable index will thus have nothing in banks, but the global index will have a large banking sector—from 20 to 40 percent for most countries.

When all the differences are added together, the tracking error of the investable index relative to the global index is 11.39 percent. That is, the returns to the IFC Investable and the IFC Global indexes in any given year could differ by 1,139 basis points.

Why the big difference? **Figure 1** shows that country weighting is the reason investable and global indexes are so different from each other. Country weights were responsible for 63 percent of the predicted variance between the two indexes. Only 6 percent of variance was because the industries were different, and only 5 percent was because of risk characteristics—P/Es, size of company, yields, and so forth. The countries responsible for the difference were primarily Malaysia and Mexico on the upside and Taiwan and Korea on the downside. Those four bets pushed the indexes dramatically away from each other. If the country weights had been similar, the indexes' performances would have been similar.

Table 4 presents the correlations among emerging market indexes. (These series begin and end at different times, so they cannot be compared during one consistent period.) The figures indicate that the three investable, or free, indexes move with each other 90 percent of the time. The correlation between the IFC Investable and the IFC Global indexes, however, is only about 0.55. Thus, at some level, all the

Table 3. Differences between IFC Investable and IFC Global Indexes

Country	Fundamental Beta	Predicted Tracking Error
Argentina	0.99	2.60
Brazil	1.04	7.40
Chile	1.00	1.80
Colombia	1.02	3.50
Greece	1.09	5.60
India	1.02	2.40
Indonesia	1.00	0.50
Jordan	1.09	5.70
Korea	0.99	0.70
Malaysia	1.00	3.30
Mexico	1.00	2.10
Pakistan	1.00	7.90
Philippines	1.05	6.90
Portugal	1.07	6.50
Taiwan	1.00	0.30
Thailand	1.01	2.20
Turkey	1.00	1.10
Venezuela	1.18	17.20
Composite	1.10	11.39

Source: Derived from BARRA's emerging markets model.

Note: Fundamental beta and tracking error of the investable index relative to the global index.

Figure 1. Sources of Differences between the IFC Investable Composite Index and the IFC Global Composite Index

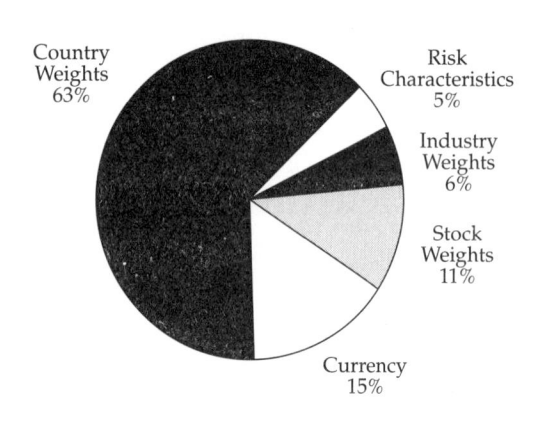

- Country Weights 63%
- Risk Characteristics 5%
- Industry Weights 6%
- Stock Weights 11%
- Currency 15%

Source: BARRA's emerging markets model.

Note: Proportion of predicted variance between the two indexes.

Figure 2. Emerging Markets Investable Index Returns

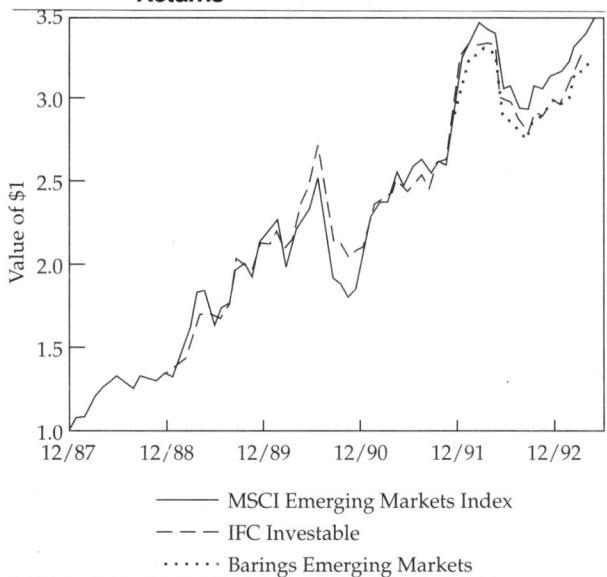

— MSCI Emerging Markets Index
– – – IFC Investable
· · · · · Barings Emerging Markets

Sources: Arjun Divecha, based on IFC, MSCI, and Barings Securities data.

investable indexes are more similar to each other than they are to their respective global counterparts.

Another way of looking at correlations is performance of the indexes over time. **Figure 2** shows emerging market returns for the three investable indexes from December 1987 through December 1992. The cumulative return has been 200–250 percent. The correlations are high; all the indexes moved closely together.

Figure 3 shows the IFC Investable versus the IFC Global indexes for approximately the same period. These two indexes performed significantly differently from each other. The investable outperformed the global index for four reasons—Mexico, Malaysia, South Korea, and Taiwan. During this period, Korea and Taiwan plummeted, and Mexico and Malaysia soared.

As **Figure 4** shows, the IFC Global and MSCI Global total returns track each other closely. Although one index has 20 countries and the other has 14, capitalization weighting of both makes the returns similar. For example, when Argentina is up 300 percent, whether an index has 300 or 320 percent does not matter, both figures are in the same ballpark.

Conclusion

The obstacle in the way of finding good performance benchmarks is that the global benchmarks that have long been in use do not reflect an investable universe. The problem with using the investable indexes is that they usually have so much weight in a few countries that active managers have difficulty using them.

Table 4. Correlations among Emerging Markets Indexes

	IFC EM Investable[a]	IFC EM Global[b]	MSCI EM Global[c]	MSCI EM Freed	Barings EM Index[e]
IFC EM Investable	1.00				
IFC EM Global	0.55	1.00			
MSCI EM Global	0.63	0.97	1.00		
MSCI EM Free	0.89	0.53	0.60	1.00	
Barings EM Index[e]	0.89	0.69	0.80	0.90	1.00

Source: BARRA.

Note: EM stands for Emerging Markets.

[a] Data available from January 1989 to April 1993.
[b] Data available from January 1985 to April 1993.
[c] Data available from January 1988 to June 1993.
[d] Data available from January 1988 to June 1993.
[e] Data available from January 1992 to May 1993.

Figure 3. IFC Investable Index versus IFC Global Index: Total Returns

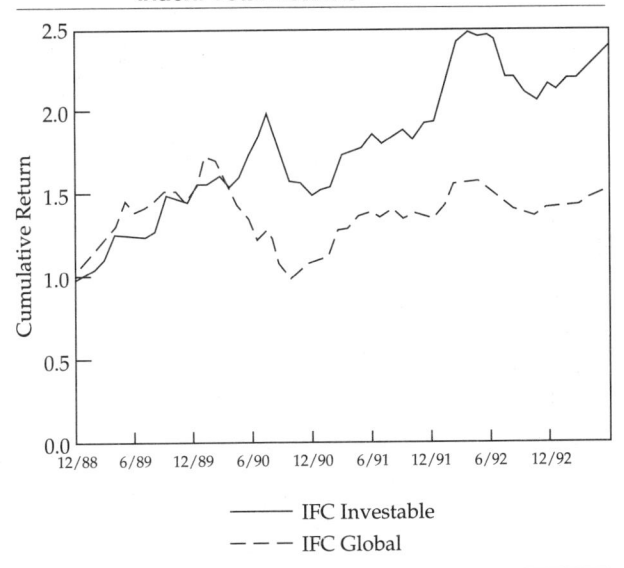

Source: Arjun Divecha, based on IFC data.

Figure 4. IFC Global Index versus MSCI Global Index: Total Returns

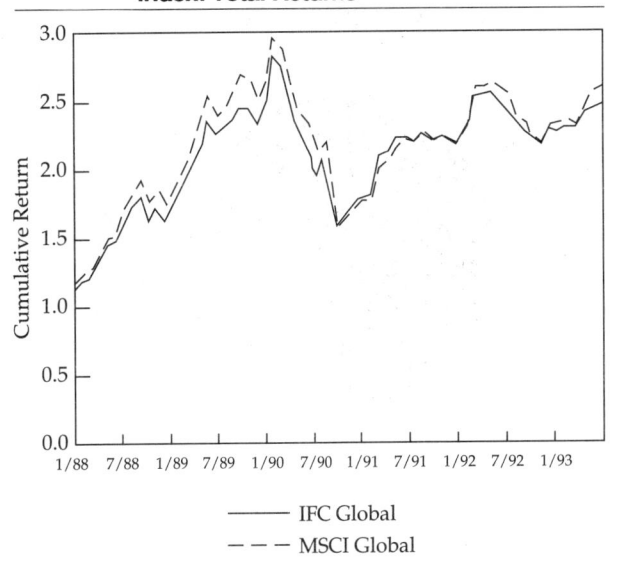

Sources: Arjun Divecha, based on IFC and MSCI data.

Therefore, a useful distinction may be the investable set versus the opportunity set for a particular investor. The investable indexes address the investable set, but a portfolio manager cares primarily about the opportunity set.

Question and Answer Session

Arjun Divecha

Question: To what degree are the historical data of the global and investable indexes consistent?

Divecha: The data are consistent in that they reflect what was available at the time. For the IFC indexes, the data are consistent as far back as, perhaps, 1985 because the indexes were constructed then. The Barings Index goes back only to January 1991, so in a sense, it is a live index. I don't know about the MSCI indexes.

Question: Why should a plan sponsor consider emerging market benchmarks differently from developed market benchmarks?

Divecha: The emerging market benchmarks are less precise and quantifiable than those for the developed markets. Five years from now, a set of well-established benchmarks may exist that everyone accepts, but that has not happened yet; so, much uncertainty surrounds the question of which benchmark is the appropriate one to use.

Question: Do you think that the difference between the performance of the IFC Global and Investable indexes reflects the impact of foreign investment?

Divecha: Intellectually, that is an appealing argument, but I do not know whether it is true. Carried to its logical conclusion, it says that all one needs to do to be successful is to invest where the foreigners invest. Obviously, that prescription is not completely valid.

Question: What type of weighting scheme do you recommend—capitalization weighting, equal weighting, some other weight?

Divecha: In an ideal world, I would use minimum-variance weights (i.e., the mean–variance-efficient portfolio). In the real world, I would settle for capitalization weights.

Question: Do the IFC and MSCI indexes have the same drawback for the foreign investor as do local indexes, namely, that the indexes do not reflect the investor's potential universe?

Divecha: The answer depends on the size of the investment. A small investor (under $50 million) has a much larger potential universe than a large one (because of liquidity constraints). Thus, the indexes are constructed for the large investor.

Question: Given that sophisticated emerging market investors are targeting and investing in 20 or more markets, isn't the broadest index the best performance measurement benchmark?

Divecha: Ideally, one should tailor the benchmark for the manager based on the habitat in which he or she invests. Practically, one of the indexes will probably become the de facto benchmark for everyone.

Self-Evaluation Examination

1. A key disadvantage of investable (or free) emerging market indexes is:
   a. Inclusion of developed market stocks in the index.
   b. Heavy weighting in only a few countries.
   c. Excessive volatility because of the rapid changing of securities composing the indexes.
   d. Impossibility of investing in the stocks composing the indexes.

2. Most emerging market country funds share which one of the following characteristics?
   a. Tendency to trade at net asset value.
   b. Expense ratios approximately the same as for domestic mutual funds.
   c. Denomination and trading in the underlying currency of the relevant country.
   d. Active management to achieve superior investment returns.

3. Goupillaud advises that, from a plan sponsor's viewpoint, the most important research consideration about a specific emerging market should involve:
   a. Reading books about that market.
   b. Attending seminars about that market.
   c. Traveling to and within that market.
   d. Analyzing historical risk and return relationships for that market.

4. Prior to entering an emerging market, an investor should examine the following:
   a. Data sources, accounting characteristics, custodial facilities, and settlement procedures.
   b. Historical stock returns, language requirements, and economic policies.
   c. Restaurants, country clubs, and airports.
   d. Population characteristics, politics, regulations, and inflation.

5. According to O'Brien, European investors have shown increased interest in:
   a. Emerging market fixed-income investments.
   b. Currency investments in emerging markets.
   c. Derivative securities on emerging market assets.
   d. Selling short the stocks of emerging countries.

6. The investment in emerging market currencies typically involves:
   a. Hedging away part of the risk with the use of derivative securities.
   b. Taking the total currency risk.
   c. Larger portfolio amounts than for either stocks or fixed-income securities.
   d. Excessive risk with extremely low expected returns.

7. The World Bank defines an emerging market as one having:
   a. A GNP less than US$10 billion.
   b. An inflation rate exceeding 25 percent.
   c. Per capita GNP under US$7,910.
   d. A stock market capitalization less than $5 billion.

8. The International Finance Corporation (IFC), as of December 31, 1992, included how many emerging markets in its Global Index?
   a. 12.
   b. 14.
   c. 18.
   d. 20.

9. All of the following factors support the continuation of some of the high growth rates in emerging markets *except*:
   a. Low-cost, skilled labor.
   b. High rates of inflation.
   c. Abundance of underexploited natural resources.
   d. Low tax rates.

10. The most important trading consideration with respect to emerging market securities is:
    a. Selection of a satisfactory broker.
    b. Considering only stocks with large market capitalizations.
    c. Ensuring that the stocks have American or Global Depositary Receipts available.
    d. Ability to hedge away the foreign exchange risk.

11. A Brady bond is usually:
    a. Denominated in U.S. dollars.
    b. Uninvestable because of the small amounts outstanding.
    c. Issued by a public corporation.
    d. AAA-rated because of governmental backing.

12. The most important accounting consideration in analyzing the financial statements of companies in emerging markets is:
    a. Tax rates.
    b. Liquidation values.
    c. Inflation.
    d. Earnings per share.

13. Given the difficulties in obtaining a satisfactory custodian for emerging market securities, Summers recommends the following:
    a. Use only a U.S.-based custodian.
    b. Avoid emerging market stocks that do not trade on an exchange in a developed country.
    c. Use several custodians in each emerging market to spread the risk.
    d. Select an attractive custodian in an emerging market after examining key custodial issues.

14. Tata suggests that investing in emerging markets is expanding beyond equity assets to encompass which of the following groups of assets?
    a. Currencies, real estate, and commodities.
    b. Debt, real estate, and venture capital.
    c. Currencies, commodities, and venture capital.
    d. Debt, real estate, and commodities.

15. The IFC sees all of the following as major trends among emerging markets *except*:
    a. Expansion of the investor universe.
    b. Higher future rates of return.
    c. Expansion of the asset class.
    d. Deepening of the markets.

16. Wagener contends that, to be a successful stock picker in emerging markets, an investor should use a growth style and concentrate on:
    a. Absolute valuation, management quality, and country environment.
    b. Management quality, inflation, and foreign exchange rates.
    c. Custodian services, settlement procedures, and regulations.
    d. Interest rates, relative P/Es, and risk premiums.

17. The size of the emerging markets' debt market is estimated to be almost:
    a. US$10 billion.
    b. US$150 billion.
    c. US$400 billion.
    d. US$1 trillion.

18. According to Faber, investors in emerging market stocks should devote considerable attention to:
    a. Political considerations.
    b. Market cycles.
    c. Regulatory environment.
    d. Historical risk–return considerations.

19. Which of the following portfolio weighting approaches has experienced the best risk and return results in recent years?
    a. Equal weights.
    b. Market-capitalization weights.
    c. Trading weights.
    d. Forecasted returns.

20. Which of the following is *not* a characteristic statement about emerging markets?
    a. The individual markets show high volatility.
    b. Correlations of returns among the separate markets tend to be high.
    c. A diversified portfolio of emerging market stocks has lower risk than the risk for most of the individual markets.
    d. Emerging market returns vary considerably from year to year and from country to country.

21. The largest (smallest) market capitalizations of the individual emerging markets included in the IFC Investable Index are:
    a. Mexico (Jordan).
    b. Japan (Sri Lanka).
    c. Malaysia (Chile).
    d. Taiwan (Thailand).

22. Information for effective company valuation in emerging markets should be gathered from all of the following *except*:
    a. Various published sources.
    b. Participants in the local markets.
    c. Historical detailed data bases.
    d. Country and company visits.

23. The objectives of financial-sector regulations in emerging markets should include the following:
    a. Fairness, efficiency, and ethics.
    b. Rules, accounting standards, and fairness.
    c. Ethics, customs, and political factors.
    d. Market integrity, fairness, and efficiency.

24. The concept of the sovereign policy cycle, or "virtuous circle," suggests that:
    a. Investors should invest only in the sovereign debt of emerging countries.
    b. Stock prices in emerging markets follow predictable long-term cycles.
    c. Emerging countries experience periodic political and economic shocks that affect securities prices.
    d. Sovereign policy decisions by politicians affect inflation, interest rates, and currency values.

25. The estimated market capitalization of emerging market stocks is:
    a. Approximately $1 billion.
    b. More than $50 billion.
    c. Between $15 billion and $25 billion.
    d. Unknown.

Self-Evaluation Answers

1. b. Divecha (Table 2) shows that Mexico and Malaysia, together, make up more than 50 percent of the IFC Investable Index and approximately 45 percent of the MSCI Free Index.

2. d. According to Gill, the primary objective of managers of country funds is to achieve superior performance.

3. c. Goupillaud recommends that the best approach for investing in emerging markets is to know the countries by traveling to and within them.

4. a. Krueger explains that the search for good data sources, analyses of accounting characteristics of the country, examination of existing custodial facilities, and the study of the settlement procedures are prerequisites to investing in an emerging market.

5. a. O'Brien points out that European managers, in their search for higher yields, have increasingly moved to emerging market fixed-income investments.

6. b. Because of the limited derivative products, investment in emerging market currencies involves taking total currency risk (see Portillejo's presentation).

7. c. The World Bank defines a developing country as one with a per capita GNP of less than US$7,910 (see Paulson-Ellis's presentation).

8. d. The IFC includes 20 emerging markets in its Global Index but only 18 markets in its Investable Index.

9. b. Paulson-Ellis indicates that low-cost and skilled labor, underexploited natural resources, high savings, pro-business policies, cheap land, and low tax rates support the continuation of high growth.

10. a. According to Peña, of particular importance in the trading of emerging market securities is the selection of a satisfactory broker. In choosing a broker, investors must assess the advantages and disadvantages of using local and global brokers, issues of confidentiality, and transaction costs.

11. a. Brady bonds refer to rescheduled bank debt securitized under the Brady plan announced in 1989. Most Brady bonds are U.S. dollar denominated (see the "Overview" and Wenhammar's presentation).

12. c. Schieneman asserts that, although many accounting considerations are important to the evaluation of emerging market companies, foremost among them is inflation.

13. d. Summers contends that an investor must analyze key custodial considerations, including the characteristics of the custodian bank, the extent and quality of the subagent network, the custodian's foreign exchange capabilities, the custodian's corporate actions department, and the custodian's fee schedule.

14. b. Tata suggests that investing in emerging markets is expanding beyond equities to encompass debt, real estate, and venture-capital investing.

15. b. According to Tata, the IFC sees three major trends in emerging markets: expansion of the asset class, expansion of the investor universe, and deepening of the markets.

16. a. Wagener argues that successful stock pickers in emerging markets must be growth managers and concentrate on absolute valuation, management quality, and country environment.

17. c. Wenhammar estimates the size of the emerging markets' debt market to be almost $400 billion, of which only approximately half is considered investable.

18. b. Investors must be aware of the cycles in emerging markets. Faber believes that opportunities are falling in countries that rely on exports of industrial products and rising in markets with large resource bases.

19. d. Table 7 in the Davis presentation shows that an approach using forecasted returns has experienced the best yearly return (29.1 percent) at the lowest risk (12.2 percent).

20. b. Despite the volatility of individual countries' markets, emerging markets offer a huge diversification benefit to portfolios. Davis's Table 3 substantiates the low or negative correlations among these markets that provide the diversification benefits.

21. a. Table 4 in the Davis presentation indicates that Mexico has the largest market capitalization ($130 billion) and Jordan has the smallest ($5.2 billion) among the 18 countries composing the IFC Investable Index.

22. c. Jimenez contends that researchers must gather information from various published sources, participants in the local markets, and most importantly, country and company visits. Analysts will have to build their own data bases.

23. d. Van der Bijl posits that the special characteristics of the financial sector in emerging markets require that the objectives for their markets include market integrity, fairness, and efficiency.

24. c. The sovereign policy cycle in Figure 2 of the Purcell presentation asserts that every emerging country suffers shocks and crises from time to time.

25. c. The size of the emerging stock markets' capitalization is estimated in the "Overview" to be between US$15 billion and US$25 billion.

Order Form 031

Additional copies of *Managing Emerging Market Portfolios* (and other AIMR publications listed on page 144) are available for purchase. The price is **$20 each in U.S. dollars**. Simply complete this form and return it via mail or fax to:

> AIMR
> Publications Sales Department
> P.O. Box 7947
> Charlottesville, Va. 22906
> U.S.A.
> Telephone: 804/980-3647
> Fax: 804/977-0350

Name _____

Company _____

Address _____

_____ Suite/Floor _____

City _____

State _____ ZIP _____ Country _____

Daytime Telephone _____

Title of Publication   Price   Qty.   Total

_____   _____   _____   _____

_____   _____   _____   _____

Shipping/Handling
- ❏ All U.S. orders: Included in price of book
- ❏ Airmail, Canada and Mexico: $5 per book
- ❏ Surface mail, Canada and Mexico: $3 per book
- ❏ Airmail, all other countries: $8 per book
- ❏ Surface mail, all other countries: $6 per book

Discounts
- ❏ Students, professors, university libraries: 25%
- ❏ CFA candidates (ID #_____): 25%
- ❏ Retired members (ID #_____): 25%
- ❏ Volume orders (50+ books of same title): 40%

Discount $_____

4.5% sales tax
(Virginia residents) $_____

8.25% sales tax
(New York residents) $_____

7% GST
(Canada residents,
#124134602) $_____

Shipping/handling $_____

Total cost of order $_____

❏ Check or money order enclosed payable to **AIMR**   ❏ Bill me

Charge to: ❏ VISA   ❏ MASTERCARD   ❏ AMERICAN EXPRESS

Card Number:_____   ❏ Corporate   ❏ Personal

Signature:_____   Expiration date: _____

Selected AIMR Publications*

Franchise Value and the Price/Earnings Ratio, 1994 Martin L. Leibowitz and Stanley Kogelman	$20
Investing Worldwide, 1993, 1992, 1991, 1990	$20 each
The Modern Role of Bond Covenants, 1994 Ileen B. Malitz	$20
Derivative Strategies for Managing Portfolio Risk, 1993 Keith C. Brown, CFA, *Editor*	$20
Equity Securities Analysis and Evaluation, 1993	$20
The CAPM Controversy: Policy and Strategy Implications for Investment Management, 1993 Diana R. Harrington and Robert A. Korajczyk, *Editors*	$20
The Health Care Industry, 1993 James Balog, *Editor*	$20
Predictable Time-Varying Components of International Asset Returns, 1993 Bruno Solnik	$20
The Oil and Gas Industries, 1993 Thomas A. Petrie, CFA, *Editor*	$20
Execution Techniques, True Trading Costs, and the Microstructure of Markets, 1993 Katrina F. Sherrerd, CFA, *Editor*	$20
Investment Counsel for Private Clients, 1993 John W. Peavy III, CFA, *Editor*	$20
Active Currency Management, 1993 Murali Ramaswami	$20
The Retail Industry, 1993 Charles A. Ingene, *Editor*	$20
Equity Trading Costs, 1993 Hans R. Stoll	$20
Options and Futures: A Tutorial, 1992 Roger G. Clarke	$20
Improving the Investment Decision Process—Better Use of Economic Inputs in Securities Analysis and Portfolio Management, 1992 H. Kent Baker, CFA, *Editor*	$20
Ethics, Fairness, Efficiency, and Financial Markets, 1992 Hersh Shefrin and Meir Statman	$20

*A full catalog of publications is available from AIMR, P.O. Box 7947, Charlottesville, Va. 22906; 804/980-3647; fax 804/977-0350.